GOVERNMENT REIMAGINED

Leading Through New Realities

www.thinkers50.com

enquiries@thinkers50.com

Thinkers50 Limited
The Studio, Highfield Lane
Wargrave RG10 8PZ
United Kingdom

First published in Great Britain 2020

Design by www.jebensdesign.co.uk

ISBN:
PDF Edition 9781838076559
ePub Edition 9781838076566
Kindle Edition 9781838076573
Print Edition 9781838076504

ABOUT THINKERS50

Thinkers50 (thinkers50.com) is the world's most reliable resource for identifying, ranking and sharing the leading management ideas of our age. Since 2001, we've been providing access to ideas with the power to make the world a better place.

The Thinkers50 definitive ranking of management thinkers is published every two years. Its Distinguished Achievement Awards, which recognise the very best in management thinking and practice, have been described by the *Financial Times* as "the Oscars of management thinking".

CONTENTS

ACKNOWLEDGEMENTS

I wish to thank my loving and supportive wife Yasmin and beautiful children, for keeping me grounded at all times, and for being my inspiration.

The eminent contributors, whose personal experience and insights have been both highly informative and hugely influential on writing this book.

I would also like to thank Haneen Qatamesh, Ade McCormack, Des Dearlove and Victoria Jebens for their continuous dedication and support throughout the evolution of my ideas.

INTRODUCTION

Approximately two hundred and twenty generations ago, human beings created the wheel. Twenty-four generations ago we developed the printing press. One generation ago we invented the smart phone. Each of these technologies changed the world beyond recognition. We cannot anticipate or even comprehend the impact on society of emergent technologies associated with concepts such as artificial intelligence (AI), blockchain and the Internet of Things (IoT); let alone the impact of new technologies that are only just leaving the laboratory, and those yet to come. What we do know is that change is now exponential, moving at a speed that is unprecedented in human history, with huge implications for jobs, health, education and just about every other aspect of our daily lives.

At the same time, global threats – everything from financial crises to natural disasters, pandemics and global warming – are fuelling uncertainty and insecurity. Social media and a more connected world fan the flames. Governments everywhere are struggling to keep up with technological developments and protect their people from an increasingly unpredictable world.

The simple fact, however, is that government as we know it was not designed to cope with the sheer velocity and ferocity of change that we are now experiencing. The cracks are already starting to show in the form of citizen dissatisfaction and the rise of populism. Unless the cracks are addressed, they will only grow wider. Government is no longer fit for purpose and needs to be reinvented to reflect this new reality. That is the central premise of this book and I believe it is timely.

THE END OF SYNTHETIC CERTAINTY

The existing literature assumes that societies generally operate in a steady state. From time to time, they are subjected to destabilising forces, for example war or economic depression. The traditional role of a government was to return society to the earlier steady state. This model had a simple, even innocent feel to it, much like Newtonian mechanics before the advent of quantum mechanics. In this old model, these forces were somewhat linear and isolated. Society generally enjoyed what might be called "synthetic certainty". Or at least that was the case for those societies that enjoyed the benefits of the industrial age.

This was a world where governments could make plans in the knowledge that they would still be relevant in, say, five years' time, and that society would continue relatively unchanged. Governments the world over believed they could rely on business as usual - or rather government as usual.

Today, however, we live in what has been described as a VUCA world, an environment characterised by volatility, uncertainty, complexity and ambiguity.[1]

In the last 25 years we have seen a series of major disruptions to government as usual. There was the Asian financial crisis in 1997, the dotcom bust in 2000, the SARS crisis in 2002, the tsunamis in 2004 and 2011, the global financial crisis in 2008, the Arab Spring of 2011, the Ebola outbreak in 2014 and covid-19 in 2020. All of these were what Nassim Nicholas Taleb in his 2001 book *Fooled by Randomness* calls Black Swans – unexpected events that have a huge impact.[2]

Add in the threat of global warming, oil price volatility and a refugee crisis around the world, plus the coronavirus pandemic, and it is clear that the disruptions are incessant.

Whether we like it or not, we have to accept that the era of synthetic certainty is over. What has replaced it is a growing awareness that we cannot hope to control events but must learn to be better at responding to them.

We need to build resilience and agility into our lives, including the way our governments operate. Change is now a constant, disruption is to be expected, and requires an adaptable response. At present, too many governments are reactive rather than responsive.

TRANSFORMING GOVERNMENT

I have spent the last 30 years working with government transformations in the Middle East. I have led policies and strategic programmes at the institutional and national levels in a number of countries in the region including my home country of Oman. The projects I have overseen have spanned education, technology, business and leadership development. As a result of those experiences I thought I had a reasonably good grasp of how governments work.

Until very recently, I would have said that every transformation is a journey with a beginning and an end; but I was wrong. Continuous transformation is now the operating system for government. Government must be reinvented on an ongoing basis to remain relevant and responsive to the fast-paced environment it operates in. Government cannot remain separate from its context.

It was that realisation that inspired this book. The title is a heartfelt plea to the leaders of the world to open their minds not just to the inevitable threats and challenges we face, but to the incredible opportunities that reimagining government also presents. I believe that the governments of the future will work in close collaboration with business and private citizens to be more responsive to the societies they serve, and generally more responsible for serving the best interests of us all now and in the future.

PLANTING A SEED

When the late Sultan of Oman, His Majesty Qaboos bin Said Al Said, created the Public Private Collaboration (PPC) Task Force in 2013, it was with the express aim of creating a greater role for the private sector in Oman's economy. The Task Force included senior government officials and private sector leaders, and I was overseeing its work. But I noticed that on both sides, the government and the private sector leaders, were not ready for a real partnership. There were trust issues between them, with each side suspicious of the other. As a result, the efforts were fragmented. It was clear to me that building trust and aligning misaligned agendas was the key to creating a more collaborative relationship.

Governments cannot move the economy forward on their own; the private sector has to create jobs for citizens and provide innovation, and citizens must provide the skills and talents required to create value. Government leaders need to have the mindset of a partner, rather than a dominant player. Becoming more citizen-centric is also crucial. Most importantly, in a fast-changing world, governments need to foster an ecosystem where all actors – government, business and citizens - can contribute and thrive.

LEADERSHIP NEEDS A RESET

Government Reimagined is my attempt to make sense of this changing world. The rapid advance of technology, global supply chains and even the climate have led to an unprecedented level of global interconnectedness. This is a breeding ground for chaos. The forces acting on countries are no longer isolated and linear but compounded in their impact.

This is having a profound effect on social contracts – the tacit assumptions that act as glue to hold societies together and legitimise the relationship between citizens and governments. The VUCA world is causing traditional social contracts to fray and, in some cases, tear. Citizens, many of them with access to social media, technology and connectivity, have become more aware of what is happening around them. This is a cause of increasing frustration and insecurity as they long for the steady state conditions of the past. At the same time, technological progress, particularly in respect of robotics and AI, is creating uncertainty in labour markets. These are fertile conditions for social unrest.

To address these concerns, we need to create societies and governments that can operate effectively despite the uncertainty. Indeed, we need governments and nations that can thrive on it.

HUMAN ADAPTABILITY

Covid-19 is a stark reminder of how quickly the world can change and events can escalate. Many governments were caught unprepared even though a pandemic had been predicted for years. Yet despite the mistakes that governments made, there were examples where business and citizens showed their willingness to play their part, whether it was firms reorganising production lines in order to supply personal protective equipment, or citizens voluntarily self-isolating to protect the vulnerable members of their communities.

What this demonstrates to me is the adaptability and ingenuity of human beings. The crisis brought changes to the way we live, work and learn as we embraced social distancing, working from home and virtual communication. It shows that just because we have done things a certain way in the past does not mean we cannot reimagine them and do them differently in the future.

Take education, for example. Schools and universities moved to virtual classrooms. This was not new knowledge; we already had the capability to move education online and reap the cost savings, but the pandemic created the necessity, and going forward, we will see new experiments in blended learning.

Even something as dreadful as a pandemic can alert us to new opportunities to reimagine our world. And reimagine we must because the world is not going back to the old normal. Even without the pandemic, the changes taking place are so fundamental and so fast moving that standing still means going backwards.

IS THIS BOOK FOR YOU?

I'd like to think that *Government Reimagined* is of interest to anyone concerned with the future direction of government. I believe it is essential reading for those driving state transformation. It is my attempt to corral and codify the learnings of leaders who have led successful government transformations, flavoured with my own first-hand experiences. As such it will have particular appeal for ministers, under-secretaries and those aspiring to such roles. The tools and frameworks in Part II of the book grew out of a need for a new language and lens as well as a desire to reconceptualise the role of government.

MEET YOUR GUIDES

Your guides on this transformational journey are experienced public leaders who have served at the highest levels of government: a former president, two prime ministers, a deputy prime minister and two cabinet ministers. I am grateful to all of them for their thoughtful contributions.

- **John Bruton** - Taoiseach (Prime Minister) (1994 to 1997), Ireland
- **Toomas Ilves** - President (2006 to 2016), Estonia
- **Lim Hwee Hua** - Minister (2009 to 2011), Singapore
- **Supachai Panitchpakdi** - Deputy Prime Minister (1992 to 1995 and 1997 to 2000), Thailand
- **Alexander Stubb** - Prime Minister (2014 to 2015), Finland
- **Ed Vaizey (Lord Vaizey of Didcot)** - Minister (2010 to 2016), United Kingdom

I am also profoundly grateful to **Zhang Ruimin**, chairman and CEO of the Haier Group, for granting me access to his remarkable and highly innovative reimagining of a business organisation.

As the lead author, I have endeavoured to make sense of all their leadership journeys alongside my own - to analyse and extract the common ground, and to distil the learning so that government leaders everywhere can benefit from our collective experiences.

For my part, I currently lead the Omani government's socioeconomic-focused Think Tank Unit. In this role, I am blessed with the opportunity to develop solutions that will benefit the Omani nation and people. As well as conceptual thinking around policy creation and decision-making, I also take the lead on implementing a variety of national initiatives around public and private sector leadership and the skills development of young people.

I have held key positions leading and advising on strategic government initiatives and programmes across the Middle East. The initial phase of my career also exposed me to the private sector through my work with international consulting firm, Booz Allen Hamilton (BAH).

To this day I maintain close ties with academe. This serves to ensure that my work has rigorous underpinnings. At heart, my interests, experience and research lie in the area of public sector transformation.

THIS BOOK IS DIFFERENT

This book builds upon my previous book, *Leading Smart Transformation: A Roadmap for World Class Government*.[3] Back then, I realised we needed a new approach to government. Its central messages remain valid, that governments need to raise their game to deliver world-class services to their citizens and create an environment that empowers the private sector by removing unnecessary obstacles.

With *Government Reimagined*, however, we look at the wider state ecosystem, examining the symbiotic relationship between government, business and citizens (GBC) as a force for innovation and national wellbeing. It is a clarion call and I hope perhaps even a catalyst for change. It is also a plea to the government leaders of today and tomorrow to reimagine a future-proofed government.

True transformation is both challenging and ongoing. This book aims to encourage you to think of government leadership as an operating model, a way of being and doing, as opposed to a programme or initiative. The good news is that while there is no "one-size-fits-all" solution, there are generic principles to guide you through what is uncharted territory for both government leaders and public servants.

Perhaps most importantly, this book will drive home what real transformation is and isn't. Sprinkling existing government processes with AI is not enough. A faster, smarter, cheaper version of an unfit for purpose model will simply serve to accelerate its demise. The following chapters will provide you with a vivid collection of real transformational journeys and the associated lessons learnt.

REIMAGINE GOVERNMENT LEADERSHIP

The contributors highlight the linkages between government leadership and the two other primary actors in this drama, namely business and the citizen. At its best, the response to the covid-19 pandemic exemplified what can be achieved when these three essential parts of society work together.

But we should not think only of how they can work together in times of threat and crisis. There are huge opportunities for government leaders who can engender the trust, innovation and collaborative energies of the government-business-citizen triumvirate.

There are plenty of books on government leadership, but they are set in the context of a steady-state world. In some cases, transformation is perceived as simply a new technology refresh. This is a dangerous assumption.

The leadership coach Marshall Goldsmith wrote a book called *What Got You Here, Won't Get You There*[4]; today that is true of not just leaders but entire nations.

The digital age is a new era for government and for leadership; one where value trumps experience and where formal education cannot keep up with the pace of change. The capabilities that have made you successful in the past are not guaranteed to ensure you are successful as a leader going forward.

By reading and acting on this book, you will become part of a growing cohort of people-centric leaders who are engendering the citizen-followership needed for a state to thrive in these increasingly uncertain times. It is strong on facts and reality, not on airbrushed or theoretical opinion. It is grounded in hard-earned experience. The compelling transformation stories you are about to read also include actionable next steps in respect of your own leadership development. You will hear from senior figures who were participants at the epicentre of these transformations and not merely observers from a safe distance.

THE BOOK ARCHITECTURE

From a structural perspective, the first part of the book provides you with the perspectives of former presidents, prime ministers and ministers who share their nations' transformative journeys to date along with their leadership experiences. Each story culminates in a set of recommendations, and the chapters are interspersed with case studies of six other countries that have undergone significant national transformations.

The second part of the book builds upon these shared transformation stories by offering my own perspective and prescriptions for reimagining government. This represents a distilled analysis of the leadership challenges associated with state transformation.

The concluding chapter draws all the key learning points together to provide you with what might be called an empirically tested "grand unified theory" of government leadership. It is a model that I hope will serve you well regardless of the unforeseen challenges and opportunities that lie ahead.

OPTIMISE YOUR LEADERSHIP JOURNEY

You can read the contributor chapters in the order they appear to develop a visceral feel for transformation in practice, as well as acquiring the associated insights. However, the book is structured so that each chapter is self-standing and you can choose the transformations that most relate to your situation.

Whilst the book aims to tell the stories of transformation from those who led them, it is also a reference book, which you can revisit as you take your own leadership development journey.

THE FUTURE STARTS HERE

Prime ministers, ministers and under-secretaries reading this book are at or fast approaching the pinnacle of their government careers. As such they might be forgiven for thinking that there is not much more to learn. However, the unprecedented rate of change we are experiencing means that those skills that served us well in the past are at best necessary but not sufficient.

This book is in many respects a wakeup call. But most importantly I hope it will inspire, invigorate and empower you to become a transformational government leader, and someone that other people will feel compelled to follow.

Ali Qassim Jawad, Muscat, August 2020

Part I

In the following chapters, you will hear from a diverse panel of six global leaders regarding the paths that they and their nations have taken on their journey to transformation.

These are interspersed with uplifting case studies to further enhance our understanding of what transformation looks like from a global perspective.

Digitialising a Nation - a Personal Account

"Some people see things and ask why?
I see things and ask why not?"
John F. Kennedy

Toomas Hendrik Ilves
President of Estonia, 2006 to 2016

1

In 1938, the last full year before the second world war, Estonia and its northern neighbour Finland were calculated to have the same GDP per capita. Neither country was particularly well off, but their levels of development were quite close. In contrast, in 1992, the first full year after the restoration of Estonian independence, Finnish GDP per capita stood at approximately US$24,000 and Estonia's at US$2,800 per capita, an eight-fold difference; so much for the wonders of communism.

Yet by 2006, after 15 years of independence, a democratic government, and economic reform, Estonia's growth rate was a remarkable 12%[5] and GDP per capita was US$19,310.[6] In 2008, Estonia ranked 12th out of 162 countries in the Index of Economic Freedom, which covers 12 economic freedoms from property rights to financial freedom; the best performer of any former Soviet republic. By 2018, Estonia's GDP per capita had surpassed US$36,000.[7]

In this chapter, I will shed light on how Estonia rose from economic misery to a free-market success story and became the world's "first digital country".[8]

For the past three years I have lived in the middle of Silicon Valley, considered the world's centre of IT innovation. Within a 12-kilometre radius of my office at Stanford University you find the headquarters of Tesla, Apple, Google, Facebook, Palantir and YouTube. This prime piece of Californian real estate is rightly seen as the centre of the digital revolution that in less than three decades has completely remade our world - a world that is scarcely recognisable to anyone who was alive before it. Nearly all of these Silicon Valley companies provide us with services we use day in, day out, morning to night. Remarkably, 20 years ago, none of them existed; moreover, just 30 years ago, at the end of the cold war, they would have seemed quite fantastical.

Yet there is a paradox here: despite living in the heart of Silicon Valley, if I need to register a child for school or obtain a driving licence or, indeed, have any interaction with any level of government – local, state or national – I would almost certainly have to travel to a government office. Once there, I would have to wait or stand in line for hours, then fill out forms and applications by hand, stand in line (again) to hand them in and then wait for weeks for it all to be processed.

In short, unlike the wonders of the digital lives we live with our smartphones and apps, our public services and means of governance hardly differ from the 1950s and 60s. This is true in most of the world today, not just in developing countries, but in the heart of Silicon Valley and in many other rich and otherwise "most advanced" nations.

Attempts have been made to bring governance into the 21st century. Yet these have, on the whole, been inadequate. At best, it is occasionally possible to accomplish a government or public service-related task online using a shaky and inevitably insecure website, based on an email address and an easily hackable single password. If my data are stored on a government server, I don't know how secure they are. Or if, in the case of 23 million past and present United States federal employees in 2015, and another 200,000 in early 2020 at the Defence Information Security Agency (which manages the IT systems of the White House), my data are simply stolen, presumably by a foreign power.

In other words, digitalisation of governance is not just about "putting government online". Nor is it merely turning paper records into PDFs. Digitalisation of government is more than converting analogue to digital; it is using digital technologies to transform how work is done and revolutionise processes and practices. Ultimately it means rethinking and reimagining how governance works - a point I shall come to at the end of this chapter.

In contrast to the United States and most of Europe, in my own country, Estonia, an individual who needs to interact with the government or public services is required to show up in person in only three instances: to get married, to get divorced, or to transfer physical property. The latter, incidentally, is to prevent anonymous shell companies with dubious owners from buying up real estate, as we have seen happen in the United Kingdom, Canada and the United States, including in the skyscraper that is the home of the current United States president.[9]

All other interactions and transactions in Estonia between citizens and the state, agencies and ministries, are digitalised and can be - and in almost all cases are - dealt with online at the highest levels of security currently available. In the almost 20 years this system has been operating, it has never been "down" or suffered from any breaches. Moreover, the Estonian system is set up so that the government can never ask you for any information it already has; this is our so-called "once-only" regulation and applies to your address, date of birth and anything else.

In 2007, a series of Distributed Denial of Service (DDOS) or cyber-attacks hit Estonia. A DDOS denies access to servers by maliciously flooding them with thousands of near-simultaneous queries. Such attacks do not, however, constitute a breach or a compromise of data; no one gets inside. They began to occur after the removal of the "Bronze Soldier" (a statue of a Red Army soldier) from the centre of Tallinn.[10] Estonian appeals to Moscow for help with the cyber-attacks were ignored. They lasted several weeks and were targeted at the online services of Estonian banks, media outlets and government bodies. However, our e-governance systems remained intact.

If we take Carl von Clausewitz's definition of war as the "continuation of policy by other means" and take this incident as the first public instantiation of employing a cyber-attack as a policy measure, the cyber-attacks on Estonia could be taken to be the world's first case of cyber war. Yet Estonia's digital government was not affected.

Let me address another paradox. Whenever I talk about digitalisation of governance I inevitably hear about "Big Brother", government surveillance, the KGB, the Stasi, Gestapo and, since 2013, Edward Snowden's revelations at the United States' National Security Agency (NSA). Fears of government surveillance are legitimate, if you don't get digitalisation of governance right.

The paradox, as Shoshona Zuboff describes in her book, *Surveillance Capitalism*, is that what we fear of government surveillance pales before the gathering of data by the private sector services and social media that we all use every day. The collection of data on each and every one of us via Google searches, Facebook, the free apps on our phones (there are no free apps) and the cookies on almost every commercial website, is simply astounding. That's without even mentioning the location data used by Google maps. Add to this that in the United States, where governance and public services are basically un-digitalised, there are new and undeclared forms of public-private partnerships at work. The United States government is not Big Brother - it does not spy on you. Instead, Immigration and Customs Enforcement (ICE) finds you by simply buying location data from private sector surveillance companies.

It is important to point out that with all the scraped metadata and digital exhaust we produce, which goes into creating the highly granular profiles of each of us that tech companies sell for advertising and which is the primary source of their income, you yourself do not know what information exists. Nor do you know who has it, to whom it has been sold, or who is using it.

Digital governance, when done properly, is quite different from all the data tracking and scraping carried out by private sector social media platforms, web page cookies, and smartphone apps, in that knowing who accesses your data is a key feature of its success.

ESTONIA'S CASE FOR DIGITALISATION

How and why did Estonia embark on this path to digitalising government? Primarily, it was a question of development or more precisely developmental economics. The country was trying to catch up with the West. In 1991, after fifty years of Nazi and then Soviet occupation, Estonia regained the independence taken away in 1939 by the Molotov-Ribbentrop Pact between Nazi Germany and the Soviet Union.

We, along with the rest of the former communist bloc that emerged from Soviet domination in 1989 to 1991, faced an enormous problem: we were free but extremely poor. We now faced a development problem: how to get out of the poverty imposed by 50 years of totalitarian rule and catch up with the far richer countries that had not been occupied. As is the case with all developing economies, Estonia faced Zeno's paradox of the fleet-footed Achilles who must catch up with the slow tortoise that started the race before him. Like Achilles, we would never catch up, though, because the tortoise (in this case the Finns), and more broadly, the developed nations of the world, would continue to develop and so forever remain ahead of us no matter how hard we tried.

For me, the solution lay in the digitalisation of the country. Inspiration came from two sources, one from my own life and the second from understanding a major leap in technology: the first internet browser.

I was lucky enough to learn computer programming at what at the time was an unheard-of-age, in 1969, as a 15-year-old, in a one-off experiment by my mathematics teacher who was pursuing a PhD at Columbia University. Fifty years ago, learning to programme entailed renting a stand-alone teletype machine that ran perforated tape and a large modem that involved sticking the telephone receiver into 10-centimetre wide suction cups, which in turn were connected to a mainframe computer some 30 miles away. Yet our small group of high-school students all learned to code in BASIC, a simplified version of FORTRAN. Writing a program to print a graph of $y=x^2$ and to see the parabola printout was one of the wonders of my tenth grade.

Later, in college, I saw an advertisement on a bulletin board to programme a laboratory computer for 10 hours a week. Thinking to myself "what could be so difficult?" I applied and soon found myself before a coffee table sized box. The computer was a PDP-8, the earliest of the commercially sold small computers, used in 1970s laboratories and so named because of its maximum memory capacity of 8 kilobytes. Today, this would be the size of an empty email message. Because of this limitation, all commands had to be written in ASSEMBLER language, a hexadecimal (base 16) programming language with all commands written in alphanumerical code. Yet with my knowledge of programming from high school, it was not an insurmountable challenge. Twenty-five years after learning to code and, despairing over how Estonia could ever catch up with western Europe, I hit upon the idea that if I could learn to do this as a high-school student, then all children can and should learn to use computers.

The second source of inspiration for digitalising Estonia came in 1993 when the first-ever web browser, Mosaic, came out. Mosaic went on sale for around US$29.95. Back in 1993, you physically had to buy the browser in a store and boot it up to your computer with floppy discs. Being a geek, I did just that. What struck me, when I finally got the browser to work, was that here was something so new, so different, yet at the same time so promising. I knew then and there that although it would take time, the internet would take off and dominate life. Countries both rich and poor - the United States, Finland, Estonia, Germany, Japan - were all in the same position and starting out on a level playing field. Sure, the West had its interstate highways and autobahns, its developed infrastructure in general, but here was something that would be a part of everyone's future, and no one had the advantage of being ahead of Estonia. But we had to get on board quickly. That was when I realised that Estonia needed to digitalise.

Out of these two insights, I proposed to the government that it begin digitalisation. Knowing that this would take years and based on how quickly my classmates and I had learned to programme, I thought the best way was to begin with young people. I proposed Estonia bring computers and computer education to all students. The idea came to be called "Tiger Leap", to connote that through computerisation the country, or at least its education system, would make a dramatic leap into the future. Fortunately, at that time in 1995, Estonia had an enlightened minister of education, Dr Jaak Aaviksoo, who was willing to take risks and who pushed the government to accept my proposal to put computers in all schools and connect them to the internet.

The idea was not met with universal approval, however. The teachers' union were vehemently opposed, saying that computers in schools would ruin education. For almost a year, not a single issue of the teachers' union weekly publication appeared without an article lambasting the idea or me. Indeed, for much of the next 20 years, opposition parties seemed to pick on digitalisation as something to criticise.

Yet the government proceeded, using a 50-50 matching scheme I put forward, whereby municipal governments that were willing to pay for half the price of a computer would have the other 50% paid for by the national government. By 1998, all Estonian schools had computer labs and were online. Estonian banks noticed the success and popularity of the project and decided to get involved too. Their motivation was simple: they had bricks and mortar banks in every tiny village, which was simply not sustainable and digital banking would help get around this. Along with some government financing and strong NGO participation, the banks developed a programme to ensure that every village had access to computer banking in municipal offices or libraries and could connect to the internet. In addition, the banks supported an educational programme for older people and those in rural areas to learn to use computers and to bank online.

THE BIG LEAP INTO DIGITAL GOVERNANCE

By the end of the 1990s, Estonia was fairly advanced, with online banking, access to the internet and commercial web services. Yet we were all using the standard forms of security: an email address, password and rickety architecture that made the web as insecure and clumsy as it still is in most of the world today.

By the turn of the millennium it had become clear that digitalisation was indeed a way to develop - but it had to be executed altogether differently, to take account of the myriad issues that would arise were we genuinely to digitalise governance. First, we needed the trust of a population that had just emerged from a half century of totalitarian control. Estonians had experienced the very police-state surveillance and privacy violations, with disastrous consequences for those discovered to harbour the wrong opinions, which people in the West cite as objections when I talk about digital governance.

The challenge was: how do you build a "digital democracy"? You know you have certain tools that previously did not exist, but how do you actually do it? It's not simply a matter of technology. The technology existed; the question is how do you do it politically? Digitalisation, after all, is a political decision. Do you start from scratch? Is it merely replicating the paper world in digital format by putting paper documents into PDFs? What kind of social contract do you need? How can you re-design governance that, since the invention of bureaucracy 5000 years ago, has always been a serial or sequential process, with a document going from one office to the next to be stamped or signed off? These were just some of the questions that arose when trying to take digitalisation of governance to the next level.

Most importantly, to make sure your citizens are willing to use the system, how do you guarantee trust? If there is no trust, there will be no uptake by the population. Trust is critical: the *sine qua non*.

WHAT PROVIDES TRUST?

When it comes to guaranteeing trust, the first and foremost requirement is transparency. Long before one addresses the concrete issues of which technology to use, trust in digitalisation above all means that you as a citizen have to know who can look at your data: what is legitimate to look at, what is not legitimate to look at and who in fact is looking at your data? From this basis you can begin to build trust. You need to define clearly which agencies may or not look at your data. Rushing to "buy a solution" will not resolve the legal and regulatory issues that inevitably will arise, and upon which trust in the system will depend.

Nor must a country treat data as merely a legal or regulatory issue. What is culturally acceptable to make public can vary. For example, in northern Europe we tend to favour transparency and hence consider something such as property ownership public information. But in southern Europe, this is taboo. In Estonia, even before digitalisation, anyone could access someone else's property records; in Greece you cannot. You need to design your system to follow your laws but also to meet the cultural expectations of your population.

THE ELEMENTS OF ESTONIA'S SYSTEM

Secondly, trust is based on the security of your identity. You need to trust that no one can impersonate you or change your data; that online only you are you. What, then, are the essentials of Estonia's system, which the United Nations rates as Europe's most cyber secure?

- A secure and unique digital identity for every resident.
- An architecture that is based on legal as well as culturally acceptable norms about what is private and what is public, along with mutual, reciprocal transparency. You can log on and find out who has been looking at your data.
- Data integrity, meaning data cannot be changed without authorisation.

These essentials demonstrate why we have had no breaches in the 20 years since they were implemented. The technology will change over time and indeed can vary from country to country, but the essential principles around which it is built remain the same.

DIGITAL IDENTITY

First, identity: what is a secure digital identity? In the first place it belongs only to one person, i.e., it is unique. It cannot be duplicated; it cannot be forged. As opposed to the classic New Yorker cartoon, where one dog sitting in front of a computer screen says to a second dog: "On the internet no one knows you're a dog", digital governance cannot work without a secure identity. Funny as the joke was 27 years ago, this remains today the fundamental problem of any interaction that is not face-to-face: you do not know who you are dealing with. Is it the government? Is someone impersonating you? Are you as a user dealing with a public service or your bank? Or is it some other entity pretending to be the government, a bank, or credit card company?

Every resident of Estonia is issued a unique, secure digital identity that is used to access all government services, be they health records, automobile registration, taxes, social services, property records and a myriad of private sector services (predominantly financial services) securely.

Currently, until better technologies emerge, the most secure system is one where all communications are encrypted throughout the process of digital connection, known as end-to-end or E2E encryption. E2E encryption uses a public key infrastructure, a mathematical encryption model so unbreakable that when it was invented, the United States National Security Agency and the CIA tried to ban its publication in a scientific journal.

The second component to a secure identity is to require two-factor authentication. In order to guarantee that someone on the internet is who he or she says they are, it is necessary to use a chip, possessed uniquely by the user, that matches a code known only to them. The principle here is that something in your possession - a chip ID - and something only you know - your code - match. Only then will you be able to connect.

The unique digital identity is used to access all services through two-factor identification using a chip, either in an ID card or using a smartphone, which of course also contains a chip in the SIM card, which needs to be programmed uniquely for the user. Communication with a certification authority authenticates each interaction and allows access to all government and many private sector services through E2E encryption using public key infrastructure. The digital identity allows legal signing of documents equivalent to a wet signature, together with a time stamp.

I should add here that, sadly, the unwillingness of the governments of even the most highly developed countries, including the United States, to implement this initial *sine qua non* of cyber security - a unique ID with 2FA and E2E encryption - means that even elementary cyber security of the public sector and critical infrastructure is doomed. Unencrypted communication with a single password linked to an email address cannot be the basis of any e-governance system.

A final aspect of digital identity necessary for a digital governance system to work is a political decision. Digital IDs must be mandatory. EU countries, for example, are currently mandated to offer citizens digital identities in addition to their government-issued ID documents. Unfortunately, in most, digital identities are voluntary. As a result, uptake rates are low - typically 20-25% of the EU population possesses a digital identity. This in turn means there is no incentive for either government agencies or the private sector to invest in developing digital services. If 25% of citizens possess a digital identity, then 75% don't and that proportion of the population therefore will continue to demand and require analogue services and staff to process their paper applications and needs. The private sector, too, will opt not to undertake the investments required to offer digital services when a cost/benefit analysis shows minimal savings.

This is a catch-22. Without enough users there is no incentive to develop services; without services there is no incentive for citizens voluntarily to procure digital identities. This is one step where the government needs the political courage and will to make digital identities part of any mandatory ID, either an ID document as in Europe, or the driving licence in countries such as the United States.

ARCHITECTURE

A secure digital identity, however, is only the first step. The second crucial aspect of any digital governance system is the architecture. Secure communication is too unwieldy and expensive for every government agency to implement on its own. Ministries and agencies need a single gateway that certifies the user's identity, and then allows him or her to access what it is that they need. This is not as easy as it perhaps sounds. How do you connect the various ministries and agencies with the citizen? Who should be permitted to see what? Which agency can see tax records? What should the police be able to see? What is completely public information? What is strictly private?

This is not a trivial problem; solving it means designing and connecting all the various public and private sector entities in a way that corresponds to the nation's laws. Indeed, this is the most time-consuming task: building your digital data access architecture and ensuring the data sought are in the proper digital form. It depends on the country's legal, regulatory and cultural constraints. Yes, the citizen must be allowed to see his or her own data (health care, tax and property records). But you also need to ensure that agencies can legally access the information they are entitled to and cannot access what they are not entitled to.

To achieve this, a country needs to keep logs of all access so regulatory agencies and the citizen can always check to see who has looked at someone's data. The key here is transparency for the citizen. It is based on the principle that I as a citizen can see who has accessed my data, which largely solves everyone's biggest fear: violation of privacy. I know who looks at my data. It is also necessary for the government to access data in order to police its own officials.

Ministries and agencies also need to digitalise their own records so that citizens and agencies can access them. Records that remain on paper represent data that people cannot access. This process of digitalising records takes time.

THE ONCE-ONLY RULE

Once data and records are digitalised, however, a government can implement an additional and crucial benefit of a well-designed architecture where access requires identification with a strong ID: the once-only rule. This regulation means that no citizen can be asked for personal data that already exists in the system. A database that depends on a unique identifier eliminates duplication of interaction with the government. The standard procedure in most countries where various public services constantly ask for one's address, phone number, date of birth etc, is eliminated. When I fill out my tax form, all relevant data is already there: my salary, my tax-deductible charitable donations, my dependent children. This is a fundamental source of citizen satisfaction with digital governance.

One final point on the architecture of data exchange: the architecture adopted by Estonia - an open-source, non-proprietary digital data-exchange platform called X-Road - has now been implemented in varying degrees by another 15 countries. Indeed today, Estonians and Finns can collect their medical prescriptions in any pharmacy in either country. This, I believe is the way of the future: connecting services across borders and doing so on a highly secure interoperable platform. This would begin to take public services to the level of the private sector.

The particular architecture used, however, is not important. Since the creation of X-Road almost 20 years ago, a number of other systems have been devised. All governments need to decide which is best for them, although open-source, non-proprietary software offers far more flexibility and at a lower cost. What is important is that connections between agencies and citizens follow the laws and regulations of the country, exactly as traditional paper-based bureaucracies should.

PRIVACY AND DATA INTEGRITY

Probably the greatest concern raised by people when discussing e-governance is the question of privacy. Generally, I answer by saying that, given the mutual and reciprocal transparency of the Estonian system, where I can see who has looked at my data, I feel more secure about my privacy with a digital system than with a paper system. Why? Because with a paper system there are few if any records of who has accessed them.

Consider the case of the Formula One racing car driver Michael Schumacher, one of the best-known public figures in Europe, who suffered serious brain damage in a horrific ski accident in 2013. Within hours of the accident the "yellow press" was full of pictures of his x-rays and medical records. It was impossible to trace where these came from because the records were paper not digital. In a properly digitalised system, this wouldn't have happened because access to digital records is restricted to authorised doctors via their ID, and each person who accesses a record is logged.

Privacy, in other words, relies on transparency and the understanding that all access is traceable. It is the same with records that are already made available to the public; if all access to them is logged then transparency is reciprocal. In Estonia, for example, where property ownership records are public, anyone can look at what property I own. Indeed, when I was in government, journalists frequently peered at my property records, perhaps in the hope of finding a scoop. I, however, also knew who was curious enough to look.

People's emphasis on, if not fears about, privacy in digital governance, however, misses a far more serious issue that accompanies digitalisation: data integrity. This is the third pillar of trust and security in public services. Privacy is the principle that no one without your permission can see your data; data integrity means that no one without your permission can change it. Too little attention is paid to this crucial difference. Yes, privacy is important, and you would be right to be concerned if someone accessed your health-care records or your bank account. What, though, if someone changed your health-care record? What if your blood type, for example, were changed, or the amount of money in your bank account? We should all be far more concerned about data integrity than we are.

This does not simply apply to personal data. It also applies, for example, to laws and court cases, which in Estonia exist only in digital form. Imagine if someone changes a law or the particulars of a court case. How would anyone know if it has been changed? Since 2008, Estonia has put all critical data on a private or permissioned, distributed ledger, or private blockchain as it is commonly known. The population register, health, property, court, tax and pension records are all secured too. This is a vital step. Attention to data integrity is integral to digitalisation, in case systems are breached.

DIGITALISATION CHANGES 5,000 YEARS OF GOVERNANCE

The key to understanding how digitalisation represents a dramatic change in governance lies in the nature of the "state". The development of the state occurred 5,000 years ago when China, Mesopotamia and Egypt emerged in parallel with writing and record keeping. Indeed, we can posit it was record keeping, necessary for management of the proto state, that led to the development of writing. Proto governments needed to collect taxes, needed to know how much grain was grown, how many men were available for military service and so on. All functioning states needed to keep records. Writing as literature, be it the Epic of Gilgamesh or the Analects of Confucius, came later.

To understand the magnitude of the potential revolution digitalisation offers we need to understand how governance, or, in other words, the management of the state - which in this case could be a city, a province, or a parish - has always been a serial process. All documents, records, statistics and orders have always been processed sequentially, or one step at a time.

Consider what parents have to go through when a child is born. First, one has to obtain a paper birth certificate. To do this you may have to provide a marriage certificate. Once you have the birth certificate, you can apply for health insurance. In many countries you need to register the new-born as a resident; you need to register with a doctor. You may need to apply to social services for paid parental leave. The necessary approvals are processed in serial fashion, but not by the government. Rather, you have to do it yourself.

However, in a digitalised society, all the serial steps are processed in parallel. Each agency, department or sub-department receives the information at the same time and does whatever needs to be done. The birth of a child is registered digitally by the hospital; all the parent has to do it tell the hospital the name of the child. From there, the state issues a birth certificate, registers the child's place of residence, offers a doctor, all relevant social and health services are automatically put in place and the parents indicate whether the mother or father will take family leave. It all happens instantaneously. The relevant data for the parents is already in the relevant registries and the computer merely makes a binary decision as to whether the parent or child is eligible for one or another service.

Parallel processing is the key to understanding why digitalisation of governance dramatically increases efficiency and reduces time wasted on bureaucratic, human-mediated, sequentially performed administration. This is where the time saving comes from - by dramatically reducing the work needed to run governance and, more importantly, the time and labour required by citizens. This is probably the most important lesson for governments and their leaders to take on board because it will change governance forever.

MY LEADERSHIP JOURNEY

So far, I have discussed what is required for digitalisation of governance in terms of technology and architecture but there is, of course, another vital ingredient: leadership. My leadership style is very open. I have an idea and I try to get people to follow me, rather than impose my will on them. I allow people to argue with and challenge me and the people who are under me know they can yell at me if they need to; I have found that through candid discussions you get better results.

My first experience of leadership was in 1988, when I was working in Munich as a journalist for Radio Free Europe as head of the Estonian desk. One of the lessons I learnt early on is that when people talk to you and reason things through, you end up doing them. But when people order you to do something, you do the bare minimum. It's not that you want to subvert the process, but if you don't believe in it, you're not going to do it well.

So, my approach for 30 years was to meet frequently, talk things through, make proposals and have robust discussions. Since much of what I was proposing involved fairly radical departures from the way things had been done in the past, it was important to get people on board.

Estonians are usually passive or reticent in relations with managers; it's not common for them to raise their voices. So, the times when that happens stand out. It's not that my meetings were usually confrontational, but on certain occasions there were some people who went ballistic. I didn't mind though, because you want your people to be involved, and you don't accomplish that by ordering them to do things. You want them to feel like they are part of what you are trying to achieve and not simply fulfilling something they don't understand or don't believe in. You also need to be willing to change your mind and your ideas if people offer a better solution.

Estonian culture is naturally a little dubious of authority, which is a healthy way to be. People may do what they are told to, but that's not the best route to success. I knew that running the government would be a team effort, so I had to build the team. As the leader, you're not going to do it alone. There will be a lot of people working with you and you want to stimulate independent thinking on their part. As the leader you cannot figure it all out. If you encounter a problem, then maybe you have to change course a little bit.

I see too many people in leadership positions who argue by fiat; they just say, "I'm the boss therefore that's how it is." Maybe that works for a private company. But as we see from numerous examples in contemporary politics, a leader that simply stamps their authority results in policies that are not well thought out. (We've seen that with certain leaders during the covid-19 crisis.)

Being open to challenge shouldn't be confused with being overly cautious though. The policies I've been involved with have been quite radical. When I was ambassador to the United States, for example, Estonian foreign policy was focused on joining NATO, and membership of the EU was an afterthought. But I was convinced that this was the wrong way around. As long as Estonia was not in the EU, the EU members who opposed our NATO membership would veto us. Once we were in the EU, however, they could not veto another EU member.

The top tiers of leadership of the foreign ministry were resolutely opposed to my argument. But, when I became foreign minister, I opened up the discussion and asked: what are the advantages? What are the disadvantages? What should we do? People argued very strongly but eventually came around to my way of thinking. You need to have that robust debate. If you have sullen, angry people who have been overridden, you will get only a half-hearted commitment.

Estonians voted to join the EU in 2003 and we joined both the EU and NATO in 2004.

My personality is such that I'm not dictatorial. On the one hand, I try to be cooperative, but on the other hand, I am someone who is constantly coming up with radical ideas. That can also be challenging. Today, no one questions the importance of being digital, yet in the early 1990s when I was first talking about it, many people treated the idea as completely insane. However, I had this vision of the future; I was convinced it was the way to go and that we should go early.

The thing with vision is that if it works out, you are a great leader, and if it doesn't then people question your leadership. Living in Silicon Valley I can draw some comparisons with the 95% of startups that fail. The entrepreneurial leader comes up with a visionary idea, but if it doesn't go anywhere then the vision is just a mirage. In politics, too, visions can lead to dead ends.

Shifting Estonia's foreign policy to prioritise joining the EU involved far more people in government than were initially involved in the digitalisation process. Persuading 500 people inside a ministry is hard. To get what you want, you have to be willing to revise your position, or at least the details, for the sake of the bigger goal. If something doesn't work, it doesn't work, and you need to try doing it differently. It's always a collaborative effort.

With the change in Estonia's EU policy and an upcoming referendum, there was a lot of painstaking explaining to do through the media. Likewise, the process of digitalisation was slow going. Setbacks occurred - mostly technology glitches - which affected public attitude. The big glitch I remember was with digital prescriptions in 2007 to 2008. They were rolled out but there were problems. This led to some hostile press and ultimately the minister of social affairs, who was responsible for the roll out, resigned. But once the problems had been solved the service became very popular and we very quickly reached a point where 99% of prescriptions in Estonia were digital. So, although there was a failure at the implementation stage, the setback was overcome simply through the popularity of the service.

It helped that I was familiar with technology. I had grown up programming computers, so I had a deeper knowledge than other politicians might have had. There's a famous essay by C.P. Snow written in 1959 about his experience at Cambridge University. He was a physical chemist and therefore he could talk to the other scientists about quantum mechanics. But he was also a literary novelist (in fact he coined the term "the corridors of power"). It meant that he was familiar with the worlds of both arts and science so, after having dinner at his college with the scientists, he would go over and sit with the literary people on the humanities table. His point was that he was the only one who could walk back and forth between the two tables. The scientists weren't interested in the humanities, and the literary crowd didn't have the background to converse with the scientists.

I was the C.P. Snow character moving between the technology table and the politics table. I could sit with the geeks and understand what they were talking about because I understood the fundamentals of digital technology. Then I could go and talk to the politicians. You also need to be able to explain to the tech people that unless they could guarantee for example, absolute privacy, their idea was a no-go. The inability to move comfortably and credibly between these two worlds is a big problem in politics, especially in democratic societies. We saw that when Mark Zuckerberg was called before the United States Senate Finance Committee and the committee chairman didn't understand how Facebook was making its money.

RECOMMENDATIONS FOR LEADING TRANSFORMATION

Based on my own experience, my recommendations for leading a nation undergoing a transformation (or a crisis for that matter) would be:

1. **Offer a vision of a better future**

   The leaders I admire most are visionary leaders. A vision is the starting point for uniting people on a shared journey. In the case of President Franklin Roosevelt for example, it was clear that the economic model in America during the Great Depression of the 1930s was not working, so he offered an alternative vision. Similarly, it wasn't enough in Estonia to merely digitise governance by replacing paper records with PDFs; we had to offer citizens a vision of a better functioning government.

2. **Bring people together**

   A strong vision also helps to create a language of unified identity. Great leaders offer messages of hope and togetherness. Roosevelt used the radio, which was the new technology of the day, to communicate with the American people with his famous fireside chats. It's hard to do that without a vision and a broad appeal. During the covid-19 crisis some leaders had no alternative vision to offer. Boris Johnson and Donald Trump, for example, operate in highly polarised environments - of their own making. That means that half the population does not consider them to be a legitimate leader. So, in a crisis they have to worry about their voter base, the ones who do see them as legitimate. They revert to trying to get their supporters on board, which means the decision-making isn't about what's best for the country, but what are my voters thinking?

3. **Take the public pulse**
   Leaders also need to exercise judgment and get their timing right. You can be a little ahead of the mass of the population, as I was with the digitalisation in Estonia, but you need enough people with you to create momentum for change. Being too far out of step with public sentiment is dangerous. With the coronavirus, for example, Trump didn't gauge public opinion sufficiently well and made some bad decisions. People were frightened to go back to work and chose to take the repercussions, rather than risk dying.

4. **Listen to expert opinion**
   As well as taking the public pulse, good leaders are erudite enough to see the big picture and also to recognise when they need experts. (Populists typically dismiss experts.) I'm reading a book called *The Fate of Rome: Climate, Disease, and the End of an Empire* by the historian Kyle Harper. His thesis is that the fall of Rome was not down to bad leadership or politics but due to climate change. The Roman optimal climate, which allowed the Romans to prosper, in turn also enabled disease: smallpox and, later on, bubonic plague. These diseases decimated the population of urban centres and undermined the Roman Empire.

   Of course, the Roman leaders did not have the advantage of science. They had no clue what was going on. People were dying and they were dying very quickly. The bubonic plague was interpreted as the wrath of God. Even good leadership would have stood no chance.

   To transfer that experience over to the modern day, you can see that the countries that understood how the coronavirus was proceeding made the right decisions. Others had the science but decided to ignore it.

5. **Stay agile**
   A crisis like covid-19 or even a cyber-attack comes out of nowhere. The business of governance is usually a slow process but, in a crisis, you have to act fast. Clearly, authoritarian regimes are better at this. But the other side of authoritarian regimes is that they can manipulate statistics and falsify numbers, so it's hard to judge them.

With coronavirus, some countries, like Italy and Spain, were taken by surprise, because it came so quickly. Their health systems were overwhelmed. Other countries, especially in northern Europe, which had not been hit yet, managed to take action earlier.

Yet, in other democracies the leaders dithered. In the United Kingdom, Boris Johnson's government initially pursued a herd-immunity strategy but reversed that decision when they realised how many people would die. The United States was slow to confront the reality of the pandemic. The *New York Times* reported that epidemiologists and statisticians at Columbia University had calculated that if the government had started the lockdown a week earlier some 36,000 lives would have been saved.[11, 12]

The point is that small differences in timing can make a big difference. And you can act quickly in a democracy, as Jacinda Ardern proved in New Zealand.

6. **Don't wait for perfect information**
   This point connects to the previous one. The problem with being a leader is that you have to make crucial decisions with far less than the optimal amount of information. Henry Kissinger said that leaders are locked in an endless battle in which the urgent impinges on the important, so public life becomes a continual struggle to make decisions in the face of insufficient information and changing circumstances.

   It's easy to go back and criticise someone for making the wrong decision when it turns out that they did not have enough data. But as a leader you will always have to make decisions without all the information. If a disaster is looming, you have to act.

   During the cyber-attack on Estonia we made the decision to close off the country. In retrospect, that enabled us to reboot everything inside the country. It was a tough decision and we didn't have enough information to be absolutely sure this was the right course. But we had to do something – and fast. Since the attacks were coming from external sources, we closed down anything that wasn't from an Estonian web domain. It worked. But we couldn't be sure at the time that it would.

7. **Favour slow thinking over gut instinct**
   The next point may appear to contradict the previous one, but leadership is, after all, paradoxical. Daniel Kahneman's book about fast and slow thinking is a warning that leaders should be wary of listening too much to their instinct.[13] I try to use slow

thinking as much as possible because I know I can get into trouble with fast thinking. That's why you have advisers and why you listen to them. Their job is to think things through and use their slow-thinking capacities. Your job as leader is to weigh the options. This brings me to my final leadership recommendation.

8. **Create an environment where you can be told you are wrong**
   Good leaders surround themselves with people who can tell them if they are making a mistake. The best leaders seek out people who are smarter than they are or have different skills or knowledge. It's about the culture you cultivate and allowing people to speak up. If you surround yourself with sycophants and toadies who simply agree with you, you will make some bad mistakes.

CONCLUSION

What can be learned from all of the above? Here are my five takeaways.

1. Digitalisation of governance will work if it has the support of the public. Not all of the public will necessarily come on board, but it is important to have the support of key actors in the private sector and among segments of the population such as the youth and the technical elite - engineers, scientists and academics. Banks are a natural ally, for two reasons: digitalisation led by the government makes transactions more secure than the methods banks alone could use and, equally importantly, it allows banks to cut both labour and rental costs. Indeed, the banking sector is and will be the one part of the private sector for which digitalisation offers the greatest advantages in security as well as savings.

   The support of the younger population helps with mobilising society and it is always good to harness their energy and willingness to modernise and try new things. All elements of society, from academics and the technical elite to the private sector and the nation's youth, were instrumental in building popular support for digitalisation in Estonia.

   Governments need to make digitalisation a public priority. They succeed when digital transformation is a stated policy goal, led and articulated as a priority from the top. Because digitalisation is an all-government process, all ministers and senior officials need to be on board to make it work. Too many countries fail at digitalisation because they push the task on to one entity, appointing a "digital minister". This almost guarantees failure as other ministers will ignore what the digital minister says, hampering efforts to digitalise their own ministries by blaming slow progress on the digital minister ("not my problem"). The only way to avoid this is for the *primus inter pares* in the government to be at the head of the process, at least politically. Practically and technically, the head of state or government should be the political driver, while an appointed expert project director manages the process.

2. Digitalisation succeeds when governments quickly offer public services that the population likes, such as easy tax filing, digital prescriptions and anything that simplifies interactions with bureaucracy (registering births, securing health insurance, registering a car, or renewing driving licences). Simply digitalising government so that ministries themselves are more efficient but without offering better services to the public has little public appeal. One way to determine what will be most popular is to look at which government offices have lots of citizens waiting for something, or where the backlog for processing citizens' applications is long.

3. Digitalisation stalls when there is a lack of political will on the part of the government. Governments fear to take the initial steps that may not be popular and so demur. For example, many governments in Europe and in the United States were, or are, afraid of issuing mandatory secure digital IDs. Since this is a *sine qua non* for any kind of secure form of digital governance, this simply means that digitalisation will fail. A second failure is the inability to communicate adequately to assuage irrational fears, such as loss of privacy and "Big Brother" surveillance, and explain that, if digitalisation is implemented the right way, these fears are groundless.

4. This is where political courage and leadership come in. Changing the way people do things is always difficult. Political leaders may feel unsure of themselves and don't want to take steps they fear will be unpopular. Civil servants used to one way of doing things will be reluctant to change, and citizens will not necessarily understand what the new policies mean.

   For this, the political "leadership" of a country needs to show genuine leadership, explaining what digitalisation means, how it works and what it will do for people. This also means leaders should at least have an understanding of the basic aspects of what is entailed, and if called upon explain why the steps are being taken.
   None of this will be easy. I personally was lambasted for Estonia's digitalisation plans for almost ten years, beginning with when I started promoting computerisation in schools. Generally, the criticism was from the political opposition. A decade later, however, all of the changes enacted in Estonia had come to be considered "normal"

and, as is inevitable, the initial arguments against digitalisation were quickly forgotten. It is a fact of political life that the transformational leader often puts in the hard yards only for the next steward to take the credit. Two decades after proposing school digitalisation, Estonia was celebrated as "the world's first Digital Republic".

5. Finally, digitalisation will happen around the world. The covid-19 crisis and the need to reduce physical contact and crowding in government offices is already pushing digitalisation faster than before. Governments that move quickly will be ahead of those that stall and drag their feet. Those countries that act now will also be better ready to deal with new challenges that will inevitably arise, digitalised or not.

RWANDA

In the last 20 years, Rwanda, a small landlocked nation situated in the heart of Africa, has emerged as the continent's unexpected success story. From being a nation devastated by one of the worst cases of genocide and ethnic violence in modern history, Rwanda has undergone a remarkable transformation into growth and economic prosperity.

In 1994, a plane carrying the Hutu president, Juvénal Habyarimana, and the Hutu president of neighbouring Burundi, Cyprien Ntaryamira, was shot down as it came into land at Kigali airport.[14] The assassination sparked mass genocide. Bands of Hutu militia set out to eliminate the minority Tutsi group and over the course of 100 days, around 800,000 Tutsi and moderate Hutus were slaughtered. Revenge killings led to the deaths of a further 100,000 Hutus.

The violence was halted by the arrival of the Rwandan Patriotic Front (RPF), a Tutsi rebel group backed by the army of Uganda and led by Paul Kagame, Rwanda's current president. The RPF defeated the militia groups and drove the Hutu assailants out of the country, thereby allowing exiled Tutsis to return. Paul Kagame was sworn in as the vice-president. He became president in 2000.

Although the massacre had been successfully quelled, there was still a risk of a second wave of violence, motivated either by revenge killings initiated by the Tutsis, or Hutus aiming to eliminate the remaining Tutsis. It was of vital importance for the new government, therefore, to create social harmony and national unity. Hutus and Tutsis were encouraged to come together with one purpose – to rebuild the nation.

The genocide left Rwanda one of the poorest and sickest countries in the world. Life expectancy had dropped from 55 to 27 years and the under-five mortality rate was higher than anywhere else in the developing world. Moreover, the country's health infrastructure lay in shambles. Most health workers had been killed or had fled. Widespread rape resulted in the rapid dissemination of HIV and a massive cholera epidemic swept refugee camps. Vaccination for polio and measles was abysmally low.

Economically, the country stood pretty much at stage zero. The violence had decimated Rwanda's economic base, which had already been fragile from extended drought, declining world prices of coffee and tea, and fiscal constraints imposed by international financial institutions.

Since the late 1990s, however, Rwanda has made significant progress and economic and social outcomes have improved dramatically. By 2011, Rwanda had reached an economic growth rate of 8.2% and has since been lauded as the model African nation for economic development. Poverty declined from 59% in 2001 to 39% in 2019. Foreign direct investment has increased from US$2.5 million to US$1 billion. In the last two decades, Rwanda has undergone rapid economic expansion and structural transformation. Rwanda's economy is predominantly agrarian. In 2010, agriculture contributed about 80% of economic activity. Through a wide range of development and economic restructuring programmes, however, including the elimination of trade barriers, the industrial and services sectors have been on the rise. Manufacturing is still relatively small but growing steadily, at an annual rate of 7% as of 2019.

Human development indicators have also improved dramatically. By 2018, vaccination coverage stood at 97% and ante and post-natal health care was widely available. Between 2000 and 2013, maternal mortality ratios decreased by 77%. In 2018, 97% of Rwandan children attended primary school – the highest rate in Africa - and the country is listed among the top three in the world for improved access to education.

In terms of infrastructure, considerable progress has been recorded in energy, transport, water and sanitation. Some 52.8% of Rwandan households now have access to electricity. In addition, water systems have been improved through public-private partnerships. The road network has been expanded significantly and Kigali International Airport modernised. The construction of a new airport in Bugesera began in 2018. According to the 2019 World Bank's Ease of Doing Business index of the world's most business-friendly economies, Rwanda ranks 29th out of 190. It is the best performing African country over the last 10 years.

Rwanda has also made great strides towards women's empowerment and gender equality. According to the World Economic Forum statistics for 2019, 95% of girls attend school, compared to 92% of boys. Female participation in the labour force stands at 84% - one of the highest in the world. Moreover, Rwanda has the highest number of women in politics anywhere as more than half the members of Parliament in the country's lower house are female.[15]

Political stability has contributed significantly to Rwanda's rapid growth. Consistency of vision, continuity of reform policies and implementation efforts have enabled a conflict-ridden population to heal, move forward and work together, putting aside the ethnic rivalries that fuelled conflicts in the past. In the 2019 Global Peace Index, Rwanda had the fifth largest improvement in peace and moved up 24 places in the rankings.[16]

Crucially, Rwanda has sought to craft a forward-looking narrative and foster a growth culture that instils respect for individuals, creating a foundation for cooperation. The government has successfully established a shared vision for the nation amongst business and citizens alike. Independent problem solving and teamwork has been encouraged to streamline implementation of new ideas. While Kagame is the head of the government, his entire team is involved in refining the vision and developing reform plans.

To achieve the shared vision of stability, self-reliance and prosperity, people have been empowered at all levels (organisational, regional and sectoral) to ensure that institutions are sustainable and dynamic and maintain momentum to drive the country forward.

The Nordic Economic Miracle

"There are no shortcuts to anywhere worth going."

Finnish proverb

Alexander Stubb
Prime Minister of Finland, 2014 to 2015

2

In the second half of the 20th century, Finland underwent a rapid transformation from an agricultural to a knowledge-based economy. It led the way in mobile communications and today remains a centre of technological and entrepreneurial excellence.

From relative economic obscurity in the 1970s, Finland now features consistently high in the annual WEF Global Competitive Index[17a], is rated one of the top three least corrupt nations by Transparency International[17b], sits in the top 10 of the 2018 Environmental Performance Index[17c] and ranked number one in the United Nation's World Happiness Report[17d] in both 2018 and 2019.

In this chapter, I will share my insights on how Finland has bounced back from a series of major disruptions it has faced in its recent history.

FINLAND'S THREE TRANSFORMATIONS

There's a Finnish word *sisu*, which means perseverance and grit, and never giving up. *Sisu* is at the heart of the Finnish transformation.

On December 6th 1917, Finland gained full independence from Russia, and since the end of the second world war has navigated its way through an unprecedented period of societal change; a remarkable journey that can be divided into three distinct phases or transformations.

1945 – 1989. In the first phase, amidst the ruins of war, Finland needed to rebuild structurally, economically and sociologically. It also needed to avoid any unwelcome incursion from its aggressive neighbour, the Soviet Union.

1989 – 2008. When the Berlin Wall fell in 1989, signalling the end of the cold war, Finland seized the opportunity to focus on a major economic transformation that, within less than 20 years, saw GDP per capita increase from half that of Sweden's to equal levels.

2008 – present: In 2008, when the global economy plunged into financial crisis, the Finnish economy suffered along with the rest of the world. But the challenges of the banking crisis also provided the impetus to introduce much-needed reforms - a phase of transformation that continues to this day.

THE FIRST TRANSFORMATION: 1945–1989

It is tempting to look back at the Finnish experience and assume that transformation was always going to succeed. But the outcome could easily have been very different. Situated in the far north of Europe, Finland lies between Scandinavia and Russia and has strong historical links with both, having been ruled by one or the other from the 13th century until gaining independence in 1917. In the latter half of the 20th century, with the cold war tensions escalating between East and West, Finland had to make some very strategic choices about the path it would take.

At the end of the second world war in 1945, Finland was, to all intents and purposes, a very poor country. A 1300-kilometre border with the Soviet Union's authoritative communist regime meant that the nation had to find a balance as a buffer between East and West. It had to walk a tightrope between its natural inclination to open up to the democratic West and the need to placate an aggressive eastern neighbour. The Finns made a strategic decision to hunker down and concentrate on rebuilding their war-torn country. In the years that followed they remained neutral and, in somewhat isolation, diligently applied their reserves of *sisu* to the hard work and sacrifices of reconstruction and the creation of a welfare state.

THE SECOND TRANSFORMATION: 1989–2008

In 1989, with the Soviet Union imploding, it was decision time once more; times had changed. The political map of Europe was shifting. Finland lost almost 20% of its trade with the Soviet Union. Should it now integrate into western institutions and become more international, or try to hold its own independently?

In hindsight the choice might seem obvious: why would a relatively poor country not want to open up to trade and treaties with the big economies of western Europe? But not everyone in Finland agreed. There were some still in fear of turning their back on their influential eastern neighbour. Ingrained positions can be slow to shift and traditional mindsets hard to influence.

Fortunately, the Finns chose to look west and it was this decision - along with joining the European Union and pouring heavy investments into education – that set the nation on the path to success. A country that had been a backwater of Europe throughout the 1970s and most of the 1980s rapidly transformed itself into what became known as the Nordic Miracle.

THE NOKIA EFFECT

Integral to the economic success of Finland post-1989 was the emergence of the Finnish firm Nokia as the world's preeminent mobile phone company. By the start of the 21st century, Nokia and Finland had become synonymous with mobile technology expertise.

The Nokia story mirrored the Finnish economic miracle. With a history dating back to 1865, the company had transformed from a forestry and rubber boots business in the 1970s into the global leader for mobile handsets, overtaking Motorola in 1998 to become the best-selling mobile phone brand in the world.

In 2003, Nokia introduced the first camera phone. By the fourth quarter of 2007, the company enjoyed a market share in mobile phones of 50.9%, and its mobile operating system Symbian commanded a market share of 62.5%. Microsoft's Windows held just 11.9%.

However, 2007 also saw the launch of the new Apple iPhone.

In 2008, the financial crisis bit hard and Finland, like other economies, felt its teeth. The recession that followed was compounded by the faltering fortunes at Nokia. The mobile phone giant that had been Europe's most successful and highly respected technology company saw its market dominance undermined by the arrival of smart phones. In a double whammy, while the iPhone impacted Finnish telecoms, the arrival of the iPad two years later also hit Finland's paper industry - Nokia's original core business. Over the next five years, Nokia's market share fell to just 3.1% and in 2014, the company sold its mobile and devices division to Microsoft. This marked a low point in Finland's recent history.

Since then, Nokia has rediscovered its ***sisu****, reinventing itself as network hardware and software provider and positioning itself as a leader in the transition to 5G wireless technologies. The resurgence of Nokia has also spawned a slew of startups in the gaming industry and elsewhere. Moreover, in 2016, the company re-entered the mobile phone business with a licensing agreement that allows it to sell phones again under the Nokia brand.*

THE THIRD TRANSFORMATION: 2008–PRESENT

The 2008 financial crisis and its fallout provided the trigger for Finland to re-evaluate and transform itself once again. It was the third big transformation in less than 70 years, a single generation. This time, with the economy hit hard by the global crisis, the transformation was about long overdue structural reforms in the financial system, the labour market, local government, health care and pensions.

Finland took the decision to go "full Keynesian". Increasing the nation's levels of debt to keep the economy moving funded big infrastructure projects, such as roads, metros, railways and airports.

In contrast with the transformation of 1945 to 1989, when there was very much a feeling that individuals were contributing for the good of the country, in 2008 it was more about citizens demanding from the state, in a classic reversal of the famous Kennedy question: ask not what you can do for your country, ask what your country can do for you.

But the necessary reforms required in the various systems (financial, legal, health care) proved excruciatingly slow to identify, execute and take effect; by June 2014, the Finnish unemployment rate had reached 8.7% and was still rising.

It was at precisely this point that I became prime minister of Finland.

MY JOURNEY THROUGH POLITICS

My career in politics began in 2004 when I was elected to the European Parliament as a member of Finland's National Coalition Party. In 2008, I was appointed minister for foreign affairs, just as the financial crisis hit. In 2011, I stood for election to the Finnish parliament for the first time and was elected with the second highest vote count. Subsequently, I was appointed minister for Europe and foreign trade. When Prime Minister Katainen stood down, I became chairman of the National Coalition Party and was appointed as prime minister on June 24th, 2014.

I sometimes joke that everything started to go to wrong when I became foreign minister in April 2008. The war in Georgia in August 2008 was followed by the Lehman Brothers' crash. The Finnish economy, along with the rest of the world, was plunged into financial crisis. That crisis turned into a structural crisis, which turned into a euro crisis. That was followed by the asylum crisis and the rise of popularism. I left politics in 2016, just as employment started to improve and the Finnish economy started growing again.

They say it's good to live in interesting times, and my period in politics was certainly one of those. I learned a lot about transformations and leadership.

THE TRIGGERS FOR TRANSFORMATION

Transformations have a trigger. And these triggers are usually quite dramatic. They have to be in order to galvanise people into action. You don't start a transformation unless there is a crisis or an urgent need; there is no appetite for reform during the good times. In the EU there was no push to reform the euro, or asylum policy, until the euro and asylum crises hit. As people, we usually only change when we are forced to: a sudden diagnosis of a health condition, for example, triggers a change in lifestyle. It is that moment of realisation or diagnosis that triggers the change. Nations are no different.

In Finland's case its three periods of national transformation were each triggered by different circumstances. In 1945, the country lay in ruins after the war and was in desperate need of reconstruction. In 1989, the end of the cold war and the collapse of the Soviet Union created the need for new trading partners. In 2008, the trigger was the banking crisis.

EXAMPLES OF TRANSFORMATION DURING MY TIME IN OFFICE

Some of the biggest transformations that I was involved with in government were during my spells in the Ministry for Foreign Affairs and as Europe and trade minister.

These transformations were about opening up the administration and diplomatic services. My argument was that we were a public service and needed to be more transparent and proactive. Going forward, I argued, it wasn't going to be enough just to write reports to each other and our political masters. So, I forced people out of their civil service bunkers to give interviews, or to go on Twitter or Facebook, to be accountable and to be the diplomats of public service.

I also oversaw a generation shift in nominating ambassadors. This wasn't very popular in some circles where people were still wedded to the old, hierarchical, age-based system. But again, it was important to be seen to be open in how we nominated and selected public servants.

BRAND FINLAND: A TEAM EFFORT

Another important step during my years in government was to commission a report on what Finland stands for as a brand and create what we called "Team Finland".

The strategy for Team Finland followed the same logic about being transparent and proactive: that it was not enough anymore for a trade ministry to deal only with trade agreements, IPOs, intellectual property and the like. We had to do more to promote Finland to the rest of the world as a brand and an idea. All of our embassies around the world needed to be active in trade promotion. In the beginning, this type of change was met with reluctance – people are naturally fearful of change - but with the right information, the right communication and the right strategy in place, new roles and functions can be adopted and accepted.

To create the "brand" of Brand Finland, we used a competitive identity consultant called Simon Anholt. But I knew the project had to be properly inclusive and really embrace civil society, so we also brought in people from business, NGOs, labour unions, industrialists and academics to form a delegation.

The delegation was charged with the task of thinking and exploring ways to make Finland more visible, more relevant and more valued on the global stage.

This culminated in the publication of a 365-page report entitled Mission for Finland,[18] which concluded that Finland should promote itself as a global problem solver in a number of key areas where it has particular strengths. Examples include functionality - Finland offers the world functionality and sustainability in the form of both products and services, as well as a functional society; water – Finland offers the world clean water, clean food and related expertise; and education – Finland offers the world better education and teachers.

Team Finland is now an active network of organisations that offers support and services from research to funding, to help promote Finland and Finnish businesses at home and overseas.

OBSTACLES TO TRANSFORMATION – AND OPPORTUNITIES

Transformations come with challenges, as you can't get everyone to agree with change. Resistance can come from political parties, the private sector, public service or groups of citizens. And change can simply be very hard work.

In Finland the three transformations that started in 1945, 1989 and 2008 respectively all came with their own unique contexts and brought their own challenges and opportunities.

In the 1945 to 1989 period, the country was so badly affected by the war that there was no significant resistance to transformation. There was little choice but to re-build, restructure and forge a new way forward, however difficult. There was a shortage of resources, of course, and it was a hard grind, but the defeat of fascism had created an ideological willingness and drive to succeed.

In 1989, however, the country was more ideologically divided and binary. Simply put, there were sections of Finnish society who had always believed in communism and were distraught that the Soviet Union had just collapsed. Their old order had just crumbled, and they were not supporters of Finland opening up to internationalisation and the democratic capitalism of the West. There was a lot of tension between those who wanted Finland to join the European Union and those who were opposed. It was very much liberals versus the conservative left – and this created a resistance to change.

The third transformation, which was triggered in 2008, came with three big obstacles to change. Without a doubt the number one impediment to reform was the labour unions and the confederation of industries. The old corporate structure that was based on labour versus industry or management - rather than jobs versus growth or innovation - was a major obstacle. Typically, the people who are resistant to change are the ones who benefit from the current system and societal structures.

The second major impediment was, and still is, the nature of politics in Finland. We always have coalition governments, which force compromise and can stifle new legislation.

From 2007 to 2011, it was still fairly easy to push through reforms because there were only four parties and they were held together by an ideological glue: all four were centre right. But from 2011 to 2015, there were six parties in the coalition government - three from the left and three from the right - and that became a major problem. It's hard to get much done with that sort of ideological split.

The first two and a half years of the 2011-2015 government were simply about trying to build up trust between parties that naturally did not trust each other. And then once sufficient trust had been established for agreements to be made and reforms to be enacted, the chairman of the Social Democratic Party, who was the finance minister, lost a leadership challenge to a labour unionist, which put an end to the trust-building exercise and destroyed the collaboration that had been over two years in the making.

This is where I landed as prime minister. And I had just one year to try to reform the labour unions: a mission impossible. The only new legislation that we were able to push through at that time was pension reform.

The third hurdle to overcome in the post-2008 transformation was the stringent legal structure. We had and have a democratic system of governance, but there were a lot of legal experts who kept seeing problems in anything that we were trying to reform. Consequently, the planned changes for local municipalities and health care have been slow. There are reforms on the table in Finland that were started as long ago as 2003 and 2004 but have been delayed for years because of so-called constitutional objections.

I'm not saying that we should go against the rule of law or the constitution, of course, but the way the law is interpreted can be an impediment to change.

In summary, in Finland we had three things acting as the main obstacles to reform after the 2008 financial crisis: unions, politics and the legal system. The labour unions and industrialists protect their own interests. Coalition governments, which are often messy, might be geared towards compromise, but that compromise results in suboptimal solutions. And the legal system can be used to block change.

MY LEADERSHIP JOURNEY

As a leader, one of my greatest assets was that I was an outsider. I was considered to be apolitical. I didn't join a political party until 2004, five months before election for the European Parliament. My campaign drew on my expertise in European affairs - gained from my time as a researcher and adviser at the EU – and allowed me to focus entirely on issues, not on bashing other political parties. I was voted in with a landslide.

In many ways, I was a very modern and different politician. I said what I thought and was very open and frank. In Finland I was very unusual, too, because I smiled a lot – Finns are typically very dour! I was also very international; I spoke five languages and featured in a lot of international press. All of this meant that I very quickly became the darling of the Finnish media because I was able to tell a positive story about Finland to the rest of the world - in a concise and understandable way.

Success breeds success and my popularity continued when I became foreign minister, which happened very suddenly in 2008. I was called back to Finland from Brussels with just 24 hours' notice, after a scandal forced the resignation of my predecessor. It was very bold of the then finance minister, who later became the prime minister, to offer such a high-level role to me – a relative newcomer to Finnish politics.

In 2008, Finland held the chair of the Organisation for Security and Co-operation in Europe (OSCE) and as foreign minister one of my first important missions was to chair the peace negotiations in the Russo-Georgia conflict. This helped to raise Finland's profile and status with its European counterparts and gave the Finnish people a new sense of pride and dignity. I felt I had their support and encouragement.

Another chief mission of mine was to open up the Foreign Ministry and make this similarly more democratic and transparent. This proved to be a popular move and I quickly became the most popular politician in Finland. But when that happens you also make enemies among the political class, and some were just waiting for a chance to stab me in the back.

When you raise your head above the parapet you invite criticism. People ask:

- "Who is this guy who thinks that he's special?"
- "Who is this guy who is transparent in his leadership?"
- "Why does he give so much responsibility to other people?"
- "Why doesn't he stamp his authority on the situation?"
- "Why does he dress the way he does?"
- "Why does he smile so much?"

When I became prime minister in 2014, again I came in as a complete outsider, not as one of the party faithful. But I soon discovered that as the leader of the country everything changed. Being prime minister was not the same as being a member of the European Parliament, or minister of trade for European Affairs, or even foreign minister. That is when I should have realised that I needed to make some adjustments in the way I behaved. The role of prime minister needed to be taken absolutely seriously, especially as we were all faced with a global financial crisis, and I should have presented a more appropriate demeanour to the public. What had helped to create my popularity before was not going to help me on the next phase of my political life. I should have started behaving in a more prime ministerial way.

When I didn't, I left myself open to attacks from the media. Whether it was a casual tweet on some sports event, being seen playing with kids in an amusement park, or wearing shorts in the summer for a press conference, these behaviours became a diversion from the job I was doing. They had nothing to do with substance; they were all about image. But image is important for a leader.

I should have realised that I could not simply be myself anymore; I had to be more nuanced and strategic in how I presented myself in public. I still believe that you have to be genuine and you have to be yourself, but you have to modify and moderate that to the context. If you are a bit quirky, be quirky. If you are difficult, be difficult. If you're positive, be positive, but be yourself in a thoughtful and strategic way.

So, I needed to change, to transform my own behaviour and image as a leader. From the moment I was selected as prime minister I should have understood that such a position changes things. It's not about putting on a mask or pretending to be someone else, it's about adapting to the role and toning down some of your behaviour. It's about gravitas. You have to accept that with high office comes certain responsibility.

I fully understand and realise that I was pushing the limits of ministerial behaviour in my previous posts, and when I became prime minister, I should have toned it down. But it's difficult. We all have our own personalities and some of us don't like to take ourselves too seriously. I had a hard time adapting.

RECOMMENDATIONS FOR LEADING TRANSFORMATION

Based on my experience of leading a nation undergoing a transformation, here are seven key pieces of advice:

1. **Have a clear strategy and mission statement of what you aim to achieve**
   Under the mission statement you need a one-pager outlining the strategy for how you're going to achieve the mission. This is very important first step. It gives a very clear message to the civil service and the general population of what you want to do and how you're going to do it.

2. **Move quickly**
   Make most of your changes in the first 100 days. The sooner you get things done the better. Procrastination is not the way to bring about change. You just have to get on with it, take whatever criticism is thrown at you and keep driving forwards.

3. **Communicate at all levels**
   You must communicate what you are doing, and you need to do it at the lowest levels with the people who are the implementers - the people making the changes on a day-to-day basis - and you also need to communicate at the higher level - with the people you are working with - and with the general public.

   If you have a mission statement and a strategy that you start pushing through in the first 100 days, and you communicate effectively with all your stakeholders, then you are halfway there.

4. **Be transparent**
   I know this doesn't suit all governments, but I do believe that the more transparent you are the less gossip you have to contend with, and that makes it easier to push through changes. In a society as open as Finland, it is essential.

5. **Engage all actors across government, private and public sectors, media and citizens**
   When a government is meant to be transparent, you can't rely on traditional hierarchical power to get things done. You need to consult and discuss not only within government but also with the private sector, the civil service and, to a certain extent, with the media as well. You have to involve civil society - ordinary citizens - as well as government. I call this being transnational.

6. **Get the civil service on board**
   As a former civil servant myself, I know that without the proactive support of the civil service you will not be able to affect change. Civil servants know that politicians come and go and that you will be gone in a few years' time, so they may try to slow things down. If you can convince them that the transformation is necessary and in the best interests of the nation, they will be much more likely to push reforms through.

7. **Create an ideas lab to come up with out-of-the-box ideas**
   Bring in people who think differently; these are the ones who come up with crazy ideas and sometimes even offensive ideas, but they are completely detached from government ministers and civil servants. Put them next to the prime minister's office to provide an alternative perspective.

THE CHALLENGE AHEAD

A big shift is taking place in global politics. The rise of populism has seen traditional ideology-based politics being replaced by identity politics. The big ideologies that dictated the course of 20th century politics have become less relevant. Populist movements – Brexit, Trump - whether from the left or the right, are based on identity. And that identity is usually a one-issue identity, such as nationality, the nation state or the environment.

In his 2011 book, *Thinking, Fast and Slow*, Daniel Kahneman – winner of the Nobel Memorial Prize in Economic Sciences – outlines two ways of thinking. When we think fast, we are instinctive and emotional. When we think slow, we are more deliberate and more logical.

And I think that democracy is going through a transformation from slow thinking – contemplative, rational, taking time over decision-making – to an age which demands fast thinking, which leaves us exposed to error and prejudice.

In 1945, the West cheered the death of fascism. In 1989, we welcomed the end of communism. In 2008, we questioned the capitalist tenet of liberalism. And then in 2016, with Brexit and the election of Trump, you could argue that some people were starting to question democracy and its basic values. Post-2008, many democracies are less influenced by issues of ideology and much more by issues of identity; with the populist power behind Brexit and Trump it is identity rather than ideology driving change.

In 2010, the Mission for Finland Country Brand Report set out to address several global-level challenges, including how to:

- Find a sustainable way of life.
- Find ways to reduce poverty.
- Produce fewer disposable solutions and provide more robust problem solving.

These challenges remain and we need to be able to engage our slow thinking systems in order to come up with rational, long-term solutions. In Finland, we believe we can.

"Finland's greatest strength is the unbiased, solution-focused approach to problems, which derives from our history and culture. When faced with an impossible situation, we roll up our sleeves and double our efforts… By 2030, Finland will be the problem solver of the world."[19]

NEW ZEALAND

In the last 40 years, New Zealand's economy, once characterised by extensive interventionism and protectionism, has undergone a radical transformation. As a result, economic performance has improved dramatically, with the country going from being one of the most interventionist in the OECD to one of the most open and market based.

From the early white settlement of the 19th century right up until the mid-20th century, New Zealand's economy was based on natural resources. Even in the 1950s and 1960s - considered to be New Zealand's golden years - economic activity was centred around the production and processing of primary products. Wool was the main export and Britain was the main trading partner, thanks to New Zealand's former status as a British colony. This high dependence on primary products and very narrow export base meant that exporters had little control over pricing and were sensitive to developments in international commodity markets. In the late 1960s and 1970s, the global price of wool declined significantly, and this led to the beginning of a turbulent period for the nation's economy.

National income deteriorated and by 1979, GDP per capita in New Zealand had fallen to around 90% of the OECD average (down from 120% in 1966). Unemployment, current account deficits and inflation increased substantially. By 1984, the country was facing unsustainable fiscal and current account deficits (ranging as high as 40% of GDP), inflation of over 12%, foreign debt at 46% of GDP and a foreign exchange crisis.

In 1984, the newly elected Labour government designed a comprehensive series of reforms to turn the economy around. The aim was to move away from the inward looking and interventionist framework that had evolved during the previous half century. Subsidies and other support mechanisms for agriculture were withdrawn, financial markets rapidly liberalised, and an extensive privatisation programme kick-started.

Public sector reforms were also initiated. In 1984, government spending had reached 44% of GDP, investment capital was exiting in huge quantities, and government controls and micromanagement were pervasive at every level. Under the new programme, changes were put in place to facilitate better management of budgeting and accounting across government departments. Department heads were employed on five-year contracts, based on specific performance metrics and a strict departmental budget, and were given more authority and discretion to determine their own staff sizes and staff remuneration levels. Key sectors were privatised including telecommunications, airlines, irrigation schemes, computing services, government printing offices, railways and bus services. Fiscal control improved, government spending decreased and, by 1998, New Zealand was one of the few OECD countries running a genuine fiscal surplus.

In the social sector, the government focused on housing and health. Subsidised rent and homeowner loans for low-income households were replaced by supplements in the form of cash grants or vouchers. In health care, a "contract system" similar to that in the United Kingdom was put in place to pass more control to local authorities. Planning for health and disability support was regionalised with the creation of 21 new district health boards, which were comprised of locally elected members as well as appointed officials, all of whom were accountable to the minister of health.

These sweeping reforms had a dramatic effect on the budget position. Net government indebtedness declined sharply from more than 50% of GDP in 1991 to below 30% in 1997. Inflation decreased from 10–20% during the 1970s and early 1980s to 2% by 1997. The current account deficit also improved over this period.

Labour productivity increased strongly (especially in the agricultural sector) and overall employment levels improved. Quantitative import restrictions were eliminated completely, substantially reducing tariffs, and export subsidies were abolished, which improved taxation structures and freed up the financial system.

The reforms also laid the groundwork for long-term economic growth. New Zealand's GDP grew from US$46.3 billion in 1993 to US$182.5 billion in 2013, a four-fold increase. The unemployment rate peaked at about 11% in 1993 but had fallen to less than 4% by 2008, when the global financial crisis hit. The expansion of economic freedom and reduction in private sector regulations led to New Zealand consistently topping the World Bank's Ease of Doing Business ranking in the four years between 2016 and 2019.

Minority groups benefitted from the improvements in income distribution resulting from the strong performance of the labour market. Unemployment among the indigenous Maori and Pacific Islanders dropped by 10%. In 1995, Maori employment growth doubled that of the non-Maori population. In the early 2000s, noticing a widening gap between rich and poor, the government introduced measures to increase spending on health, education and public housing, with a focus on the Maori and Pacific Islander communities. Social indicators such as life expectancy and infant mortality rates continued to improve.

One of the critical factors behind the success of New Zealand's reforms was the speed in which they were devised and implemented. Roger Douglas – the finance minister from 1984 to 1988 - has been lauded as the main architect of the nation's turnaround. He clearly set out his economic objectives and quickly set about implementing the changes - in case he did not get elected for another parliamentary term (he did, in 1987, but resigned in 1988). New Zealand's unique economic restructuring - which set the nation on the path to becoming the world's 38th most globalised economy today - became known as "Rogernomics".

Building a Social Contract on Trust

"He who does not trust enough will not be trusted."

Lao Tzu

Lim Hwee Hua
Cabinet Minister, Singapore, 2009 to 2011

3

When Singapore gained independence in 1965 it was an impoverished nation with no natural resources, a housing crisis and massive unemployment. Since then, it has pulled off one of the greatest economic transformations of the last fifty years and become a major international transportation and financial hub. Today, Singapore's central business district is crowded with skyscrapers that rival neighbouring Hong Kong and mid-town Manhattan, attracting foreign investment that it supports with a clean and efficient bureaucracy and a strong regulatory and legal framework.[20]

Stable and prosperous, disciplined, industrious and smart; Singapore's development has been spectacular. In 1965, its nominal GDP per capita was around US$500 – the same level as Mexico and South Africa. In 1990, its GDP per capita had risen to around US$13,000, surpassing South Korea, Israel and Portugal. By 2015, it had reached US$56,000; Singapore had caught up with Germany and the United States,[21] and celebrated 50 years of independence with an economy that was almost 40 times larger than in 1965.[22]

In 2020, Singapore had the fourth highest GDP per capita of any nation;[23] ranked highest in the world in the World Bank Human Capital Development Index (2018);[24] was first in the World Economic Forum's Global Competitiveness Index (2019)[25] and topped the 2020 Index of Economic Freedom - making it the world's freest economy.[26]

In this chapter, I will share my insights on how Singapore reinvented itself after independence and continues to reinvent and renew itself.

The people of Singapore have been described as paranoid – and with good reason. Their unwillingness to take success for granted or rest on their laurels is integral to the country's remarkable economic transformation. Without the nation's healthy caution, the story could have been very different.

On all counts, Singapore should not have survived this long. A tiny cluster of islands between the Indian Ocean and the South China Sea, it has no hinterland to speak of and no meaningful domestic economy. Totalling just 724.2 square kilometres,[27] the country is also severely restricted in terms of space and its complete lack of natural resources.

However, Singapore is blessed on two fronts: its strategic geographical location at the crossroads of trade flows between East Asia and Europe and its resilient, hard-working population. Singaporeans have always risen to the challenge in the face of adversity as demonstrated first, following the withdrawal of the British, and then in Singapore's separation from Malaysia. The nation's founding father, Lee Kuan Yew, and its pioneering generation of leaders refused to accept the fate of an impossible nation.

Ironically, the country's difficult start formed a crucial genesis of shared history that anchors the social contract between the government and the people of Singapore to this day. The government and people have a common heartbeat and common cause, constantly thinking ahead about the challenges and agonising over how to address them. The way the country responds to crises, including the covid-19 pandemic, is a good illustration of the social contract, and something I will discuss later.

A lasting relationship between government and citizens has to be built on nothing less than trust, however. A social contract that endures the test of time for longer-term macro-economic policies and sustains the nation through crises is founded on the underlying shared values of meritocracy, prosperity through hard work and thrift and a collective responsibility for - and ownership of - the country's future and wellbeing of its people. To foster these values, the Singaporean government and citizens needed a shared vision, a plan they could work towards together.

VISIONARY LONG-TERM PLANNING

In the 1960s, the only naturally occurring economic activity in Singapore revolved around trading, thanks to its strategic location. Faced with this single attribute, the cabinet conceptualised a "hub strategy" for the newly independent nation, running the gamut of transportation, financial services and trading activities, to substantiate and entrench the local economy at a time when the country had no financial means or natural resources to speak of. Attracting foreign investments became a top priority. An Economic Development Board was established, with the sole aim of promoting investment and developing industry to create sustainable economic growth.

The aspirations of an open hub strategy demanded certain conditions upon which it could operate, in particular trust (integrity), efficiency and effectiveness. At that time, bar the occasional re-fuelling of ships, there was no compelling reason for the world to stop in Singapore. The government of the day adopted a multi-pronged approach, which included the formulation and enforcement of strict laws to rid the system of all traces of corruption; to inspire Singaporeans to be well educated and equipped to serve the world; and always to endeavour to do their very best.

Pinning your economic strategy on becoming a global hub comes with its innate challenges. The manifold benefits of being a transportation hub motivate many governments to aspire to be the major hub of their respective region. Any semblance of one hub leading all others will be met with fierce competition from neighbouring airports or seaports. Financial and business services were traditionally derivative activities of transportation hubs. However, over time, once they are established and critical mass achieved, financial hubs become an anchor unto themselves.

How does Singapore maintain its market position as both an open transportation hub and an international financial services centre? The answer is through hard work, painstaking long-term planning and commitment to the vision. This requires a huge amount of strategic forethought and pre-emptive innovation to ensure that the country is always able to offer the most innovative services at globally competitive rates.

Four elements are vital to the country's shared long-term plan:

1. **Developing talent within the public sector**
   From the outset, Singapore's government recognised that in order to plan and execute its strategy competently, priority should be given to the attraction and retention of local talent within the civil service. State scholarships overseas were identified as a powerful lever. Earlier generations of Singaporeans were fairly impoverished and appreciated the value of scholarships, especially for an education overseas. Today, even though many families are affluent enough to afford education, these awards are still sought after as a mark of accomplishment. They are seen as a badge of honour, with their recipients returning to Singapore to "serve out a bond", as we call it, and to give service within government.

   Over the past decade, Singapore's government has granted around a hundred scholarships per year for under-graduate and post-graduate education, across a wide range of subjects and countries.[28] Such a pipeline of talent ensures competent continuity in the formulation and execution of long-term macro-economic and social policies.

2. **Human capital equipped for purpose**
   Human capital development is the second vital ingredient in Singapore's recipe for economic success. This has taken on greater emphasis with shortening business cycles resulting from increasing globalisation and technological disruption. This is of

national importance and not limited to the public sector. All stakeholders have to regularly update their skills and be able to create goods and services that meet fast-changing needs, regardless of how long ago they left school. Life-long learning has become a mantra and taking charge of this responsibility at the individual level is vital to creating a coherent and appropriate collective national response.

The value of a pool of human capital that is able to respond in a dynamic manner cannot be over-stated. This need can be seen in the efforts to sustain Changi Airport as a world-class transportation hub and Singapore Airlines as one of the world's top-performing airlines. This same requirement – the continual development of individuals so they can respond to changing needs - is repeated in almost every sector that is being disrupted. The financial services industry is a classic example, being constantly transformed by digitalisation and fintech innovation, as are manufacturing activities, which are being disrupted by artificial intelligence and robotics.

As human capital is Singapore's vital resource, the government performs the much-needed role of champion and facilitator of constant skills upgrading and, more importantly, innovation and creativity.

Over the years, this has taken on various permutations with breathless urgency – from a productivity drive in the 1980s, computerisation in the 1990s, internationalisation in the 2000s and, since then, to career mobility by staying relevant. Whereas a career was once secured by simply graduating with a good degree, Singaporeans now focus on continual learning and upgrading and, with the recent massive transformations in industry, re-skilling, to be able to facilitate a complete switch of career. Constant learning has become a part of the national DNA.

Such transitions are not without their challenges. Efforts at re-skilling have to include the necessary counselling elements as well as an active matching of available job opportunities to these newly acquired skills. Job losses and redundancy unfortunately tend to afflict the more mature and more expensive employees to a greater degree. The difficulty of mid-career switchers adapting to new technology or work environments should not be under-estimated. Cultural norms mean that older people often struggle mentally to work under younger but better equipped bosses. Patience and perseverance are needed for a successful outcome. It can be argued that this is merely a generational problem, as younger people are more adaptable to a changing work environment. Ultimately, it boils down to trust in the government of the day, that all the hard work at adapting and building human and intellectual capital will lead to a greater good for the individual and their family.

3. **Agile macro planning and execution**
   The third element vital to Singapore's shared long-term planning is its agile approach to macro-economic strategy.

Given the pace of change, which is enabled by technology and brought on first by globalisation and now rising nationalism, the government is constantly reviewing its macro-economic strategy to remain competitive and relevant.[29] Private sector involvement has always figured prominently, reflecting the underlying importance of private capital to Singapore's economy, including foreign direct investments (FDIs).

These holistic strategy reviews are not just academic exercises but contain specific recommendations. The purpose is clear: to secure the buy-in of all stakeholders. Once there is ownership, motivation helps drive efforts towards stretched goals. The common thread running through all these government reviews is the quest to define a sustainable economic strategy for the wellbeing of a stable, harmonious society. Thorny issues around foreign participation, whether as cheap foreign labour or direct investments by multinational corporations or cultivating indigenous enterprise against the odds of a small domestic market, must be addressed head-on with no ifs or buts.

These dilemmas never quite go away and will require slightly different responses over time. Again, securing the buy-in of all stakeholders is vital to foster a solid social compact to see through some otherwise unpopular policy changes. A case in point is the express intention to reduce the use of cheap foreign labour, which smaller contractors in Singapore rely on to fill the jobs that locals shun, or devoting a large part of the budget towards building infrastructure, which can take years to materialise.

In parallel to these regular macro-economic strategy reviews, government agencies work hard to establish free-trade agreements or double-tax avoidance treaties with as many jurisdictions as possible. Such efforts are not lost on the population in terms of the overall economic benefits. Singapore's government adopts a completely transparent approach towards all these endeavours and takes pains to educate the public on progress or, occasionally, the need for a revision to strategy.

Somewhat perversely, the Singaporean public has come to expect the government to be ever more effective and efficient. Foreigners often fail to understand why locals complain incessantly about over-crowding on what is a relatively well-functioning mass rapid transit system. Or why they criticise an older public housing unit that is actually more spacious than a private apartment in Hong Kong.

There is a context to this apparent dissatisfaction. It goes back to the DNA of paranoia that comes from a keen sense of survival. Singaporeans set very high standards and expect constant improvement. Complaining is something they enjoy doing - and even have a laugh over. It is an ironic expression of the social compact between the government and the people and is rooted in the notion that open praise leads to complacency, whereas criticism motivates better performance.

4. **Solidarity in a crisis**

The final crucial element of Singapore's long-term planning strategy is ensuring solidarity between government and people in times of crisis.

Singapore's economic success depends on its ability to deal with disruption. The mettle of any government will be tested whenever there is a crisis, be it triggered locally or extraneously. In Singapore's case, the last few crises have been the result of regional or global factors, which rendered the country vulnerable because of its huge exposure to the global economy. These include the Asian financial crisis (AFC) of 1997 to 1998, the dot-com crash of the early 2000s, the Severe Acute Respiratory Syndrome (SARS) outbreak in 2003, the global financial crisis (GFC) of 2008 to 2009 and the covid-19 pandemic that started in late 2019, which all inflicted great pain on Singapore's economy and people.

For each crisis, the government dug deep into its reserves, giving real meaning to the idiom "saving for a rainy day". Funding was targeted at mitigating job and income loss, shoring up business survival and providing cash flow relief to households. The investment of public funds required to resuscitate the economy was jaw dropping and justifies the practice of painstakingly squirrelling reserves away in good years. Around S$12 billion (US$7 billion) was ploughed into the economy to revive businesses during the AFC, and the onslaught from the GFC dented national coffers by almost twice as much at S$23 billion (US$16 billion). By June 2020, stimulus packages for the covid-19 pandemic already totalled just under S$100 billion (US$72 billion).

Singapore's government has consistently shown its willingness to act decisively to counter an economic downturn and help the economy recover as quickly as possible. Not surprisingly there is great curiosity over the size of the national reserves to fund such rescues time and time again. Despite the occasional campaign by detractors to have this statistic revealed, the majority of Singaporeans simply trust that there are sufficient savings whenever a crisis presents itself. More importantly, notwithstanding the associated hardship whenever livelihoods are threatened, there is willingness on the part of the citizens and businesses to throw their support behind the government's recovery efforts. This is obviously not a given in all countries, as the violent protests in many other economies undergoing painful restructuring have demonstrated. In Singapore, however, such solidarity comes from a cultivation of trust over a long period of time.

Rallying behind the government of the day has proven, time and time again, to be key to mitigating financial and non-financial crises. The SARS outbreak and the covid-19 pandemic both entailed the imposition of strict measures on businesses and restrictions to personal freedom, which required the full cooperation of residents. Likewise, there is general acceptance in Singapore of the need for intensified surveillance to counter the rise of terrorism, even though this might be deemed to be intrusive in other parts of the world.

As well as the deep-seated trust that the government acts in the best long-term interests of the people, Singapore also benefits from the shared values that come from being a meritocracy.

SHARED VALUES

Singapore has evolved over the years as a migrant nation: a majority of the population is Chinese (76%), many of whose forefathers hailed from the southern provinces of China; indigenous Malays (15 %), and South Asian immigrants with roots mostly from the southern states of India (7.5 %). A wide range of religions overlay this multi-racial melting pot, from Buddhism and Taoism to Islam, Hinduism to Christianity as well as, of course, atheism. For a young nation, this would be a potentially explosive mix unless there is acceptance, not just mere tolerance, of the diversity of races and religions.

Singapore's first political leaders recognised very early on the need to share a common economic vision and values that were applicable to all citizens, regardless of race or religion. This "national glue" that holds Singapore's different social groups together is not something that can be taken for granted, however. Both vision and values remain a work very much in progress, as increasing globalisation and social fragmentation show that a common vision founded purely on economics may not be sufficient to foster a uniquely Singaporean identity. It is the shared values of meritocracy, hard work and thrift and intolerance to corruption that help to bind Singaporeans together in common cause.

MERITOCRACY: WALKING THE TALK

It is an indication of Singapore's meritocracy in action that a whole generation of children from low-income homes were awarded scholarships to study at top foreign universities and then returned to Singapore to formulate and execute public policies. This principle of meritocracy undergirds many policies, from admission to secondary and higher levels in schools based on transparent criteria, to career progression in the public sector; it is based on equal opportunity for all races. No one should get ahead by virtue of relationships or the ability to line the pockets of people in positions of influence. Corruption is a strict no-no.

HARD WORK AND THRIFT

Values, such as hard, honest work, thrift and meritocracy, are more enduring than specific promises stemming from political ideologies. Though it is often argued that thrift is a typical Asian trait, Singapore's government realised that the habit of saving (for a rainy day) does not always come naturally. Having also seen how national pension plans can pose substantial fiscal challenges over time, Singapore opted for individualised "forced savings".

To this day, the Central Provident Fund (CPF) represents a very important and sustainable pillar of personal financial sufficiency in old age. Unlike the pay-as-you-go pension models seen in other countries, which can leave individuals vulnerable to poor fiscal balances, Singaporeans can manage their own forced savings accounts. These CPF accounts can be used to meet mortgage payments, medical expenses, or health care insurance and, post-retirement, can be a source of finance.

The separation between state and individual finances is a conscious and important construct. It represents a safeguard for the public's retirement savings and prevents them from falling prey to rogue government attempts to spend what does not belong in the public coffers.

INTOLERANCE TO CORRUPTION

Endemic corruption would obviously be a real scourge to the underlying economy of Singapore. As it aspired to be a trusted hub for transportation and financial services, the country simply could not afford to have its image tarnished. Having no hinterland of its own – Singapore is simply a port city - the ability of the country to play a hub role successfully pivots on integrity: the rule of law, the integrity of the Singaporean people and sound business practices. The Prevention of Corruption Act, enacted as far back as 1960, is therefore much more than just a legacy of British rule. It is the centrepiece of empowerment of law against all kinds of corruption in both the public and private sector. The zeal with which the act is enforced and updated for relevance speaks volumes about how seriously the government takes the issue. It wants to minimise, if not eradicate corruption altogether. Even offences that might be viewed as petty elsewhere, such as bribes to the police for a speeding ticket or a civil servant for a favour, attract heavy punishments.

The Corrupt Practices Investigation Bureau (CPIB) is empowered to investigate all corruption cases, regardless of rank, seniority or political affiliations. There are notable examples in Singapore's history to demonstrate that no one is above the law.

TRUST AND TRANSPARENCY

In Singapore, there is a strong (implied) social contract between the government, the business sector and the public. In my experience, trust and integrity are of the utmost importance to that. When you make mistakes, you can correct your style or revise your plans. As long as your intentions are consistent with that vision, most people will accommodate setbacks and missteps. If they understand what you're trying to achieve they will be willing to embrace change. The government needs to chart the vision about where the country wants to go, but ultimately what holds the nation together is the trust between the government and the people.

MY LEADERSHIP RECOMMENDATIONS

So, here we come to my recommendations for effective leadership:

1. **Trust is your greatest leadership asset**
   Above all, leaders should be trustworthy and above corruption. In Singapore there is a long-running debate about government salaries which, on paper at least, are among the highest in the world. But we have a system of what we call "clean wages". So, what you see is what the members of government actually get. It's very transparent.

In other countries, salaries are more opaque: politicians have travel allowances and other perks like housing and household help, which means the total amount they receive can be way in excess of what is reported as their salary.

2. **Create a virtuous circle**

   In Singapore, the government has served the people well over the long term and that is why they trust their government. I know some people say there is more cynicism culturally towards government in the western democracies, but I don't think people are so different in Singapore. It's just that we've had many years of the same government being allowed to carry out its long-term plans and so people have seen the benefits – that's why they find it easier to trust.

   The difference in the West, perhaps, is that politicians lean towards short-term populism. Because people know they won't be in power for long, they are more interested in what the government can give them today rather than trust it to deliver benefits in the long run. They decide whether to re-elect the politicians based on whether they delivered in the short term.

   Just as trust creates a virtuous circle, so distrust becomes a vicious cycle that feeds on itself. Politicians focused on the short term will pick and choose policies they think will get them elected in a few years' time. They know they won't be around to face the music later, or for that matter, to get the credit either.

3. **Prioritise in a crisis**

   Trust becomes even more important in a crisis. In Singapore, we went through the precursor to the covid-19 pandemic with SARS back in 2003. I was already serving as a member of Parliament then, so I had to deal with the issues on the ground. It brought home to me the importance of having enough reserves, in terms of both financial reserves and the store of trust that people have in you. You cannot do everything, so you have to prioritise and manage your reserves: financial reserves, reserves of trust and goodwill, and your personal reserves of energy and wellbeing as a leader.

   To me that was the most important lesson and one that was repeated during the global financial crisis in 2008 and 2009. The cabinet then undertook a lot of the work behind the scenes, trying to get the right schemes up and running. In a crisis, there's no shortage of things to do and people trying to help; the challenge is to prioritise. How do you gain control at a time when everything is in complete chaos?

You need a clear head and strong solidarity, not just within the top echelons but also with the people. These are important leadership lessons.

4. **Communicate consistently**
   If you look at the way Singapore has dealt with crises, including covid-19, there is a consistency to the approach. We have been very mindful about the cost to the economy and the impact of any sort of stringent measures. But at the same time, public health must take top priority. The wellbeing of the people is paramount. It's always going to be a difficult tussle in terms of what should and should not be done and when. Sometimes you can be blindsided because certain situations don't present themselves immediately. And once it starts escalating it can get a little out of control. In Singapore we had a problem with a surge of coronavirus transmission in the foreign worker dormitories, where thousands of migrant workers live in close proximity. Aggressive testing led to a spike in the number of infections, which horrified people. But the government endeavoured to be honest at every step of the way. To tell it as it is. To say what needs to be done, both temporarily and permanently, and get on with it. In June 2020 they announced the type of new dormitories to be constructed henceforth to reduce the density of migrant worker housing.

5. **Renew to remain relevant**
   As a leader you can never afford to rest on your laurels. It is vital to remain curious about the world and seek new answers to the important questions. Outside of a crisis, for example, there are leadership challenges that are more applicable to Singapore as a small country than other nations, namely, how do we stay competitive, and compelling as a hub?

   As a leader, you always have to think ahead. It's not good enough just to maintain what you have; you have to always strive for better. We can't afford to take anything for granted. That's why the Singapore Government built and continues to expand Changi Airport ahead of time, not because the existing airport had run out of capacity – it had just been expanded - but because it anticipated that it would. Not many countries would be prepared to do that, but the government of the time knew it had to because aviation capacity is integral to our survival as a hub. And thinking ahead is a never-ending process. To mitigate the effects of ageing infrastructure, Changi is continually being upgraded.[30]

CHANGI AIRPORT [31]

When Changi Airport opened its doors in 1981, it ranked alongside Tokyo's Narita Airport as Asia's largest. It was built in record time, just six years from when the government announced its construction. The decision of the Singaporean government to undertake such an ambitious new airport project back in 1975 – when the current airport had only recently been expanded – is a testament to the nation's belief in forward thinking and long-term planning.

Singapore's previous civilian airport was Paya Lebar, which opened in 1955, eight kilometres from the city centre. In 1961, a $2.25 million,[32] five-storey administration and operations block was completed at Paya Lebar and, in 1962, the runway was extended by another 1,000 feet – at a cost of $3 million - making it one of the longest runways in Asia at the time. A new parking apron was completed in 1963 for a further $1.6 million. The $3.5-million permanent passenger terminal (the terminal had been housed in a temporary building since 1955) finally opened in 1964.

By 1971, however, Paya Lebar – considered a state-of-the-art airport at the time - was already reaching capacity thanks to rapid increases in passenger and aircraft volume. The terminal was expanded but, by 1975, the government realised that for Singapore to pursue its vision as a major global transport hub, an ambitious new plan was needed. Not only was a much larger site required for a new airport, it needed to be located away from the new high-rise housing developments and it had to be built as rapidly as possible.

The decision was made to build the new airport in Changi. Out on the east coast of Singapore Island, 24 kilometres from the city centre, Changi was considered suitable to meet not just current aviation needs but also – crucially - future expansion requirements: with a construction plan based on a scheme of a massive land reclamation, additional runways and terminals could be added in the future by reclaiming more land.

The original airbase at Changi was built between 1943 and 1944 by British and Indian prisoners of war. The POWs were kept in nearby Changi Prison and the occupying Japanese intended their new airbase to be the largest airfield in the region. After the end of the second world war it was taken over by the British RAF and, in a reversal of roles, Japanese POWs were put to work to improve both runways.

In April 1976, the massive land reclamation project for the new airport got underway. A total of 8.7 kilometres of land – 60% of the site - was reclaimed from the sea. Initial construction works also included ground levelling, swamp filling and the building of canals to divert water from existing streams.

Following its inauguration in 1981, Changi Airport gained a second terminal in 1990, its third in 2008 and fourth in 2017. There is also a privately-run luxury VIP terminal JetQuay CIP, which opened in 2006 and is available to all passengers, for an access fee.

Around 7,400 flights arrive or depart at Changi each week – about one every 80 seconds. In 2019, it became the world's seventh busiest airport, with over 68 million passengers passing through. Changi is also one of the busiest freight airports in the world, handling over 2 million tonnes of cargo in the same year.

To attract passengers both corporate and leisure, Changi provides probably the most tranquil, seamless and pleasurable airport experience in the world. Not just content with high-quality facilities and efficient design, Changi has gone a step further by creating beautiful, tropical gardens both inside and out; spectacular water features; and impressive artworks.

In 2019, the new Jewel Changi Airport opened. A neo-futuristic, nature-based entertainment complex that connects three of the terminals, this joint-venture project with CapitaMalls Asia comprises underground parking, over 300 retail and dining outlets and a host of attractions for all ages including the world's tallest waterfall - the 40-metre Rain Vortex; bouncing nets; a canopy bridge; discovery slides; "foggy bowls" and mazes. The Jewel project was first announced by the government in 2013 as a part of its plans to double Changi's capacity by the mid 2020s.

A fifth "mega terminal" has also been planned since 2013, to open in the 2030s. Set on 1,080 hectares of reclaimed land the new terminal is designed to handle a whopping 50 million passengers a year.

Singapore's success story with Changi Airport is reflected in the number of awards the airport has won: 622 and counting. In 2020, Changi was announced the World's Best Airport by Skytrax – for the eighth consecutive year. Changi has also been voted best airport multiple times by international travel publications including ***Business Traveller, Travel+ Leisure, DestinAsia*** *and* ***Wanderlust****, as well as by organisations such as the Airport Council International.*

The bold decision to build a new airport back in 1975 is indicative of Singapore's mission to take ownership of the future, while the rapid execution of the project is confirmation of the nation's commitment to prosperity through hard work and thrift. The continuing focus on improvements and expansion at Changi are a reflection of Singapore's belief in its vision as a major transportation hub and commitment to continual renewal, to stay ahead of the game.

For Singapore as a nation that spirit of continual renewal and reinvention is integral. You can think of Singapore as a lean startup – that startup mentality is very much in our DNA. Hence the paranoia I mentioned earlier. We are restless and never satisfied.

6. **Develop personal resilience**

   Resilience is another critical element of leadership. Resilience requires keeping a really open mind, which is easier said than done. As much as we keep telling people you need to re-skill, you need to be open to challenges and so on, as a leader you have to exemplify that. You have to demonstrate it in your own behaviour. You also have to be resilient enough to fight your corner. What I really enjoyed in government were the sessions where I had to persuade colleagues of an argument that was not immediately obvious. There continues to be the evergreen debates over the best use of our limited financial and other resources, or human capital. For example, because Singapore is limited for space, how land is to be used is always hotly contested. There's no shortage of champions who will say it should go to manufacturing, or it should go into transportation and so on. What's important is that the robust debate ends with a collective decision to be made, defended and executed.

7. **Beware of populism**
   In a country with long-term horizons like Singapore, there's no room for a purely populist message. It isn't enough to say something because you think it will sound good on social media this week. It has to sound good ten years from now. That is always the true test. And it's essential for a country like Singapore because we have very little room for mistakes - from the physical resources point of view, as well as human capital.

8. **Persevere to prosper**
   As a leader there is no substitute for commitment and hard work, and you can never take your eye off the ball or think that the job is done. Singapore aspires to be a meritocracy, for example, but we will always consider it to be a work in progress. If I had to give us a score on meritocracy right now, then we are probably a seven out of ten. There are still areas that we need to look at. However well the system is constructed and conceived, as long as human beings execute it, there will always be some bias even if it is unconscious. So the government's role, as well as that of the employer, is to look out for these biases and try to address them though policy positions or through regulation. For example, the government has an important part to play in helping the private sector be more inclusive by employing people who are less advantaged.

9. **Create a leadership culture**
   The national scholarships have been extremely important in fostering a culture of leadership. Not only were they pivotal in developing a cadre of highly-educated global citizens to lead the government and civil service, they also inculcated a culture of national service and duty. The state scholarships have been very valuable in this regard and for different reasons over the years. They started with the administrative services (the core policy formulation pool) and then eventually a lot of the statutory boards started to generate their own scholarship schemes as well. So, scholarships became a much wider offering.

   In my time, a scholarship was purely about the financial means because without it, I wouldn't have been able to study even in Singapore, let alone outside the country as I did. Nowadays, however, there are a lot more affluent families who can afford to give their children a good education but still regard the scholarships as highly prestigious.

Because we've always had a pool of talent in the civil service to help with policy formulation, execution and so on, Singapore has created its own culture of giving and contributing to the country. The scholarships helped position working for the government as the highest level of national service. There is huge prestige to being selected as part of that group. So today we have scholarship recipients who don't really need the money to study, but who will nonetheless take up the scholarships because they have earned it on their own merit. That enables them to be their own person, to be independent of parental support and contribute in their own right.

So the scholarship scheme has been extremely valuable to Singapore. That's not to say that all the recipients are now affluent. There are still many who actually need the sponsorship and the scholarship policy still serves that purpose.

The other aspect of the national scholarships is that by sending people abroad rather than studying in Singapore, the government creates a core of highly-educated global citizens who are familiar with the way that other countries work, which is a double benefit. Even now, I still keep a close tab on what's happening in the United Kingdom and in the United States, because I went to universities there.

OWNERSHIP OF THE FUTURE

Inculcating a sense of collective responsibility is vital for the long haul. Unless all Singaporeans pull in the same direction, there can be no viable future. Government strategy centres on the country's ability to partner with foreign stakeholders in order to realise sustainable growth, while building a stable and harmonious society. Prosperity and stability are built on trust and sharing the fruits of the country's labours.

RACIAL AND RELIGIOUS HARMONY

Given the diversity of Singaporean society, maintaining racial and religious harmony is no small matter. Access to equal opportunities for education and employment necessitate a detailed analysis of how each citizen can be fully developed to his or her fullest potential. Inequality gaps, partly generated by the low birth rate and ageing population, have to be plugged.

The converse is equally important: Singapore's government devotes an inordinate amount of attention to removing barriers and causes of friction to achieve racial and religious harmony. From the outset, the need to foster a unique Singaporean identity, regardless of race, was recognised. Ethnic quotas were applied to public housing blocks, which some commentators may regard as social engineering, but the aim was to ensure integration. Places of worship for more than one faith are systematically planned into new towns to get people used to non-segregation by race or religion. Likewise, deliberate efforts are made to expose terrorism operating under the guise of religion.

SHARING THE FRUITS OF LABOUR

Unless citizens can enjoy the fruits of their labour, it will be hard to inspire enthusiasm or motivate perseverance. That's why Singapore's government has adopted a multi-pronged approach.

On the economic front, measures range from:

- Attracting sound FDIs to anchor themselves in Singapore for the creation of good jobs.
- Establishing a collaborative tripartite alliance among the government, employers and unions to represent employees.
- Emphasising life-long learning to ensure employability.

On the social front, priorities include:

- Providing affordable public housing for the majority of the population (currently more than 80%).
- Ensuring access to schooling at minimal fees, through the compulsory education policy.
- Planning for a sustainable health care delivery system that is within the reach of all citizens.
- Dealing with rising inequality through specific targeted measures to lift low-income households and a redistribution at each budget, whenever surpluses allow.
- Addressing the challenges of an ageing population in terms of quality of life, financial sufficiency and, on a macro basis, the extent of immigration required for sustainable economic growth.

CONCLUSION: BUILDING TRUST CONTINUALLY

Building trust is always a work in progress even if efforts have hitherto borne fruit. Every generation emerges from a different set of circumstances and will relate to the government differently. Expectations are also influenced by external factors. To this end, communications and continual engagement by the government are extremely important.

To engender collective ownership of the country and their own future, the government recognises that Singaporeans now expect regular engagement through multi-channels. This goes beyond the traditional channels that most governments have employed. Formal speeches, for example, remain important but are no longer the sole means of communication. Social media, for better or worse, now dominates the attention of not just the younger stakeholders but anyone with a mobile device. Presence on social media is therefore no longer optional but must be a given. It is increasingly important, too, to direct efforts at both publishing news and correcting fake reports.

In short, building trust requires long periods of consistent hard work, honest intentions and humility. This is something Singapore's government understands well. Trust has been vital in creating a social contract and realising its vision to make the impossible possible.

VIETNAM

Just over 30 years ago, Vietnam was one of the poorest countries in the world. Since 1986, however, Vietnam has undergone an extensive political and economic reformation and within a quarter of a century has transformed into a middle-income country (MIC), as rated by the World Bank.

At the end of the 20-year war in 1975, Vietnam's economy faced considerable difficulties in terms of production, supply-and-demand imbalances, inefficiencies in distribution and circulation, high inflation and rising debt. Industry was almost non-existent and agricultural infrastructure damaged. Although the government launched multiple five-year central plans, economic growth remained sluggish. In 1984, the country's gross domestic product (GDP) was valued at US$18.1 billion and per capita income wavered between just US$200 and US$300 per year.

In 1986, the Vietnamese government introduced "Doi Moi", a series of economic and political reforms, and began to steer the nation towards a "socialist-oriented market economy". These policies symbolised a turning point in Vietnam's economic development and represented a significant shift away from the previous command-style, central-planning approach. The government's aim was to abolish the system of bureaucratic, centralised management, which was based on state subsidies, and replace it with a multi-sector, market-oriented economy. Privately-owned enterprises were encouraged and policies on collective farming and private land rights were overturned. The central tenets of the Doi Moi strategy were land reform, the liberalisation of agriculture, the attraction of foreign investment and social development. Government investments were targeted towards agricultural development, consumer goods productivity, trade and foreign investment.

Economic growth began to accelerate. By 1998, productivity accounted for a 42% increase in GDP. Between 2000 and 2010, GDP per capita increased more than three times. From 2014, inclusive growth averaged 6.6% per annum and in 2018 reached a 10-year high of 7.1%. The high inflation rates of the mid-1980s were tamed and nominal interest rates fell, generating a more stable and predictable investment climate. Industrial development accelerated and chronic food shortages were replaced by large export surpluses. Trade reforms increased investment which, in turn, brought in capital technology.

In terms of social development, poverty declined from 58.1% to 14.5% in 2008 – one of the steepest falls in the world. In health care, Vietnam has maintained its comprehensive, wide-reaching national health-care system and, between 1990 and 2008, the under-five mortality rate declined from 56 to 14 per 1,000. In 1998, the government launched the National Hunger Eradication and Poverty Reduction Program (HEPR), which included a variety of benefits including "poor household certificates" and "health insurance cards" that provided free medical treatment and partial exemption from school fees.

Education is recognised as a national priority and has received 20% of the government budget since 2008. In 2015, Vietnamese students participated in the global PISA tests for reading, maths and science and scored higher than many developed countries, including the United States and the United Kingdom.

Vietnam's turnaround in the last 30 years can be attributed to several factors, including sustained land reform, a wide-reaching foundation of infrastructure and equitable investment in human development, as well as strategic and sequenced trade liberalisation.

However, what emerges as the most critical factor is the country's strong leadership. The Communist Party of Vietnam - the ruling party that initiated the Doi Moi strategy – took a robust but pragmatic approach, encouraging internal debate, policy innovation and trial-and-error methods. Decisions, once agreed, had to carry the unanimous support of all members of the party, which made it easier for reforms to get implemented. Successful experimental initiatives that were implemented at district levels were also adopted at national level.

This focused approach led to increases in productivity and income, particularly in the agricultural sector, and the shift away from decentralised power led to the emergence of accountability mechanisms, which also helped drive the reform strategy forward. Strong, political support of the Doi Moi policies was essential to their effectiveness and success.

The Celtic Rollercoaster

"The two most powerful warriors are patience and time."
Leo Tolstoy

John Bruton
Taoiseach (Prime Minister) of Ireland, 1994 to 1997

4

In the years since it gained independence, Ireland has transformed itself from a heavily agrarian economy dependent on the United Kingdom as its primary market, to one of the most open economies in the world.

From being one of the poorest countries in Europe for much of the last century, Ireland is now among the wealthiest and most competitive economies in the EU. In 2020, Ireland was ranked 24th out of 137 countries in the World Economic Forum's (WEF) Global Competitive Index; and seventh in the WEF Gender Gap Index, ahead of the United Kingdom, France, Denmark and Germany. The Organisation for Economic Co-operation and Development (OECD) recently ranked Ireland second out of its members for GDP per capita, behind only Luxembourg and ahead of Switzerland, Norway and the United States.

In this chapter, I will explain how Ireland has ridden an economic rollercoaster, overcoming several crises that threatened to derail it, and how it is attracting large amounts of foreign investment to reposition itself as a high-tech hub.

THE IRISH ECONOMIC MIRACLE

Much has been written about the Irish economic miracle. From 1995 to 2000, the Irish economy expanded at an average rate of 9.4% (annual figures ranged from 7.8% to as high as 11.5%) and Irish GDP per capita rose dramatically to equal and then surpass all but one state in western Europe.

Today, the country enjoys a strong reputation for digital technologies, life sciences, agri-businesses and financial services. A substantial part of that success was built on foreign direct investment (FDI), but that did not happen by accident.

Not surprisingly, other countries have sought to learn lessons from the Irish experience. I was fortunate to have been taoiseach (Irish prime minister) from 1994 to 1997 and to have overseen a period of rapid growth. My own underlying belief, however, is that far from being a Cinderella story, Ireland's present-day success is the result of patient endeavour and a willingness to experiment over a long period.

A SLOW-BURNING TRANSFORMATION

In 1922, following the Irish war of independence, most of Ireland seceded from the United Kingdom to become the independent Irish Free State. The six north-eastern counties remained within the United Kingdom as Northern Ireland, creating the partition of Ireland, and leading to the Troubles, which lasted from the late 1960s until the Good Friday Agreement of 1998. Since it achieved independence, Ireland has experienced a number of distinct periods of economic growth and sloth.

Some of these periods saw exceptionally fast growth but these can largely be explained by a preceding artificial retardation of growth, such as in the 1950s, when the brake on growth was caused by two balance of payments crises, and in the period of slow growth in the 1980s that was caused by a fiscal crisis, and the recession of 2008 to 2012, which resulted from the global and local banking crisis.

Each period of economic sloth was followed by a period of rapid catch-up. But the catch-up was only possible because Ireland had gradually built up its resilience through prudent investments in education, technology and infrastructure. Social peace was maintained through social welfare income support in difficult times and this, too, can be seen as a form of investment in resilience.

1800–1922: HISTORICAL CONTEXT

Like any country, Ireland has its own unique circumstances. The first thing to say is that it is an island, and islands have some advantages. It is slightly easier for them to stay out of wars, for example, as Ireland did between 1939 and 1945. Neutrality is a more viable option for an island than for a nation physically connected to its neighbours, such as Belgium. Being an island is also helpful if you need to close your borders in the case of a pandemic.

But islands also have some disadvantages. These include the extra transport costs involved in exporting to other countries, which is especially problematic where products or raw materials have a high weight or bulk relative to their sale price. Ireland's agricultural exports suffered from this disability for hundreds of years and had to be sold at a discount.

Technology changed that. In the 20th century, new industries developed where weight and value became more disassociated. Profitable industries emerged such as computer chips, pharmaceuticals and financial services, where products had high value but low or no weight. Ireland benefitted from this phenomenon from 1970 onwards.

Another factor is that unlike many other parts of Europe, including Britain, Ireland did not have significant natural deposits of coal, so it did not develop its heavy industry during the 19th century as others did. As a result, it missed out on the growth boost that such industries brought during their heyday, but it also avoided the social costs associated with the decline of such industries from the 1950s onwards.

INHERITED ADVANTAGES

Another difference between Ireland and similar sized countries in Europe is that it is English speaking. Over the years this has been a double-edged sword. Although it has been a major advantage in attracting investment from other English-speaking countries, notably the United States, sharing a common language was one of the factors that prolonged Ireland's dependence on the slow growing British economy, preventing it from diversifying into other markets.

In a 1992 report on the Irish economy commissioned by Ireland's National Economic and Social Council (NESC), the Swedish social scientist Lars Mjoset observed of Ireland's economic performance in the 1945 to 1965 period: "Ireland was a free rider on Britain's economic decline, while Austria and Switzerland were free riders on Germany's (post-war) economic miracle."[33]

On the positive side, Ireland benefited from a good institutional inheritance from when it was part of the United Kingdom, namely a depoliticised and competent civil service and courts system, and a strong tradition of responsible parliamentary government.

EMIGRANT NATION

Another significant factor in Ireland's history is that it was a country from which millions of people emigrated. This is especially true of the years during and after the 1845 to 1848 famine, which resulted from the failure of the potato crop on which the population had become dependent.

But emigration (mainly to English-speaking countries) continued long after the famine and became a major brain drain. Other European countries like Italy and the Scandinavian nations also experienced large-scale emigration but, in Ireland's case, it became part of the culture in ways it didn't elsewhere.

This tradition has made Irish people more globally mobile than most. It has also been a safety valve when hard times hit, contributing to the country's relative political stability. Irish people have a tradition of emigrating to find work, rather than remaining unemployed and discontented at home.

All these factors played a part in Ireland's economic transformation. But they also acted as a brake on growth.

1922–1956: ECONOMIC NATIONALISM

The period immediately after Ireland gained its independence can be characterised as one of economic nationalism.

The nation's initial economic performance was undistinguished for a number of reasons. It had to recover from the damaging physical and psychological effects of civil war from 1919 to 1923 and its direct involvement in the Great War of 1914 to 1918. Many of Ireland's most talented people died in those wars. Others fled the country. This added to the existing brain drain caused by emigration.

Much of the country's basic infrastructure had to be rebuilt after the civil war at significant cost, and capital that could have been invested in expansion was devoted to rebuilding.

The Irish Free State came into being in 1922 as a result of separation from Great Britain, which was a wealthier country than Ireland at the time. Wages and pensions in the new state had been set prior to independence at levels appropriate to Britain and, as a consequence, were higher than was justified by Ireland's own wealth.

Compounding this, Ireland did not have its own currency (whilst it did print its own notes at the time, they were denominated in British pounds sterling) meaning it could not use devaluation to ease the mismatch. So actual pension cuts in nominal terms had to be made, which proved to be enduringly unpopular.

The new state was dependent on a few industries, with agriculture, brewing and distilling being the main ones and, having only minimal trade links with other countries, it was heavily reliant on selling into the British market.

Ireland also had debts to be paid and serviced. One of these was to the United Kingdom Exchequer, which had used British revenues to finance land purchases in favour of Irish farmers. In the 1920s, these debts were being repaid in the form of land annuities and were a cause of discontent.

ECONOMIC WAR

In 1932, a Fianna Fáil (one of Ireland's main political parties) government was elected in Dublin that refused to continue paying the annuities to Britain. The government in London retaliated by imposing tariffs on Irish exports, which had a devastating effect on Irish farm incomes and on the economy generally. This "economic war" lasted from 1932 to 1938. It was finally settled in 1938 on favourable terms to Ireland, with a substantial debt write-off in Ireland's favour. However, a lot of damage had been done in the meantime.

During the 1930s, Ireland adopted a policy of industrial protectionism, which was aimed at self-sufficiency by imposing tariffs and quotas and restricting overseas investment in Irish companies under a Control of Manufactures Act.

While many other countries adopted similar policies at the time, whereas most European countries had dropped them in the late 1940s, they persisted in Ireland much longer and were only abandoned reluctantly in the 1960s.

In the 1950s, 400,000 people emigrated from Ireland seeking a better life and better prospects abroad. It was only towards the end of that decade that Ireland began its tentative, and belated, journey toward economic modernisation.

1956–1980: SOWING THE SEEDS OF GROWTH

The most important initial step was taken almost accidentally. Ireland had faced a succession of balance of payments crises in the 1950s, in particular in 1952 and in 1956. The standard response to these crises was an austerity budget designed to cut domestic spending and thus reduce imports.

But in the 1956 budget a new measure, Export Sales Relief, was also introduced to boost exports. This provided that company profits made from exports would not be the subject of corporate income tax. The measure was not a central part of the 1956 budget and was almost an afterthought, yet it was to have a significant and lasting impact.

The introduction of Export Sales Relief signalled a shift away from a policy of import substitution towards one of export promotion. The original relief had been focused on getting existing domestic firms to expand into export markets, mainly Britain. But it also made Ireland an attractive place for foreigners to invest. It recognised, too, that tax policy could be used to orient business in a new direction.

Export Sales Relief was retained for the next 22 years until it was replaced in 1978 by a 10% tax rate on manufacturing profits, whether the goods were sold at home or exported.

In 1958, an official paper entitled "Economic Development" was published advocating free trade, foreign investment and growth rather than fiscal restraint. Although the document focused on agriculture rather than industrial exports and the legacy protectionist measures (tariffs and quotas) were reduced only gradually in the following years, it signalled an end to protectionism as a policy and heralded a change in direction that helped sow the seeds for future success. It would take another 37 years, however, for those seeds to germinate.

FOREIGN DIRECT INVESTMENT

An exceptional feature of Ireland's economic development story is the extent to which it has been driven, since the late 1950s, by foreign direct investment (FDI). FDI has proven to be strong in bad times as well as in good times, whereas domestic economic activity has been more volatile.

Ireland has attracted more FDI than almost any country in the world. Since 2010, 70% of FDI in Ireland has come from the United States and 20% from Europe. Foreign-owned multinationals now make up 14 of the top 20 Irish firms (by turnover), employing 23% of the private sector labour force and paying 80% of corporation tax collected.

Access to the EU market has been part of the attraction for American firms. Ireland has also become part of the global supply chain for many multinationals notably in the pharmaceutical, medical devices, financial services and IT sectors.

Domestically-owned firms are concentrated in the food sector and in engineering services. They tend to be more reliant on the British market than FDI firms. But FDI firms buy services from the rest of the Irish economy. Indeed, their purchase of Irish services exceeds their own Irish payroll costs. Wage and salary rates in FDI firms generally exceed rates in the rest of the economy.

OBSTACLES TO CHANGE

By the 1960s and 1970s, worldwide technological advances were creating new opportunities; containerisation and cheaper air travel were reducing the economic cost of being an island. Ireland's historic disadvantage became less significant.

In 1958, however, when the European Common Market was formed, Ireland missed a great opportunity by not being a founding member. Instead it remained outside the EU until 1973, joining at the same time as the United Kingdom and Denmark.

In the intervening years, Ireland remained tied to the slower-growing British economy and its currency was pegged to sterling. As a result, Ireland endured the stop/go economic policies of successive British governments, without having any say in them. This continued to inhibit the country's economic growth until the 1970s, when Ireland adopted stop-go policies of its own in the wake of the 1977 general election.

In the first 50 years of Irish independent statehood, there were other inhibitors of Irish economic performance, too. Educational policy was heavily focussed on non-material goals, like the revival of the Irish language. Large amounts of school time were devoted to this at the expense of other subjects. Spiritual and religious goals were also important in Irish education.

These were legitimate policy choices, reflecting the value system of Irish people at the time, but entailed costs as well as benefits. Chief among these was that Ireland did not introduce free secondary-level education until 1966, much later than most other European countries.

The combined effect of all these factors - civil war, over-dependence on the British market, lack of currency autonomy, protectionism, an "economic war", delays in opening the economy and expanding education - combined to delay Ireland's economic modernisation.

AUSTERITY AND FISCAL CRISIS

In the 1977 general election, a government was elected on the basis of accelerating Irish economic development financed by substantial borrowing. To appeal to voters, certain taxes were abolished. However, this collided with the contraction in monetary policy initiated by the United States Federal Reserve at the beginning of the 1980s. With interest rates high, Irish borrowing proved very costly, leading to a decade of austerity. By 1980, public sector employment accounted for a third of the total workforce. The years that followed brought budget deficits with a corresponding increase in public debt, 60% tax rates for middle-income earners and a rate of unemployment that hit 20%.

By the late 1970's, criticisms had already begun in official circles over what was seen as excessive reliance on foreign-owned industry and insufficient native entrepreneurship. Ireland had been successful in attracting foreign investment but the boost in permanent jobs and GDP was being questioned. In 1980, in response to this growing scepticism, the NESC commissioned the Telesis Consultancy Group to conduct a study of Irish industrial policy.

Published in 1982, the report found that there was indeed a rapid turnover of jobs in foreign-owned industry. It also found that there was insufficient technological development in the Irish operations of foreign-owned firms, with little being spent on research and development (R&D), and insufficient links with smaller Irish firms.

Ireland had been particularly successful in attracting companies in the pharmaceutical sector (which represented 56% of all American investment in Ireland). There were 32 of these but Telesis found that only two of them were conducting their R&D in Ireland.

On the plus side, however, Telesis found that the Industrial Development Authority's (IDA) marketing of Ireland as a location for investment was "unquestionably the most dynamic, most active, and most efficient in the world."

Telesis argued that the aim of policy should be to develop structurally strong Irish companies, rather than strong state agencies, like the IDA. It recommended: a reduction in the grants payable to foreign-owned firms; a sharp cut in grants in the non-tradeable sectors; more support for exporters; and more grants for R&D and for linkages between foreign and local firms.

INDUSTRIAL DEVELOPMENT AUTHORITY (IDA)

The Industrial Development Authority (IDA) was set up in 1949 and enjoyed a measure of autonomy from the civil service, which allowed for strategic thought and action. The IDA was to prove one of the enduring success stories of Irish economic policy. Interestingly, Sean Lemass, then in Opposition and later to be regarded as one of the architects of the modernisation of the Irish economy, opposed the setting up of the IDA and said he would abolish it if returned to power. Indeed, he was returned to power in 1951, but he did not abolish the IDA.

Once the Control of Manufactures Act was repealed in 1958 - a step which removed the formal restrictions on foreign investment that had applied since the 1930s – the IDA began to attract foreign firms to Ireland. In 1958, Leo Laboratories and Philips were among the first foreign firms to invest.

Gradually, the range of incentives offered by the IDA was enhanced, including grants for equipment and free sites. This happened at a time of growth in the world economy when firms were looking for lower-cost locations to serve the European market; something which favoured a small, independent country.

By accident or design, the policy instruments for export development and foreign direct investment (freedom from profits taxation and grants for investment) had been put in place and the IDA made full use of them.

In light of the current controversies about Ireland's supposedly low corporate tax rate of 12.5%, it is important to recall that this approach is not something that was invented in recent times to take investment away from other locations. It dates all the way back to the decision, taken in 1956, to introduce Export Sales Relief, and has formed a core part of the Irish economic model ever since.

As far as FDI was concerned, the IDA did not have a fixed list of sectors that it had decided to attract; rather, it was pragmatic. During the 1960s a wave of firms, predominantly American-owned, set up operations in Ireland with the help of the IDA. The key incentive was the 0% tax on export profits. Many of these firms transferred assembly line operations to Ireland in industries such as textiles, electrical goods and mechanical components. Few linkages were developed between these firms and local businesses, but substantial local employment was created, often in relatively remote parts of the country.

By 1973, 60,000 people were employed in foreign firms that had been brought to Ireland by the IDA.[34] *By 1980, this number had reached 80,000. It is now over 200,000. These companies helped Ireland to continuously increase its export share in foreign markets, despite unfavourable trading conditions.*

1985: THE INDUSTRIAL DEVELOPMENT BILL

I was the minister directly responsible for responding to the Telesis recommendations. My colleagues and I recognised the validity of many of the criticisms and our response was the Industrial Development Bill of 1985, which introduced a range of measures to encourage R&D and help local Irish firms.

We also recognised the need to revisit industrial policy on an ongoing basis and introduced a mandatory three-yearly review. We did not, however, accept the Telesis recommendation to reduce the maximum rate of grant that could be paid to FDI firms investing in Ireland. Such an announcement would have sent out a negative signal. Instead, we shifted the emphasis gradually away from grants for machinery towards grants for the acquisition of new technologies.

These measures helped prepare the soil for economic growth, but it was only after 1994 that the seeds planted in previous decades bore fruit.

ORGANISATIONS THAT SUPPORTED IRELAND'S TRANSFORMATION

The National Industrial Bill was the government's response to the Telesis Report. In it, we introduced a Linkage Programme to encourage more purchases by FDI firms of components from Irish sources. This proved to be a modest success. As noted earlier, FDI firms have tended to buy more services than materials in Ireland.

We also introduced a Company Development Programme under which the IDA would work intensively with indigenous firms to develop their technological and marketing capacity. This proved a great success and was taken up by Enterprise Ireland, a state body, which later took over IDA functions in respect of domestically-owned firms.[35] Enterprise Ireland also eventually took on the export promotion role of the CTT.

To ensure that small firms - and firms outside Dublin - were incentivised to grow, we established regional industry boards and made concerted efforts to encourage industrial development in smaller centres. This policy continues to this day. Generally speaking, manufacturing activity is more widely dispersed across the country than would otherwise have been the case.

But services have overtaken manufacturing as a source of FDI; exports and these service firms prefer to locate in large, urban centres where they can more easily access other services. This is part of the global trend towards urbanisation, which Ireland has been unable to avoid.

In our response to Telesis, we recognised that Ireland needed to develop its own R&D capacity. The R&D grants the IDA was able to give were enhanced. In subsequent years, much greater emphasis was placed on R&D and a specialised state body, Science Foundation Ireland,[36] was established to promote basic and applied research in collaboration between firms and universities.

We also introduced a National Development Corporation (NDC) to be a vehicle for state equity investment, on a venture capital basis, in firms developing in Ireland. The aim was to generate investment that would take a longer term and wider view than was normal among private investors. The NDC was to have a double bottom line, one financial and the other economic. Its aim was to unlock additional private investment by providing it with an equity partner to share the risk.

Great care was taken in drafting the NDC legislation to ensure that that these investments would be made on a strictly objective basis; with a view to obtaining a financial as well as a wider economic return. They were to be made without political interference. The NDC was to turn over its investments on a regular basis, as a discipline on performance, and provide a source of funds for new investments. This turnover provision was controversial with those who wanted more permanent state involvement in key sectors of the economy, but I insisted upon it.

Unfortunately, the main opposition party opposed the NDC and threatened to abolish it, which they did when they came to power in 1987: another opportunity was lost.

A body with a similar role to the NDC was established in 2014, as the Strategic Investment Fund Ireland.[37] *It has made a wide range of investments, unlocking private investment of almost twice the scale of its own investment. This is what I had in mind in 1985.*

1995–2007: THE CELTIC TIGER

Once Ireland had got through its debt crisis, the pent-up potential from the previous investment, especially the FDI, was released and the economy took off. That period – from 1995 to 1997 – coincided with when I was prime minister.

In the two decades ending in 2007, Ireland went from being one of the poorest countries in the EU to among the most prosperous. The combination of low corporate taxes, moderate wages and a young, well-educated workforce attracted multinational companies such as IBM, Dell and Coca-Cola, which viewed Ireland as a platform for exports to the EU. Pharmaceuticals companies, financial services and internet companies such as Google soon followed, drawn by the business-friendly environment.

During this period, high-tech companies poured into Ireland to take advantage of its favourable corporate tax rates, which were 20 to 50% lower than other parts of Europe. But the period was not without its scares.

In 2000, the country's fledgling IT industry was badly impacted by the dot-com crash and its tourist industry was buffeted by the terrorist attacks of 9/11. By 2004, however, when the country opened its doors to workers from the new EU members, a construction boom and a rise in consumer spending and investment meant that the Celtic Tiger economy was roaring again. In 2005, Ireland ranked first in *The Economist's* Quality of Life Index.

However, by then there were already signs that the economy was overheating. The housing boom had seen house prices double between 2000 and 2006 and was clearly unsustainable. By 2006, construction accounted for more than 12% of employment, the highest proportion in Europe. By 2007, the fault lines in the global economy were already starting to show, as the demand for new homes and other property cooled.

2008–2014: THE FINANCIAL CRISIS

It all came crashing down with the global financial crisis of 2008. GDP contracted by 14% and unemployment rose by the same amount. Rising wages and an inflationary housing market contributed to a loss of competitiveness. In September 2008, Ireland became the first eurozone country to enter recession. On 30 September 2008, in desperation, the Irish government guaranteed the liabilities of the country's six biggest banks. In the next two years, it pumped 46 billion euros into the banks, equivalent to 30% of the country's GDP.

Ireland was gripped by the deepest downturn since the Great Depression. By the end of 2010, more than 300,000 people, or one in seven workers, had lost their jobs. But remarkably, after a difficult adjustment, the Irish economy started to grow again.

2014–PRESENT: THE CELTIC PHOENIX

In 2010, Ireland secured loans from the EU and IMF totalling 67.5 billion euros – equal to 40% of the Irish economy – to be repaid over the following three years. From a peak of more than 15% in 2011, unemployment fell to less than 7% by 2017.

In 2013, Ireland exited from its EU-IMF bailout and by 2014 had begun to revive, becoming the fastest growing economy in the EU. The recovery from the financial crisis was aided by a combination of quantitative easing, a weak euro, low oil prices and a bounce back in the construction industry. The national debt and budget deficit were reduced and in 2015 the government simultaneously announced tax cuts and an increase in public spending. In 2019, Ireland's predicted growth rate was 4.1% - the second highest in Europe. The Celtic Tiger had become the Celtic Phoenix, rising from the ashes to reclaim its place as one of Europe's high-performing economies.

MY LEADERSHIP JOURNEY

I was elected to Dáil Éireann, the Irish Assembly, in 1969 at the age of 22. In 1973, my party Fine Gael entered government and I became a junior minister in the Department of Education and later in the Department of Industry and Commerce. To serve in ministerial office at such a young and impressionable age gave me an understanding of the workings of public administration and was very helpful to me later on. I came to understand how laws were crafted and official policies evolved.

My early years in politics were also marked by the terror campaign of the IRA and its Loyalist rivals, which lasted for 30 years from 1968 onwards.

Those early experiences and other key moments in my career have convinced me that leadership is contingent. In other words, it depends on the context – always. For the purposes of this book, I was asked to reflect on my own leadership style. That is something that is probably best left to others, but one characteristic I do acknowledge is that I am very persistent. I have tended to take a long-term view and I very rarely give up. I've also tried to be a good listener and develop a capacity to adapt and adopt other people's points of view, especially if that keeps the show on the road. These are some of the qualities I valued and tried to provide during my time in political life.

Experience has taught me that there are times when the best course of action for the leader is simply to try not to get in the way. But I have also been in situations where I felt strongly that the public's interests were not being served and it was necessary to adopt a more confrontational approach.

LEADING THROUGH CONFRONTATION

I was minister for finance twice, first in 1981-1982 and then again in 1986-1987. In both cases, we had a situation in which financial reality was not being dealt with properly and needed urgent action. That meant confronting Parliament and getting a budget through in 1981, then confronting Parliament again in 1982 with a budget that it did not accept, but which it eventually had to accept in substance.

And then, in 1986-1987, it meant confronting my colleagues in government with reality. What they wanted to spend and what they were prepared to raise in taxation could not be dealt with separately. They had to be dealt with in a package, and we had to have a proper examination of the two together. My point was that you can't say you want to maintain this level of spending unless you're prepared to raise the level of tax.

The result of the confrontation was the collapse of the government, as one part of it felt it necessary to leave the room. But I think I was doing my job; the job of the minister for finance, in both cases, was to confront reality and encourage or push others to confront reality too.

LEADING THROUGH CONSENSUS

When I became leader of my party, I found that the nature of the role changed with the context. To start with, in opposition, my priority was to act as a critic of the government. But when I became taoiseach of a three-party government, my challenge as leader was to promote consensus.

At that time, confrontation wasn't necessary because the economy was going well. The goal I had was to keep the government operating in a stable and consistent fashion and to deal with issues as they came along – both of which we did successfully.

This government presided over rapid economic growth. It reformed the criminal law system to combat organised crime and confiscate criminal assets. It amended the constitution to allow for divorce. It passed freedom of information and ethics legislation and abolished third-level education fees. It reduced hospital waiting lists by 58% and finished its term with a budget surplus.

I was determined that the relations between the three parties would be harmonious. I did not want this coalition to collapse as previous ones had. The success of this approach is evidenced by the fact that the three parties contested the 1997 general election on a joint platform. The good relations built up in the 1994–1997 period provided a basis on which the progressive Fine Gael and Labour could again cooperate in government, as they did after the 2011 general election.

We achieved harmony between the parties by controlling the cabinet agenda. Difficult issues were not brought to the cabinet until an agreed approach had been worked out between the party leaders and their advisers. This avoided acrimony at the cabinet table. The Finance Ministry was held by a Labour politician and this ensured that both Fine Gael and Labour felt a sense of ownership of our prudent fiscal policies.

In my previous ministerial positions, I had found that many of the failures in policy implementation occur in areas where more than one ministry is involved. Silo-ed thinking and administrative turf wars absorb an enormous amount of effort and are highly unproductive.

Breaking this down is a task in which a prime minister can be particularly effective, by bringing together ministers and the agencies reporting to them in one room with the task of solving a specific problem. I used this technique with some success in the response to organised crime and the relief of traffic congestion. It is an area of governance that deserves careful attention.

I also took a big interest, which I still do, in the success of the European Union because I think Ireland's membership of the EU and its economic success are joint products. Success is very often due to ensuring that you have a stable context in which you can implement policy, and the EU has been a stable context in which Ireland has been able to implement successful politics and policies.

Brexit is upsetting that stability. It is something that we did not want that has been imposed upon us, but we're going to have to cope with it. Covid-19 is even more disruptive than Brexit but Brexit and covid-19 have, for Ireland, a lot in common. They both involve major unproductive disruption of existing patterns of economic activity.

BEYOND THE NATION STATE

When it comes to the response to the coronavirus pandemic, I prefer the calmer, methodical approach. What was notable in the relatively successful way Ireland dealt with the crisis was the matter-of-fact approach that it adopted, taking scientific advice and taking it early, rather than the more volatile approach seen in some other English-speaking countries.

I recognise that there are limits to lockdowns and finding ways of navigating out of them was never going to be easy. In doing so, one is confronted with a really difficult values judgement because you have to balance lives against livelihoods. As a Christian, I believe that human lives come first, but if you sacrifice livelihoods too much, then lives will be lost in other ways through poverty and desperation. So, it's always going to be a very fine balance that has to be struck.

It's important, however, to take a long-term view and talk about it in a very frank way saying, as best we can, what are the scenarios in which we might be able to reopen the economy but emphasising over and over again that we don't know what's going to happen. We've got to admit it when the unknowns are far greater than the knowns and that we must be prepared to adapt.

I think voters and the public do understand that, as long as it's explained to them patiently and repeatedly. With the development of the internet and social media, I do see a more atomised society where public opinion is less uniform and there are many more separate and mutually confronting public opinions. Plurality makes society harder to manage than it would have been in my period in high office.

What we're seeing now is a series of threats that are inherently multinational - terrorism, climate change and pandemics don't respect borders. We have had massive movements of people every year from one country to another. I read recently that some 1.5 billion people visited another country last year, which is a very high proportion of the world's population travelling.

This has changed the context in which the threats we face have to be dealt with. We have to confront them in a multinational setting, however, people's frames of thought about problem solving are confined, to a great extent, within national boundaries. Their sense of identity, their sense of the community is frequently in an almost exclusively national context or a national identity. We're trying to deal with multinational problems with national instruments and that's proving very difficult.

Although our problems are multinational, even in Europe where we have so much in common with one another historically, we haven't created this supranational frame of reference, or supranational sense of shared identity or destiny.

We haven't created that adequately to give the sort of moral and emotional support to politicians who need to do things at a multinational level, which is the only level at which these problems can be solved.

This dissonance is quite acute. From the moment when I was prime minister of Ireland, one of the things I did which didn't achieve any success at the time was to promote the idea of creating a Europe-wide constituency, or a Europe-wide identity, within which one could work. We should have an election for the presidency of the European Commission as they have in

America, where all Europeans would vote on the same day about the same choice between the same individual or individuals.

That would have created the ingredients for a shared identity, for a shared emotional experience. But nobody was interested in the idea at the time. In fact, there wasn't great interest when I promoted it to the Convention on the Future of Europe in the period 2002-2004 because things then were going well, which meant people didn't see a great need for it.

But I think covid-19 is a complete gamechanger; we'll work differently going forward. There will be more working from home and more virtual conferences. Inevitably, people will become more worried about the security of supply of key commodities that we need in emergencies. I think global supply chains will come under scrutiny and there'll be a long hard look at the concentration of production of anything in any one place or small number of places.

The pandemic is such a major event that it's bound to have lasting effects. I think the best parallel is to look at the effects of the two world wars.

The first world war contributed to the emancipation of women; women who had worked in the factories demanded the vote at the end of the war. The war made people realise the importance of the contribution women make as well as the contribution of men.

The second world war came so soon after the first and the huge sacrifices that were involved made people less patient with inequality and privilege. After the second world war we saw the further development of the welfare state and a period of 30 years in which inequality between people at the higher income level and those at the lower income level was reduced. Sometime around 1980, however, that inequality gap started to widen again. It was possibly driven by globalisation and the higher rewards that people who serve a global market can get, whether they are sportsmen or chief executives.

Globalisation pushes their salaries up far faster than the salaries of people whose activity is confined to one country, and this has been driving inequality. But I think the covid-19 experience has made people impatient with that. There is a growing recognition that we are much more dependent on other people than we realised, no matter how well-off we are financially.

MY RECOMMENDATIONS FOR TRANSFORMATION

Every political career is different, so it's difficult to draw general conclusions. But based on my 35 active years in politics, here are some tentative recommendations.

1. **Don't try to do everything**
   Set yourself a limited number of goals – two or three at most. Communicate these clearly and pursue them relentlessly until they are achieved, or you have learned that they are not attainable in your time frame.

2. **Promote rigorous thinking in the pre-decision phase**
   Be open to experimentation and new ways of approaching the problems you have chosen to solve.

3. **Delegate responsibility as much as possible but have a rigorous system to monitor achievement**
   Be prepared for the resistance that arises when several ministries share responsibility. Put in place a system, if necessary, involving the prime minister, to bring all the key players together to make sure agreed policies are fully implemented by all and follow this up relentlessly.

4. **The greater your responsibilities, the more time you need to devote to personal relationships with your essential collaborators**
   Make sure they all feel ownership of decisions and are not caught by surprise. Make sure cabinet decisions are properly prepared under shared political direction.

MY RECOMMENDATIONS FOR POLICY

As for policy, from my experience, I would offer the following advice.

1. Pursue a consistent policy over time. Ireland's success in attracting FDI had this characteristic.
2. Don't take short cuts. Ireland's mistakes - for example in fiscal policy - were the result of trying to find a short cut to prosperity. There are no short cuts.
3. Remember that life is about more than money and material success. People need a sense of security and a sense of identity. In part, populism has arisen because political leaders have forgotten this. So, make sure people's emotions are engaged as well as their brains and their purses.

4. Compromise is not a dirty word. The art of politics is that of knowing when to compromise and when to stand firm. Do not allow any one issue to dominate your thinking or that of your collaborators. Try to build linkages between issues so you can maximize support for the changes you need to make.

KEY QUALITIES FOR EFFECTIVE LEADERSHIP

In my experience, effective public leadership requires the ability to:

- Choose advisers and have a willingness to trust them.
- Accept the uncertainties and contingencies surrounding all political decisions.
- Keep perspective by cultivating some outside interests.

Often, the challenges I faced in government were not the ones I expected to encounter before I took office. You find yourself making decisions on topics on which you are not, and cannot be, an expert. You must accept that. High-level political decisions are always made on the basis of incomplete information.

I also found that, in lower-level political offices, you could spend time studying and devising your own solutions and see the result of your personal insight in the final decision taken. In higher office, there is less time to think and read about issues. Instead, as a leader, you have to delegate to others and question them on their conclusions, but also trust them. So, choosing advisers is critical. In higher office, more time has to be devoted to listening to oral presentations, synthesizing in your own mind, persuading others and making difficult choices. Consequently, there is less time for original thinking.

If someone ascends to high office without learning these lessons, they will interfere unproductively, procrastinate and keep asking for further evidence rather than make decisions. There are examples of these errors in some modern leaders.

Of course, to succeed in political life, one must accept setbacks and still persist. Stamina and an ability to absorb criticism are important. The busier one is, the easier this becomes. One has less time to ruminate on slights or attacks. You just get on with it. It helps to have outside interests. When I was taoiseach, my wife and I had small children, which was great for keeping perspective. I also played quite a lot of tennis, incorporating games into foreign trips, which helped a lot and reduced jetlag.

INDIA

In the three decades following independence from British colonial rule in 1947, the Indian economy averaged an annual growth rate of 3.5%. This was often mockingly called the "Hindu rate of growth", as other Asian economies were averaging double this figure and becoming "Asian Tigers" and "economic miracles".

However, from the early 1990s, India embarked on a journey of economic turnaround, becoming the fastest-growing, trillion-dollar economy in the world and the fifth-largest overall, leapfrogging big hitters such as France and the United Kingdom to reach a nominal GDP of US$2.94 trillion in 2019.

India's rise in the last 30 years has been dramatic. But its economic success was not immediate. In the decades following independence and partition in 1947, the country's population almost doubled, while economic growth remained virtually stagnant. This led to a staggeringly high poverty rate which, by 1990, stood at 45%.

Fearing the return of imperial foreign rule and foreign economic domination from international trade and investment, economic policy was deliberately structured to be inward looking, which led to the implementation of socialist-style plans and regulations.

In the 1970s, major industries were nationalised and income tax rates grew as high as 97.75%. Imports required a special licence, which were difficult to obtain. Licences were also required for manufacturing and maximum quotas were set, which limited productivity growth. As a result, economic incentives became distorted, which gave rise to an underground economy and stagnation of government revenue. By 1985, India's share of global trade had declined to 0.5% and foreign exchange reserves were virtually empty. By 1991, the country was facing a balance of payments crisis.

In June 1991, the newly elected prime minister, Narasimha Rao, initiated a fully-fledged economic reform and liberalisation programme. Although there had been some partial liberalisation efforts in the mid-1980s, these had been piecemeal and fragmented, and had had only a small effect on growth. Rao's comprehensive reforms, however, translated into a new economic reality; as entrepreneurship surged, Foreign Direct Investment (FDI) inflows multiplied and foreign exchange reserves mushroomed. The manufacturing sector witnessed significant growth, thanks to the elimination of the licensing regulations.

Output grew by 5.7% per year in the period 1993-2005, while exports grew at almost twice that rate. Pro-competitive reforms in banking, telecommunications, insurance and transportation provided a significant boost to productivity - especially for foreign firms.

The liberalisation of trade and investment helped boost the services sector, too. Foreign and domestic competition took off, regulation was improved and consumer choice increased. In 1990, the average turnaround time for a container at India's main ports was eight days. By 2005, this had dropped to three-and-a-half days, thereby improving India's competitiveness and efficiency.

The telecommunications market also made great leaps forward, thanks to reforms in legislation coinciding with rapid advances in technology. Communication both inside India and with the outside world suddenly became cheaper and easier. In the 1980s, the government had declared telephones to be a luxury rather than a right; telecommunications were given low priority and the inefficient system was plagued with faulty lines. By 2005, however, waiting lists for telephone services had virtually disappeared in urban areas and had improved significantly in rural areas too. The number of mobile phone connections in India is now over one billion and the country boasts one of the cheapest mobile rates in the world. Moreover, India has the world's second-largest internet user base, with 661.94 million broadband subscribers.

While India continues to face development and poverty-related challenges, its economic turnaround has been impressive. Between 1995 and 2019, nominal GDP increased more than 700%. This rapid rise was powered by a number of factors including urbanisation and the rise of technologies that have enhanced efficiency and productivity. In addition, India made a bold move to incentivise the innovation and technology sector, which has resulted in a burgeoning startup "tech" scene. India now boasts more technology companies than anywhere in the world other than the United States and the United Kingdom.

Rao's skills in political leadership and foreign policy were also a key factor in India's transformation. He knew that he would need a strong team behind him to be able to convince people to support his radical reforms and one of his most important appointments was his finance minister, Manmohan Singh. Singh had immense credibility not just to convince the doubters at home but also critics in the wider world.

In foreign policy, Rao reached out to East Asian nations, particularly Japan, South Korea and Singapore and defined what is now called as the Look East policy, which paved the way for close, long-term trade agreements. He also initiated crucial talks with China to resolve border disputes, which laid the framework for rebuilding diplomatic and economic ties and, in 2008, China became India's largest trading partner. (Since then border disputes have raised their head once more, as China has sought to flex its muscles.) At the same time, Rao was looking west and, despite disagreements over India's refusal to sign the nuclear non-proliferation treaty, his conciliatory stance created an important upswing in India-United States relations. In 2016, India was declared a Major Defence Partner of the United States.

Principle-driven Transformation

"After climbing a great hill, one only finds that there are many more hills to climb."

Nelson Mandela

Supachai Panitchpakdi
Deputy Prime Minister, Thailand, 1992 to1995 and 1997 to 2000

5

Rice has been a staple of life in Thailand for thousands of years, so much so that neighbours would greet each other by calling out "*khin khao rue yang*" - have you eaten rice yet? In the 1960s, the Green Revolution introduced new high-yielding crop varieties and Thailand became the world's largest exporter of rice. Today, it is also the largest exporter of tapioca, rubber and canned tuna, as well as the third largest exporter of sugar.

The 1960s also saw the birth of Thailand's tourism industry, spurred on by the arrival of thousands of United States troops for R&R during the Vietnam War. By 2019, Bangkok had become the world's most visited city for the fourth year in a row, with over 22 million visitors, and Thailand ranked among the top five medical tourism destinations in the world[38, 39].

From this solid foundation, Thailand is transforming itself into a knowledge-based economy, including a dedicated special economic zone for new technologies, and a global health care hub.

In this chapter I will share my insights on Thailand's development journey so far and the next phase of its economic transformation.

TRANSFORMATION IN EAST AND SOUTHEAST ASIA

Thailand has followed a broadly similar development path to other countries in East and Southeast Asia. All started from economies based on primary products and commodities (such as rice, corn, cassava, coconut, rubber, tin and some precious stones) before their exports became more diversified.

In the north of the region, for instance, South Korea was still primarily a bulk exporter of animal furs at the end of the second world war. China, the largest exporter in the world today, only started its pervasive economic reforms in 1978, when leader Deng Xiaoping decided to open up its economy and began the process of re-orienting it towards the international trading system. China eventually became a member of the World Trade Organisation in 2001.

Economic development does not lend itself to a "one-size-fits-all" template, however, as countries have their own specific institutional characteristics and diverse social and cultural backgrounds. Nevertheless, despite these differences, the United Nations Conference on Trade and Development (UNCTAD) has identified two elements that are common to all the successful development strategies in East and Southeast Asia. The first is the state-led creation of a robust industrial foundation, with selected sectors playing key roles to support structural change. The second is a well-managed integration into the global economy, not with the ideology of trade liberalisation as the ultimate goal, but with the intention of making trade work for development purposes.

The development experience of East Asian countries contrasts with that of Latin America and parts of Africa, which have largely followed the Washington Consensus model based on a free market philosophy. Although market liberalisation has certainly played a significant role in our region, market forces should not take the lead on development strategy.

The fact is that unbridled market mechanisms have led to several debt crises, including the creation of bubbles in the real estate and IT sectors at the beginning of the millennium. And let us not forget either that it was excessive de-regulation of financial markets in the United States that encouraged trading in sub-prime mortgages, which led to the global financial crisis in 2008 and triggered the great recession.

CREATING A ROBUST FOUNDATION

In 1993, the World Bank published a report on the so-called "East Asian Miracle."[(2)] At the time, East Asia was enjoying the benefits of consistently high economic growth, coupled with relatively low inflation and more or less balanced budgets. According to the bank's analysis, the successes of the newly industrialising economies (NIEs) of East Asia were founded on the institution of market, pure and simple.

However, this was only partially correct. Success in the NIEs was certainly galvanised by the entrepreneurial attitudes embodied in typical Asian businesses, but the report played down the impact of a substantial level of intervention by government.

For example, Singapore, which in the 1960s was just a backwater territory of the state of Malaya, achieved its rapid economic development under the visionary "hands-on" leadership of Lee Kuan Yew. Lee pushed for Singapore's independence and adopted a specific strategy for state development, first generating massive investments in housing infrastructure and education. He then set out to define Singapore's competitive edge in the area of maritime transportation as a free port, a hub for regional headquarters of major multinationals, a global trader in commodities and a zone for high-tech industries. In South Korea, the rise of post-war manufacturing in shipbuilding, electronics and automobiles was driven by the formation of large conglomerates - chaebols – that were protected by government regulations. During the initial stage of development of the automobile industry, for example, the Korean government limited the quota for car imports to the level of car exports.

East Asian economic development can therefore be seen to have been based on a pragmatic and judicious blend of institutional reforms through market liberalisation, and interventionist policy by the state. In this way the region avoided the pitfalls and excessive borrowing encountered by developing countries elsewhere in the world.

INTEGRATION WITH THE GLOBAL ECONOMY

Integration into the global economy was an important second element in the development strategies in the region, as identified by UNCTAD.

East Asia has benefited greatly from the advent of global supply chains and the influx of foreign direct investments (FDIs) from other economies in Asia and from the rest of the world. For example, Japan's massive investments in Korea and Southeast Asia spawned new industries from textiles to automobiles to electronics. In its turn, Korea's outbound investment in Southeast Asia, particularly in Vietnam and Indonesia, has generated a strong push towards the digitalisation of these economies. China's great economic strides in the last 40 years have also benefited from unprecedented inflows of FDIs, mainly from the United States, Europe and Japan, averaging more than US$100 billion a year over several decades. Now, China is beginning to spin off direct investments into neighbouring economies.

But attracting inward investment requires caution. The efforts of developing countries in attracting FDIs must be managed within a wider, development-led industrial strategy.

The quality of inward investment is critical and should meet four minimum requirements:

1. FDIs should contribute to creating productive employment.
2. FDIs should enhance the export competitiveness of the recipient economy.
3. FDIs should contribute to the transfer of technology.
4. FDIs should enhance total factor productivity to help the economy move up the global supply chain ladder.

MANAGING GLOBAL INTEGRATION

Strategic integration with the global economy is one of the key factors in the success of the development pathway followed by countries in East and Southeast Asia. However, there are lessons to be learnt from their experiences.

1. *In opening up economies to external capital flows, caution must be exercised against the rapid capital account liberalisation recommended by the International Monetary Fund (IMF) in the 1990s. Financial liberalisation, if undertaken under unfavourable conditions, can lead to speculative capital flows taking advantage of a large arbitrage in interest rates and a de facto guaranteed exchange rate. This was one of the significant causes of the Asian financial crisis in 1997-1998.*

2. *The strategy of export-led growth supported the rise of economies in East and Southeast Asia but, with globalisation losing its shine after the great recession of 2007 to 2009, developing countries with open economies have had to adjust their trade-related strategy. While countries are advised to maintain an open economy and follow the rules of the multilateral trading system, they must also find ways to supplement the loss of income from declining trade volume. In cultivating more domestic consumption, China, for example, has taken a big step into infrastructure investments culminating in the Belt and Road Initiative, lifting the service sector from under 50% of GDP to more than 60% within a decade.*

3. *The paradigm of export-led development based on a policy of keeping labour costs low is being rethought. Competition among developing countries in producing and exporting labour-intensive goods has led to downward price pressure. If multinational firms seek to maintain their profitability levels by sourcing from the cheapest location in terms of labour costs, then global trade competition becomes a race to the bottom between low-paid labour forces from developing economies. This is already resulting in an increase in income inequality. To address this, labour must be viewed not as a cost but in terms of earnings that are necessary to support domestic demand.*

4. *The notion of the global value chain has been adopted fervently in East and Southeast Asia. However, being part of a supply chain can induce lethargy in executing structural transformation, with a country remaining captive in the role of primary producer. East and Southeast Asian cases have demonstrated that if the state plays a strong and effective role, then trade-induced structural change can be successfully implemented. Governments should adopt value chain policy in a way that ensures:*

   - *the state can always assist and support the weak bargaining position of their suppliers, particularly the farmers;*
   - *domestic suppliers are afforded opportunities to tap into advanced technology;*
   - *suppliers are enabled to upgrade themselves and move up the value chain through training, R&D and appropriate financial back-up.*

5. *From the early days of emerging market development in the 1960s and 1970s, international aid always came with conditions attached. Some of these conditions prescribed trade liberalisation, market reforms and the privatisation of state enterprises, whilst blocking agricultural subsidies (even while advanced economies applied them back home). From the 1970s, such conditions were made into international norms in the guise of the so-called "Washington Consensus" and the World Bank's "Structural Adjustment Programmes". During the Asian financial crisis, the IMF's standby loan facilities wrongly imposed procyclical macro-economic tightening policies on Asian economies, which worsened the economic recession, and led to the worst contraction ever witnessed in the region.*

EIGHT LESSONS FROM THAILAND

As noted earlier, developing countries in Latin America relied on liberalising their markets, but Southeast Asian policymakers took a more pragmatic approach by balancing market forces with state intervention. Thailand followed this path.

Structural transformation was achieved through the three-pronged approach of strategic industrial policy, export competitiveness and the promotion of FDIs.

While encouraging the private sector to make adjustments to the domestic and international markets, Thailand also implemented interventionist policies through a series of five-year national plans starting in the 1960s, to guide the economy through reconstruction. A number of lessons can be drawn from Thailand's experiences of transformation.

1. **Developmental shifts require strong, consistent leadership**

   During the 1960s, policymakers in Asian developing economies were preoccupied with feeding their populations. Some of these, including Thailand, can be typified as "monsoon economies", as they depend on a distinct rainfall pattern for their crop seasons. Historically, economic growth varied with the volume of rainfall, with high-growth years associated with an abundant supply of water.

   Thailand's agrarian economy served it well during times of crisis. Most of the labour force was absorbed by the farm sector, which was supported by government investments in irrigation systems and off-farm activities during the dry season. In the 1960s, however, with the introduction of Thailand's first five-year national economic and development plan, a nationwide road network began to be constructed. This gradually linked distant rural communities to the markets of urban centres.

   Thailand was transforming.

   It may be surprising to those schooled in democracy to learn that this development plan did not emerge from an elected government but was conceived by an authoritarian military leadership. There are parallels here with other formidable leaders in the region: Prime Minister Lee Kuan Yew's "guided democracy" in Singapore, for example. In South Korea it was the authoritarian rule of President Park Chung-Hee that launched Korea into an industrial era. Also, Malaysia's Vision 2020 - a long-term strategy to transform the country into a digital-ready state - was set out by Prime Minister Mahathir in the 1990s.

   Although it has been theorised that quality governance and inspirational leadership stems from liberal democracy, in practice, phases of strong developmental shift in Asia emerged from benevolent, but sometimes authoritarian, leadership, which guided countries out of deep poverty and enabled them to jump the middle-income hurdle.

2. **Development must be inclusive and satisfy basic human needs**
During the transformative decade of the 1960s, Thailand made a big effort to include its rural communities in development plans in order to head off the onset of social tensions. Ultimately, however, it wasn't financial assistance that brought change to these communities, but the Philippines-based International Rice Research Institute (IRRI). New high-yielding rice varieties were produced through joint international efforts and adopted by Asian nations at an unprecedented speed. This was the first Green Revolution. It helped bolster food security and demonstrated how the farming sector could be modernised through research and technology.

With both government intervention and the private sector playing important roles in enhancing food production and processing productivity, surplus labour from the rural sector migrated towards urban areas, lending support to the fast-growing manufacturing and construction sectors.

Thailand's all-out support for agriculture and food production may not have always been justifiable on purely pecuniary terms, but this form of inclusive development addressed the basic human needs of food security, human rights and equality, and brought balanced growth with a reasonable degree of equality and stability.

3. **Manage domestic demand against export-led growth**
In the 1990s, the Asian Development Bank initiated a study led by a team of renowned economists, which concluded that Southeast Asian economies could expect to enjoy rapid economic growth by linking their natural resources with expanding world demand.[40] This report had a significant impact on the future development path of the region.

At a time when Latin American economies were following inward looking and protectionist strategies, Southeast Asia began to open up. In the 1970s and 1980s, Thailand adopted export-led development policies, which produced strong growth, reaching double digits between 1988 and 1990. It gradually diversified its range of exports with rapidly growing manufacturing output and a rising service sector supported by the influx of foreign investments.

Thailand's traumatic experiences with the 1997 Asian financial crisis, however, have taught it to carefully monitor its current account balance and build up robust international reserves as a bulwark against currency fluctuations. Thailand's exposure to the global economy, while being a key factor in its growth, also left it vulnerable to the volatility of world economic conditions. Going forward, Thailand will have to be more concerned with domestic demand management.

4. **Foreign investment requires joint policy management**
Industrialisation in Thailand took off with the help of FDIs, particularly from Japan. The initial influx of foreign investments helped to spawn light industries such as textiles, clothing and consumer goods. But as the country went through several domestic and international crises, pressure increased to reform its trade policies towards greater liberalisation.

As in other parts of East Asia, policymakers in Thailand took a more pragmatic approach by balancing market forces with the enhanced role of the state. Thailand's strategy was based on close coordination between the Board of Investment (BOI) and the various economic ministries. Skills-training institutes were created for specific industry sectors, as were new industrial estates around Bangkok to help attract more foreign investors. These reforms meant that the export push after the 1997 financial crisis was more effective, having benefited from joint policy management (to ensure consistency of industrial policy with state interventions), controlled economic liberalisation, the right infrastructure (such as industrial estates) and export competitiveness.

THE THAI AUTO INDUSTRY

The complicated and convoluted saga of the rise of the auto industry in Thailand — from production of a mere 50,000 cars in 1997 to 2.2 million in 2019 — reflects the Thai development experience.

Starting simply as an assembly location for foreign car manufacturers, Thailand's auto industry went through a long period of local SME's (small and medium-sized enterprises) trading in the international auto parts sector. Yet, with government guidance and protection, which occasionally banned the import of finished vehicles and made the use of local parts compulsory, Thailand gradually grew its own auto-building industry.

The gradual shift to more liberal trade and investment policies, with less pressure on localisation, attracted more producers to the Thai market. Ultimately the push to export encouraged efficiency and rationalisation. Thailand is not yet able to compete fully in passenger cars, but it has become a leading player in pick-up trucks, exporting all over the world.

5. **Foster regional collaboration**
   To be able to buffer against recurrent global disruptions and contribute to global governance, successful regional groupings like the Association of Southeast Asian Nations (ASEAN) are an essential part of the new geopolitical landscape. China, for example, counts on ASEAN as an important economic partner in Asia, as does Europe. Thailand's strategy is to build up coalitions like these, with APEC (Asia-Pacific Economic Cooperation) being another.

6. **Ensure fiscal stability**
   Countries need to have sound economic fundamentals based on monetary and fiscal stability and discipline. To build a strong developmental state and an inclusive development policy, robust institutions that play key roles in macro-economic management must be established and maintained. Historical legacy, including intensive training of professional technocrats free from political interference, is a decisive ingredient in building up such a bulwark of creditworthy institutions.

   While in the past there have been periods of political intrusion into monetary and fiscal management, with dubious consequences, Thailand now has well-trained technocrats employed in key macro-economic institutions, such as the Budget Bureau, the National Economic and Social Development Board (NESDB), the Fiscal Policy Office and the Bank of Thailand (BoT). These institutions are the guardians of monetary and fiscal discipline.

   Monetary stability, led by the central bank, the BoT, has been at the core of the country's macro-economic management policy. The bank's relative independence from political turmoil has contributed to its solid track record. Thailand's external indebtedness is low while the total public debt is below 50% of the GDP on average, which is far healthier than most of the advanced economies of the world. On the World Economic Competitiveness Table, Thailand ranks among the top ten in the world for macro-economic prudence and discipline.

7. Social Investment

As a counterpart to sound macro-economic management, inclusive social investment policy needs strong institutions. Yet despite decades of economic growth, access to adequate social protection cannot be taken for granted in many parts of the world. It is a concern that after the financial crisis in 1997-1998, Southeast Asia readily took on substantial financial reforms but has not yet sufficiently implemented social reforms.

A complete social protection system should encompass sanitation, environmental protection, social security (pensions and unemployment support) and quality universal health care. Thailand is fortunate to have a long tradition of health care based on indigenous knowledge, herbal (ayurvedic) cures and therapeutic body massage. It has also made great strides towards providing universal health care, although the programme needs to be refined.

In March 2020, during the covid-19 pandemic, the World Health Organisation (WHO) published a global ranking of strategic preparedness and response status, placing Thailand in the second highest group of well-prepared countries. In practice, however, Thailand's response seems to have produced better results than many countries in the highest-ranking group, which included America and parts of Europe.

Thailand's public health system has been challenged before, of course, by the HIV-Aids crisis in the 1980s and SARS in 2002-2004, and it has learnt the importance of raising public awareness of the threat of pandemics. It has also learnt to cultivate groups of medical doctors and public health professionals to manage the Ministry of Public Health. Yet further reform is still needed to link social and economic investment policies to ensure equal access to quality health services, particularly in rural areas.

In the context of social development policy, education in Thailand should be a success story. The quality of skilled workers in key institutions, health care and business management, points to an effective learning system. Yet shortcomings persist in the system's adjustment to the requirement of the labour market, particularly weaknesses in the STEM (science, technology, engineering, mathematics) subjects, and with upgrading skills to raise labour productivity.

8. The role of entrepreneurs

Entrepreneurs have undoubtedly played a vital role in the economic development of Southeast Asia, but this should not blind us to the limitations of market forces. The pure market mechanism may set the right price - but rarely gets development right. The opium trade of the 1840s provides a stark historical warning of the damage that unfettered capitalism can cause and is one reason why the first few rounds of emerging FDIs in Southeast Asia were treated with caution.

In the specific case of Thailand - the only non-colonised nation in the region - foreign visitors and traders have historically always been welcomed. Some even obtained royal titles granted by the monarchs of the kingdom. Chinese traders, in particular, were seamlessly integrated into the former Siamese societies. Traditionally, Thailand has been a place where Chinese, Portuguese, Dutch and British entrepreneurs mixed easily with indigenous merchants.

In the modern era, foreign multinationals through their FDIs have found their home in Thailand and have played an important role in industrialising the economy. The joint public-private sector committee has had a long-standing role in working closely with the country's economic cabinet and shared in the decision-making process for key projects.

Nevertheless, the benevolent role of entrepreneurship should not be taken for granted. Because of the pronounced political impact of the private sector, safeguards of transparency, decency, proper conduct and anti-corruption must be established. This comes in various forms, including a national anti-corruption committee, and a special anti-corruption committee for civil servants - but the reality is that these organisations still face a mountain to climb.

At a regional and global level, competition laws will be put to an even sterner test when the digital giants of the world come to dominate the global economy, with digital gadgets being the opium of today. The national tax regime will have to be drastically reformed to be able to collect taxes from digital companies. In America, a few huge corporations rule the roost, with Amazon, for example, being exempt from state and city tax and paying virtually zero federal tax, while Boeing pays no state tax either but receives direct subsidies of billions of dollars from Washington State.[(8)]

Therefore, it is incumbent on policy makers to set out prudent market rules and regulations, especially in the areas of anti-trust and consumer protection. This is especially pertinent given the growing economic and political powers of major corporations and the emergence of giant digital platforms.

THE ASIAN FINANCIAL CRISIS

In 1997, Thailand's economy was severely disrupted by the Asian financial crisis. The crisis created a fresh impetus for reform. However, progress was sluggish and Thailand's economic performance since has been somewhat uneven, with average growth slowing and competitiveness deteriorating in the face of new players and new products.

In 2001, after the crisis had begun to subside, a new political regime took over and, although it pushed through programmes in rural health care, debt relief, and development loans, it did little to strengthen institutions and enhance productivity. According to one in-depth study of this period: "this strategy was more akin to financially unsustainable Latin American populism than to South Korea or Taiwan-style rural reforms."[11]

With a lack of pertinent effort at real education reform — there were five different education ministers from 2001 through 2004 — Thailand missed opportunities to upgrade its manufacturing sector through trade liberalisation, research and development, and technical training. Likewise it failed to modernise its agricultural sector through extension and technology improvement.

As you can see, Thailand needs to overcome certain domestic constraints in order to be able to address the challenges of transformation, specifically:

- Lack of political stability.
- The need for continuity in structural transformation policy.
- A tectonic shift in education towards serving the knowledge economy.
- A mountain of legal entanglements.
- Extreme weather conditions of heavy floods and severe droughts.
- Slow transition into a low-carbon economy.
- An expanding rural-urban income inequality gap.

THAILAND'S FOUR-PRONGED TRANSFORMATION IN THE 21ST CENTURY

Faced with the VUCA (volatility, uncertainty, complexity, ambiguity) environment of the 21st century, Thailand has had to undertake a complete overhaul of its development philosophy and vision. This is based on a four-pronged transformation of government policymaking:

1. The adoption of the Sufficiency Economy Philosophy (SEP) to provide moral leadership.
2. The creation of a 20-year National Plan enshrined in the constitution.
3. The establishment of a special economic zone akin to the technology parks in China.
4. Support for regional economic integration to bolster trade and global governance.

THE SUFFICIENCY ECONOMY PHILOSOPHY (SEP)

The first important element of the four-pronged transformation strategy is the nationwide recognition and adoption of the Sufficiency Economy Philosophy (SEP), which was first proposed by the late King Rama IX in 1974 and came to prominence in the wake of the Asian financial crisis.

Dubbed the "Development King" by the UN and presented with a UN Human Development Lifetime Achievement Award in 2006, His Majesty Rama IX's SEP infused the country's development strategy with basic "moral sentiment" - similar to that advocated by Adam Smith in the 18th century - which has been absorbed into Thailand's policymaking to shift the quality of mindset to more demanding ethical standards. The SEP is based on the King's Five Principles:

1. Know what you are doing (the wisdom of being mindful always).
2. Be honest and persevere (adopt good governance, diligence, patience and integrity).
3. Avoid extreme actions (follow inclusive growth, the middle-path and balanced development).
4. Be sensible and insightful in taking decisions (use prudence and research-based policymaking).
5. Build protection against shocks (apply contingency planning, risk management and policy space).

The Thailand Development Research Institute (TDRI) has quantified the impact of SEP on sustainable development and found that the King's Principles and SEP had a positive effect in areas ranging from poverty reduction to improving living conditions, building social capital and achieving greater equality.[14] Kofi Annan, former secretary general of the UN, has also praised the SEP as being of great relevance to communities everywhere during times of rapid globalisation, noting that the philosophy's "middle path" approach strongly reinforces the UN's own advocacy of a people-centred and sustainable path towards human development.[41]

In practical terms, integrating sufficiency thinking into economic and environmental management encompasses three stages:

1. Partial practices, reflecting a compliance frame of mind.
2. Advanced practices, which demand people's comprehension of why they are doing what they are doing.
3. Enlightened practices that transcend personal and local issues to reach an inspiration stage.[13]

From the highest level right down to village level, the application of SEP principles has made people believe in the possibility of achieving success, participating in the development process themselves and moving forward together step by step.

THAILAND'S 20-YEAR NATIONAL PLAN

The second major element in Thailand's economic restructuring is the articulation and adoption of the National 20-year Strategic Plan (2018-2037). In the past, Thailand implemented its development strategy through five-year plans, with the twelfth plan in effect between 2017-2021 and coinciding with the first phase of the new 20-year strategy.

In an unprecedented step, the 20-year plan was enshrined in the nation's constitutional law to ensure that successive governments are legally bound to follow up in the six key strategic areas, or pillars, identified by the collective efforts of parliament, the public and private sectors, and nationwide hearings with people from all walks of life.

A 20-year plan may seem paradoxical when it's so hard to predict events even a year ahead. But it is precisely because no one knows what the world will look like in 20 years that a long-term vision is needed to prepare as well as possible and to build up immunity against unpredictable events - reflecting one of the maxims of SEP.

THE SIX PILLARS OF THAILAND'S 20-YEAR NATIONAL PLAN

1. ***National Security***
   Covering the protection of the constitutional monarchy, judicial system and national defence, to international cooperation.

2. ***Competitiveness***
   Covering a wide-ranging area from monetary and fiscal discipline, support for the entrepreneurial class and SMEs, enhancing labour productivity and modernising the farming, manufacturing and services sectors, to trade facilitation, creating special economic zones, improving ICT infrastructure and enforcing Thailand's participation in international organisations.

3. ***Human Resources Development***
   Creating the necessary conditions for national development in terms of lifelong education, educational reforms, comprehensive and inclusive social protection and improvement in the universal health-care system (with the aim of making Thailand a key global medical hub).

4. ***Social Equality***
   Including initiatives to close the inequality gap in income and opportunities; access to the justice system and universal health care; and the protection of national culture, traditions and religious institutions.

5. ***Inclusive Growth***
   Preserving environmental assets; reforestation; reducing greenhouse gases; promoting renewable energy, energy efficiency, the green industry and carbon sequestration; sustainable urban development; and policy for adapting to climate change.

6. ***Public Sector Management***
   Covering the national budgeting system based on development needs; tax reforms (most intractable); linking budgetary allocation to national strategy; counter-corruption and transparency with public participation; raising public services response to public needs; and legal guillotine.

The 20-year National Plan is the most comprehensive development vision of the country and covers a massive number of projects, initially more than 6,000. Most of these are allocated under pillars two and three, with pillar three covering the largest number of projects (roughly one-third of the total).

This underlines the belief that that the necessary conditions for long-term structural transformation reside in the human resources development area. Besides setting up special funds to help equalise educational opportunities, for the first time the human development strategy will include targeted assistance, starting with pre-schooling cohorts, in promoting nutritional food and preparations for further schooling.

Reformed curricula will emphasise STEAM subjects (science, technology, engineering, arts and mathematics) and the role of teachers will be to become inspirational coaches rather than merely reciting lessons to students.

An ambitious target has also been set for reducing inequality by pushing for a targeted annual income growth of 15% for the 40% of lowest earners.

CREATING AN "SEZ" TECHNOLOGY HUB

The third element of the kingdom's transformation strategy is to move the economy up the technology ladder. A cluster of tech-based projects will create a dedicated special economic zone (SEZ) akin to the super-corridor in Malaysia and IT parks in China.

The Eastern Economic Corridor (EEC), which includes three provinces along Thailand's eastern seaboard, is a holistic effort linked to the national 20-year strategy to transform the country to a higher technology and knowledge-based economy.

The EEC is the follow-up to the successful Eastern Seaboard (ESB) project in the same region, which was implemented some 35 years ago to launch the country into an industrial era after gas deposits were found in the Gulf of Thailand. The ESB facilitated the birth and growth of a highly efficient petrochemical industry and was a joint effort between the government and private sector. The private sector became very important during the 1980s and 1990s and, without legislation for anti-trust and anti-competition, the government realised it needed to keep the private sector onside. There were regular meetings of the Joint Public Private Sector Committee and key government decisions involved private sector consultation, including negotiations to join the WTO.

The EEC will build on the successful infrastructure and industrial base that already exists and includes diverse industries ranging from automobiles to chemicals and electronics. A more advanced infrastructure will be added, comprising a new airport and an aerotropolis, including a 250 kilometre-per-hour high-speed rail link connecting the two international airports in Bangkok with the third one in the special zone.

Besides creating a digital park, ten new high-tech industries are also planned for the zone. These include electric cars, bio-industry, robotics, aviation logistics and modern medicine.

With so many ministries, public and private institutions involved, the implementation of such a large-scale project has been a major challenge. To cut through this Gordian knot a special legal act will authorise the Coordinating Office of the EEC to operate as a one-stop centre in providing the necessary licenses, public amenities and facilities to the special zone. Another legal act aims to expedite public-private sector partnership (PPP) investments. Already three of the five mega-projects in the EEC - the inter-airport speed train, the construction of the aerotropolis and the expansion of a deep-sea port - have been approved with construction starting soon. These are major investments that should help provide the needed stimulus post-coronavirus.

REGIONAL ECONOMIC INTEGRATION

The fourth element of Thailand's economic restructuring effort deals with the economic integration process in Asia to provide a counterbalance to the global malaise. ASEAN has already launched into a deeper integration by engaging in the ASEAN Economic Community (AEC), which will liberalise not only trade in goods and services but also allow free movement of capital and people.

As a single market and production base with a 650-million population, the AEC will be the seventh largest economy in the world and is meant to be a counterbalance to the rise of China and India. Further effort through Thailand's chairmanship of ASEAN in 2019 forged an agreement on the establishment of an even larger economic grouping in Asia by having the ten member countries of ASEAN form a so-called Regional Comprehensive Economic Partnership (RCEP) with China, India, Japan, Australia and New Zealand.

This mega trade deal was concluded in 2019 (although India opted to stay out for now). With one-third of the global population and output, this regional free trade agreement should be the largest outside of the EU and is destined to rise to one-half of total global output in the next 20 years.

Besides creating a cushion against global recession, the RCEP should be able to reduce the brewing geopolitical tension in the region. The deal is already creating new opportunities for Thai firms and will play a role in urging Thailand to raise its international competitiveness.

MY LEADERSHIP JOURNEY

When it comes to my own leadership journey, I was very fortunate to have a brilliant mentor at a young age in Professor Jan Tinbergen. Tinbergen was awarded the first Nobel Memorial Prize in economic sciences in 1969, which he shared with Ragnar Frisch, for having developed and applied dynamic models for the analysis of economic processes. He was very unconventional, introducing mathematics into economics back in the 1940s and 50s to make it a science. When I undertook my dissertation under his guidance for my doctorate, I told him I was on a scholarship from the central bank and had to follow a financial subject. He retorted that I would do nothing of the sort. If you do your dissertation with me, he said, finance is not that important. People come first; in fact, people come first, second and third. I have always followed what he taught me.

At the time, Tinbergen was assigned by, I think, the OECD, to work on the so-called Mediterranean Manpower Planning Group, along with some professors from Cambridge, and he said if I was interested, I should help him on this project. This turned out to be the beginning of me being pushed to think outside of my comfort zone. I thought I was going to be working at the central bank or doing economics and monetary policy. Instead, I ended up in the world of human resource planning and human capital.

Tinbergen taught me always to balance the thoughts and opinions of others by looking at their viewpoint from another angle. When people take an extreme view, for example, go and stand on the other side to look at them and see why they have this opinion. You don't have to decide whether to agree or disagree with them, just make sure you take a different perspective to ensure you balance out what they are saying.

This advice has stayed with me. When I came back to work at the Bank of Thailand, I was constantly tussling with the funding people, the IMF and the World Bank. Every year they would come to inspect us, interview us, and give us advice. And I would question if I needed to agree with everything they prescribed. I started to put my own counter arguments. When, for example, they advised us to open up our capital account, I questioned if Thailand was ready and cautioned that we needed to watch out for our debt profile, because we had been accumulating a lot of short-term debt in order to invest in long-term development.

And that was the crisis that caught us. Short-term funds flowed in without any system of exchange control. Some people don't believe in control, so we let things open up freely. I left the Bank of Thailand before the plan was put into action and became deputy finance minister, in 1986.

I had my arguments with the World Bank, too. Helen Clark, who was the chief economist at the bank, would come to Thailand and tell us to do this and do that. They would come to us and tell us when the budget deficit was going through the roof. And I would reply that if we have a budget deficit and we are borrowing for government projects, then we are doing the right thing. If we were borrowing for something that was not developmental, then it would be wrong.

Our debate went public, with the major newspapers quoting Helen Clark as saying, "don't bite the hand that feeds you." Saying that to a poorer country, while imposing conditions on us that I didn't agree with, was the core of my feud with her. She later apologised but I never forgot the "don't bite the hand that feeds you" remark. And, in fact, I bit her hand very, very strongly, making big news in Thailand and gaining myself a reputation for being unconventional.

Of course, I didn't earn many accolades with these big global financial institutions like the IMF and World Bank. I always seemed to be fighting on the other side, right up until the financial crisis hit Asia in 1997.

In the two years prior to 1997, my party was in opposition. We were sending out warnings about the speculative funds flowing into the capital account, debating the issue in parliament and holding up examples of what we called the MBA countries (Mexico, Brazil, Argentina). Rather than spread paranoia with the "d" word (devaluation), however, I was arguing that we had to be more flexible with our exchange rates.

Devaluation eventually hit Thailand in 1997 anyway. I was in Hong Kong at the time, at the handover ceremony of Hong Kong from Britain to China. For the first time, Thailand went into the IMF standby agreement.

My party was elected to power in November 1997 and I was appointed deputy prime minister in charge of economic policies and minister of commerce. I was leader of an economic programme and my friend the finance minister was leader of the economic programme with the IMF. We clashed. I tried not to argue against the IMF programme, but it was so wrong; if you look at the great recession of 2007 to 2009, it was actually counter cyclical. When you have deflationary impact slowing down because of crashes here and bangs there, you actually have to reflate the economy – you need to stimulate it.

The government in Thailand was not in great deficit and did not create the crash; the deficit was in the private sector. The private sector had been induced to borrow heavily by the opening up of the capital account, and the Thai government had not allowed the exchange rate to move.

I tried to balance the arguments of the IMF, and I understood the pressures felt by my friend the finance minister. I also tried to change some of the IMF standby agreement, which required us to privatise all state-owned enterprises. I explained that if you put that in writing it will never get passed by the Thai parliament – Thai parliamentarians would not be forced by outsiders to privatise state enterprises. I said we would have to do it at our own pace.

I also tried to forge a group of countries to set up an Asian monetary fund and went to see Zhu Rongji in Beijing. Unfortunately, we could not secure Chinese support, but I still believe we need our own Asian monetary fund. We can't simply have the IMF deciding our fate all of the time. We have more money than everybody else in the world.

It may seem that my leadership style is confrontational. However, when I applied for the director general position at the WTO, one of the objections was that I spoke too softly; I was too polite. I may have developed a habit for counter argument - for seeing things from another side – but I try not to oppose people and make enemies. My approach is to understand each other's problems and negotiate. At the WTO they said "look, here we knock heads together," so I replied that knocking heads was from the time of the Flintstones – the stone age – and I didn't believe in it. I said I like friendly persuasion and diplomacy.

During my time at the WTO I had a long discussion with Jacques Chirac, then president of France, about why America's agricultural policy was so disastrous and France's was so wonderful. I could not convince him, however, to agree that France was over-subsidising. So, I went to see my friend Chancellor Schröder in Berlin and asked if he could convince Mr Chirac to reduce his subsidies. "Look, Supachai," the chancellor said, "there's one thing that Germany would never do, and that is to have another argument with France. We have had too many arguments and too many wars. I will do my best but don't ask me to create disagreement, conflict, or friction between the French and the Germans."

My policy is to use arguments and then more arguments; try to persevere and then to persevere some more; talk again and again. If people won't allow me, I go back and I go back, and if I can't do it with them, I do it with others and ask others to help me. In this way I build my own network of people to help me in my own way of negotiation.

In times of crisis I avoid panic, but I am not necessarily calm either. When I saw President Clinton after the Asian financial crisis, I became a little agitated when he did not acknowledge what had happened or say sorry. It dawned on me that no other country in the world is going to help you, really; you have to help yourself first. You have to be strong enough. You have to be able to negotiate. And you have to be able to negotiate when you have something to exchange. One of the first people who taught me this was Henry Kissinger. Over dinner in Thailand once, he said "Supachai, believe me about one thing, no country in this world is your friend. It's only common interests that drive us into agreements. Don't ever be misled by people being friendly."

When I talk about countries being strong, I am not talking about military power. I don't measure a country's strength on how many tanks, missiles and submarines it has. A country is strong because it understands how to deal with the underprivileged. And this is something that came home to roost in the covid-19 pandemic. Thailand did not handle the crisis better than America because of a higher health-care spend, or because it is" better"; it was because we are excessively afraid. We closed the country down early but cautiously and gradually, little by little, so that people would follow, trust the leadership and understand the situation.

A leader has to be consistent and truthful. The moment you try to shift blame around your own country or the world, you're beginning to lose your sense of reasoning, rationale and reality. Post-covid-19, we have to help each other in order to come out the other side together. There is only one victory – when we are all out of it together. So, we need to strengthen our international multilateral framework, even though that is not going to be easy.

After the global recession of 2008 there were promises at the UN, the G20, G7, G8 and around the world: we all pledged financial reforms. Nothing of the sort has happened. Investment after a crisis is not investment for growth. It's investment in health care, social infrastructure, education and research. Post-covid-19 I also hope the WTO will open up intellectual copyright agreements on key medical equipment and pharmaceuticals. This is a matter of life and death for everyone; it is not a question of dollars and cents for a few American and European firms.

There is a philosophical difference between the East and the West; the West has based its civilisation on material progress, whereas the East has based its on the need to find happiness. In the East we emphasise more of what I call non-market value. When I was a monk, albeit only for three weeks, I learned that you could be happy with just two meals a day. You don't have to have three meals a day.

To have a good, happy, strong nation you need to have what Mencius, a disciple of Confucius, called a benevolent government. A benevolent government understands development in a benevolent way. Paul Kagame, president of Rwanda, is a benevolent – if authoritarian – leader. He knows how to allow people to invest in education and health care, as well as in the internet and how to connect everything. Rwanda is one of the best-connected countries in Africa.

We need democracy, but not at all costs. Democracy and laissez-faire economics must be circumscribed by rules of the game. You cannot have a roaming free spirit and free markets if people are not taught to have compassion, make sacrifices and to be public spirited.

CONCLUSION

In summary, based on past experiences for East, Southeast Asia and Thailand, there can never be a ready-made single development strategy for any economy. Economic and social circumstances influence the course of government actions.

The Asian financial crisis obliged governments to rationalise the financial system and supervisory arrangements to create a more solid system today. The corruption and competitiveness indices announced by various institutions oblige governments to meet transparency requirements and adopt digital-ready policy to enhance their competitiveness.

Notwithstanding these positive steps, we cannot allow ourselves to drift. The simple truth remains that we need a strong development-oriented government —some may say strong leadership — to form a fundamental basis for successful transformation.

In the case of Thailand, we are blessed with the King's Principles in the form of the Sufficiency Economic Philosophy. This instils ethical, non-market values that should accompany an inclusive development model, with community economics at the grassroot level as a core concept.

LEADERSHIP RECOMMENDATIONS

In the present and future VUCA world, a blend of several qualities of leaders, technocrats and entrepreneurs is needed. These include:

- Clear thinking and communication.
- The audacity to accept criticism and change.
- Absolute integrity and transparency.
- Command of a so-called "Weltanschauung" or worldview, with multilateralism and pragmatism as its guiding lights.

POLICY RECOMMENDATIONS: 10 CHALLENGES FOR TRANSFORMATION TODAY

In the previous section, some key components of Thailand's development pathway were highlighted with the emphasis on its partial success. Thailand's economic performance since the Asian financial crisis, however, has been patchy, with average growth slowing and competitiveness declining.

Nevertheless, an open society with an open trading system, strong fundamental institutions and integration with neighbouring economies remain the hallmarks of economic and social sustainability. In the last couple of decades, this sustainability has been subjected to severe challenges, some of which are ongoing and require careful management. Going forward, my recommendations are:

1. **Plan for disruption and the recurrence of global crises**
   In addition to the Asian and global financial crises the alarming spread of the coronavirus pandemic posed an unprecedented threat. Countries need to plan for similar disruptions in future – and to expect one every decade.

2. **Counter the rise of nationalism**
   Before the outbreak of the pandemic, globalisation and multilateralism were already under severe stress. Witness the non-completion of the WTO's Doha Development Agenda, for example, and the move away from some multilateral agreements by the United States. With the pandemic threat and lockdowns, countries will turn more inward, which may promote more nationalism. All countries must find ways to promote social harmony and reduce inequality.

3. **Strengthen regional alliances to offset geopolitical shift**
   A shift in economic weight from the West to the East will bring a drastic rearrangement of the traditional international order with inevitable confrontations. This is evident in the tech tension between America and China. Responses to the pandemic seem likely to drive another wedge between these two powers. The dysfunctioning of global governance will be laid bare. New regional alliances can help offset and balance this.

4. **Balance individual freedoms with state protection**
   The health crisis will tilt the political landscape towards more centralised, authoritarian rule as practiced in countries such as India, Brazil and Turkey and typified by China and Russia. This will give weight to the right-wing, nationalist-populist governments and parties in Europe. Covid-19 may be creating a world that will be less open, less prosperous and less free. The balance between individual freedom and state protection must be carefully managed.

5. **Counter deepening geopolitical divisions**
   Competing geopolitical blocs are dividing Asia as never before. China is pursuing its vision of global governance through the Belt and Road Initiative, which now covers more than 70% of the global economy, while the United States' Free and Open Indo-Pacific Forum is supported by India, Japan and Australia. ASEAN is caught somewhere in between. In the coming years, membership of regional power blocs will be vital.

6. **Take a lead on climate change**
   The world community's performance in delivering on the Paris 2016 climate change agreement has been dismal to say the least. Extreme weather conditions are becoming more frequent with devastating economic and social impact. With Asia being relatively more affected than other regions, the future of the continent as the world's food basket will be subjected to more uncertainty.

7. **Prepare for diminishing trust in the WTO**
   The free, transparent, non-discriminatory multilateral trading system will be confronted with greater non-tariff measures as economies become more aware of environmental concerns and standard setting. Calls for reform will lead to negotiations that will drive members of the WTO further apart, especially with a growing trust deficit between the industrialised member countries and the developing Group of 77 and China. Ultimately, the WTO will be less flexible and agile as the guardian of the multilateral trading system. The rise of regional trade agreements in the form of mega-deals will take away even the trade negotiating task from the WTO.[9] Developing countries need to align themselves to take advantage of these changes.

8. **Transform education systems to meet the needs of the digital age**
   The emergence of the knowledge-led digital economy is unlike any previous industrial revolution in that the speed of change will be exponential. The global labour force may not be growing as before and the world needs improved productivity through new technologies like AI and robotics that can augment human abilities. For example, Microsoft's Project Premonition, which aims to detect pathogens in the environment to protect people from transmission before an outbreak, could be a boon in the fight against covid-19 and other diseases.[(10)] At present, however, e-commerce and social media dominate the agenda. The focus should be on how to transform the educational system to meet the new requirements, and how to deal with all-powerful digital companies.

9. **Address growing inequality or risk social upheaval**
   Increasing disparities in wealth, income and opportunities between countries and within countries has become a major global issue in the last few decades. This is evidenced by the events of the Arab Spring, the "bottom billions" and other protests against unequal distribution of wealth around the globe. Oxfam reports that a falling number of billionaires command more than half the total wealth of humanity. Inequality is not only an economic problem; it will lead to destabilising social and political tension. Developing countries must address it or risk social upheaval.

10. **Build regional blocs to counter dysfunctional economic governance**
   Global economic governance has been dysfunctional since the American-led global recession from 2007 to 2008, with the G7 and G20 not being able to coordinate their macro-economic policies as easing and austerity contrasted with each other around the world. The UN Economic and Social Committee (ECOSOC) lacks serious participation by advanced member countries and developing and emerging market economies are blocked from fully participating at the decision-making levels of key international organisations. Regional blocs such as RECP offer the best way forward.

This list of transformational challenges is certainly not exhaustive, but I believe the recommendations are relevant to Thailand and all countries undergoing economic transformation.

OMAN

In less than half a century, Oman developed from an isolationist enclave on the outskirts of the Gulf region into a modern, dynamic nation and key diplomatic player in the Middle East. In 2010, Oman ranked number one in the UN's Human Development Index (HDI) as the country that had improved most in human development terms over the previous 40 years, ahead even of China.[42]

In 1970, when the late Sultan Qaboos came to power, Oman had a population of less than 750,000[43] and had little physical infrastructure, with only three schools and less than 10 kilometres of paved roads in the entire Sultanate. Access to electricity was limited to the area around Muscat, the capital. Despite the discovery of oil in 1964, the economy was dependent on fishing and subsistence farming. GDP per capita income stood at a mere US$100 between 1960 and 1966 and, even after oil exports began in 1967, very little was spent on development, while a significant part of the budget was dedicated to defence.

Realising the obstacles facing the country, Sultan Qaboos initiated large development projects soon after coming into power. New and capable advisers were engaged to oversee the great transition; the first government ministries were established and the construction of a new seaport, Matrah, (which is still Oman's principal seaport) was expedited. Roads were built and plans for a new international airport put into motion. Power generation and desalination plants were constructed, along with schools and hospitals. Funded by government revenue from oil receipts, Oman began a period of rapid economic and social development.

The share of agriculture in Oman's GDP fell dramatically from 75% in 1965 to less than 3% in 1991, while the share of industry (including petroleum) grew from 8% of GDP in 1960 to 59% by 1985. As a result of careful economic planning and modernisation, Oman's GDP grew from US$0.25 billion in 1970 to US$81.79 billion in 2014, while GDP per capita in the same period increased from US$354 to US$19,309.

In 1970, there were just three formal schools, catering to 900 students, and the adult illiteracy rate stood at 80%. Illiteracy was one of the first challenges the new Sultan aimed to tackle. Within the first five months of his accession, 16 public elementary schools were established and, for the first time, girls were included in formal education. In the following five years a total of 262 educational institutions were opened, including secondary schools and a college for training teachers. In 1986, the first higher education institute, the Sultan Qaboos University, was inaugurated. By 2017, the educational infrastructure comprised 1,647 public, special education, private and international schools, with a total of 724,395 pupils, including nursery and pre-schoolers. In 2018, the Sultanate boasted an adult literacy rate of 95%.

Health care in Oman, prior to 1970, was scarce and limited. There were only two hospitals, staffed mainly by expatriate doctors. The physician to population ratio was 1 to 50,000 and waiting lines were long. People had to travel up to four days just to reach a hospital and there was a high incidence of diseases such as tuberculosis, malaria and hepatitis. Mortality and morbidity rates were high and overall life expectancy in 1970 was just over 49 years. The new Sultan established a dedicated ministry of health and in 1976 introduced the first five-year health-care plan; the public health-care system was to become decentralised and priority given to developing health-care infrastructure. In a short span of four years, 30 new hospitals were constructed – a number that increased to 52 by 1990.

By 2009, the Sultanate had 59 hospitals in addition to 204 government-run and 787 privately-run health centres, clinics and dispensaries. As a result, infant mortality declined from 118 deaths per 1000 live births (one of the highest rates in the world) in 1972 to 7.2 per 1000 in 2018. The mortality rate of under-fives also declined drastically by 94% (11.7 per 1,000 in 2008, down from 181 in 1972). Life expectancy increased from 49 years in 1970 to 77 years in 2018 – a testament to Oman's rapid improvement in health care.

In addition to meticulous economic and social development planning, Oman has also become renowned for its tolerance, openness and harmonious relationships with other nations. From the time he came to power, Sultan Qaboos adopted a foreign policy of soft diplomacy. Understanding that in order to break into the international arena the Sultanate needed to establish itself as a diplomatic player, one of the first actions of Sultan Qaboos's government was to send missions of goodwill to Arab countries such as Saudi Arabia, Kuwait, Jordan, Iraq, Morocco, Algeria, Yemen and Lebanon. In 1971, Oman became a member of the Arab League and later the same year was admitted into the United Nations. In 1981, Oman became a founding member of the Gulf Cooperation Council.

Sultan Qaboos also managed a fine balance with relationships in the wider world, focusing on mediation and retaining Oman's neutral position. While establishing diplomatic relations with both the communist Soviet Union and China and mediating for Iran, he also maintained close military cooperation with the United States. This emphasis on a policy of being "a friend to all, enemy to no one" has done much to enhance the Sultanate's reputation, which has had positive impacts on incoming tourism, foreign investment, and the external perception of Oman as a reliable partner for diplomacy and maintaining peace. Oman ranked "high" in the 2019 Global Peace Index,[44] recording the fourth largest fall in military expenditure, and also ranked one of the lowest in the world – with 25 other countries - on the 2019 Global Terrorism Index.[45]

In 2019, Oman ranked 53rd in the World Economic Forum's Global Competitiveness Report, taking seventh place in the category of government long-term vision and sixth for workforce diversity. Amongst Arab nations, Oman ranks second for independence of the judiciary, road links and low crime (homicide) rate.[46] Through its Vision 2040 national strategy, Oman aims to become a post-oil economy.

Harmony within Oman was also a priority of the late Sultan, who introduced an official policy of religious and cultural tolerance. With the country being home to many different religious and cultural communities, Sultan Qaboos' government implemented laws aimed at guaranteeing the right to religious freedom for all. This policy has served as a unifying factor, inculcating a sense of national pride, a unique "Omani" identity and public trust in government.

A testament to this public trust was the swift, seamless and peaceful transition of power following Sultan Qaboos' death in January 2020. A unanimous vote of confidence for his endorsed successor, His Majesty Sultan Haitham bin Tariq bin Taimur Al-Said, who was sworn into power within a few hours of Sultan Qaboos' demise, was indicative of the trust the Omani people place in their government.

In 2020, in his first speech as Sultan, His Majesty Haitham bin Tariq bin Taimur Al-Said announced that, in line with the Oman 2040 vision, education would remain at the top of Oman's national priorities, providing a supportive environment for research and innovation.

Other national priorities include modernising the apparatus of government to emphasise financial balance, economic diversification and sustainability. In the business sector there would be a focus on small and medium-sized enterprises (SMEs) and entrepreneurship, particularly on firms based on innovation, artificial intelligence and advanced technology. An extensive programme of training and recruitment is planned to ensure young Omanis benefit from the opportunities in the new, global digital era.

Building a Tech Nation

"To meet the demands of the fast-changing competitive scene, we must simply learn to love change as much as we have hated it in the past."
Tom Peters

Ed Vaizey (Lord Vaizey of Didcot)
Culture and Digital Minister, United Kingdom, 2006 to 2016

6

In 1870, the United Kingdom provided 22.9% of global manufacturing output. By the 1970s this figure had fallen to 4.9%[47] and the economy was entering a long-running period of decline with rising unemployment, frequent strikes and severe inflation.

In the 1980s and 1990s the country began its transformation from heavy industry to service provider and today the service sector contributes around 80% of GDP.[48] The United Kingdom's economy is the sixth largest in the world measured by nominal GDP and the country has become a global tech hub, with London the second most connected tech ecosystem globally after Silicon Valley,[49] and Cambridge's "Silicon Fen" home to the AI research teams of global brands including Amazon, Apple, Microsoft, ARM and Samsung.

From 2010 to 2016, I served as the minister for culture, communications and creative industries in the government of the United Kingdom, with responsibilities in the departments for culture, media and sport (DCMS) and for business, innovation and skills (BIS). Within this broad remit I was also minister for the digital economy.

In this chapter, I focus on eight critical areas of attention when embarking upon government transformation. I will also share how the British government has embraced and woven the tech sector into the wider societal ecosystem. This has led to the United Kingdom becoming one of the world's leading "talent super hubs". A virtuous circle is created where the best talent attracts further great talent and in turn the super hub becomes a magnet for the world's premier employers. I believe this is the way forward in developing a 21st century economy.

I will also share my own personal leadership journey, covering what went well along with what didn't go so well, and what I learnt along the way. I'll conclude with some personal recommendations if your intention is to become a digital-age public sector leader.

CITIZEN-CENTRICITY

My own particular experience has been helping government to use technology to bring about radical change. Many businesses have had to digitally transform the services they offer to their customers because they face fierce competition in the marketplace. Any significant business that is not digital today is almost certainly failing. On the face of it, government does not face the same pressure, often because the services it offers are monopolies; the citizen has nowhere else to go. This is one of the reasons why change is so difficult.

However, governments across the world face other pressures. First, there is always financial pressure. The legacy of the financial crash and coronavirus means that there continues to be financial pressures on governments to reduce their spending deficits. Second, citizens are now used to getting services on their phones and so have less tolerance for using old-fashioned analogue services. Third, government itself needs better tools to monitor how its services are being used and therefore how they can be transformed. Fourth, digital services provide better security for many interactions. Finally, government can use digital transformation to turn government procurement into economic growth.

In the end, digital transformation is a win-win situation. Not only do citizens get simpler, clearer and faster services from a monopoly provider, the services are also much cheaper to run, so the state gets to save administrative costs and can spend more money on front-line services or reducing the tax burden.

THE BACKGROUND

Achieving government transformation in a large country is very difficult, especially when there are entrenched processes which have huge legacy systems in place. The British government has more than 300 agencies and 24 government departments. Many institutions are beyond reform. Often the only way to achieve transformation is to start at the beginning, outside the organisation, at the service level.

Transformation is far simpler in a small country, and Estonia is widely acknowledged as the European leader in putting digital transformation into effect. The key tenets of Estonia's transformation are outlined earlier in this book in Chapter 1. The Estonian government's e-portal site is visited 180 million times a month (out of a population of 1.3 million). Citizens use it to pay taxes, claim benefits, register new companies and even to vote. In total, Estonian citizens can access 160 government services online.

Estonia was able to achieve this transformation partly because after independence it was able to start with a clean slate. It also had engineering talent willing to work on the mission to create a modern state free from (Soviet) legacy. In effect, it was able to build government services from scratch, and thus make them "digital first". Now all Estonians are issued with an e-identity card, and the digital infrastructure – broadband and mobile – is universal. But many of the lessons of Estonia can still be applied in large countries, as they were in the United Kingdom.

Under David Cameron's government, which was in office between 2010 and 2016, digital transformation was a major priority and great progress was made. In 2010, public expenditure on technology was estimated to be around £16 billion. That is equivalent to about 1% of the economy. It was mostly provided by a small oligopoly of managed service providers under a set of procurement mechanisms that favoured size over capability. Outsourcing for what should have been commodity services and technology operations had reached deep into the development process, making every project over-complicated, over-priced and very difficult to manage.

The IT contract for Her Majesty's Revenue and Customs (HMRC), which is responsible for the collection of taxes in the United Kingdom, for example, cost about £1.4 billion annually, but was only able to issue two software releases a year. We were locked in, in more ways than one. One critical component of national infrastructure was running on what was called a "partial back up basis". By partial back up the vendor explained that if the system went down once it would revert to a remote back up, but if that had an issue then "you'd need a new system." Of course, this would have been understandable had the services been usable but, as many examples showed, the litany of broken user journeys indicated a common problem: services were not designed so that citizens could use them easily and – crucially for the government – cheaply.

Right at the start of the reform, as the Government Digital Service helped agencies map out their services, they found agencies were proud of their great call centres, which actually indicated that user journeys online were broken and so needed phone support. The original digital efficiency report estimated that just helping people move online would save billions.

Over the next five years, the Government Digital Service spawned a revolution in service transformation and technology reform. The GOV.UK website was the first common platform for publishing (replacing hundreds of departmental and agency sites that had only one thing in common – that they had nothing in common). Twenty-five services were selected for transformation and in 18 months, 20 of them became digital services on a par with anything in the private sector - services that understood their users' needs and met them, simply. The Lasting Power of Attorney was a particularly good example – there's a great video.[50]

The technology reforms underneath these changes were just as marked. Moving to flexible technologies such as cloud computing (Britain was the first government in the world to go "Cloud First" in 2013), strongly championing Open Standards and Open Source and introducing procurement reform to enable innovative suppliers to sell to government, all led to a seismic change in the technology marketplace.

From an oligopoly of 12 main providers the government was, at the end of 2015, buying more than 50% of its new IT from small or medium-sized businesses (SMEs). Major components of the state tech infrastructure were now stood up and supported by SMEs, in turn creating more jobs in the United Kingdom. Not only did we move from a few large suppliers to many smaller ones, we also spread the economic gain and opportunity all over the country. That helped support the tech ecosystem far beyond London and ensured every region benefited from what is a sizeable chunk of the government's budget.

To make a success of digital transformation, the government needed a clear strategy. What I highlight below includes an element of hindsight, but I have set out eight crucial areas of attention that need to be followed by anyone seeking to make the essential changes that we did.

EIGHT CRITICAL STEPS FOR DIGITAL TRANSFORMATION

1. **Prioritisation**
   The first step in any transformation is prioritisation. This sounds obvious, but it needs to be spelt out. Change must be led from the very top, and Prime Minister David Cameron was heavily invested in pushing it through. He appointed one his most effective ministers, Francis Maude, to lead the change, and ensured that his office was close to the prime minister's headquarters.

2. **Decouple the transformation**
   The second step is somewhat paradoxical. There was no way we could achieve the change we wanted by using a traditional government department, or indeed allowing traditional government departments to make the changes themselves. That route would have led to delay, duplication, waste and bad choices. So, the main driver of change had to be outside the main system of government - although still accountable to a specific minister and through him to the prime minister. The Government Digital Service was set up as if it were a startup, with headquarters based away from Whitehall, the geographical centre of government. But it was essential that it had complete control over every digital project, including the right to scrutinize and if necessary, veto every department's IT procurement policies.

The unit was headed by people who were not traditional civil servants but had been brought in to carry out the specific task of establishing digital services for the main roles of government. These were experts, not generalists – people with the specific digital skills that we needed. The headquarters physically resembled a startup, with people casually dressed, and post-it notes adorning the walls showing what tasks needed to be addressed. (I don't think there were any beanbags, though.) Background was unimportant, provided people had the right skills. Even school leavers, still teenagers, were recruited.

3. **Be citizen-centric**

The third step was to be crystal clear what the task was. The fundamental point about the Government Digital Service – and I cannot emphasise this enough - was that it asked one simple, but crucial question: what does the user need? Government is very good at thinking about what it wants, but it doesn't always think about what its citizens want. This was brought home to me when Mike Bracken, the head of the service, showed me the new government website, which was an amazing achievement - 3000 websites rolled into one. I asked, as a minister, where I could find my press releases. Cue much eyerolling. Of course, no citizen has ever gone on a website to look for the press releases of ministers.

The problem, of course, is that government tends to think of its political needs, the machinery it uses to deliver those needs, the IT system it should procure to deliver those needs exactly as it envisages they should be delivered, often before the citizen, who is the one actually using the service. So, when paying tax, it will expect the citizen to know which department to contact with any tax queries. It also assumes that every issue can be silo-ed. But many issues transcend single government departments: an education issue could also be a health issue, a criminal justice issue or a local government issue.

When constructing digital services, therefore, one should always – always - be thinking how a citizen will find and use these services. And of course, that is mainly through searching, and mainly through asking a straightforward question such as "how do I pay my tax?" (Increasingly, access will be through voice activation, and the British government now has 13,000 voice search terms that allow citizens to find a service.) Many citizens still use the telephone to call the government. In the United Kingdom, some 700 million calls are made every year to government departments and agencies (roughly 10 per head of population). About a quarter of these could be avoided if digital services were better. Telephone calls are also much more expensive, and it often takes five phone calls for the citizen to find the answer to their question or receive the service they need. It clearly makes sense to digitize a service and allow citizens to find the service they need far more easily and cheaply.

4. **Reposition government as a platform**
   The fourth step is to ensure that you avoid duplication by building one technical platform for everyone to use. We needed to think of government as a service, and therefore build one platform on to which individual components could be bolted. More than 400 services from 120 organisations have now been migrated onto the same platform. More than 44 core registers have now been uploaded, avoiding multiple duplicate registers across Whitehall.

   New government departments can take advantage of the work that has already been done. The government platform provides a suite of common tools, components and guidance which allows officials anywhere in government to draw on technical expertise and products that would be too costly to procure independently. Creating bespoke solutions is time-consuming and resource intensive. It limits the scope of transformation. Long periods of integration, costly maintenance and potentially being locked-in to a supplier can now be avoided.

5. **Recognise that digitisation is not enough**
   The fifth step is to remember that digital transformation only comes about through physical transformation. The key thing here is that you are not digitising an existing service; you are designing an entirely new service, and one that is likely to cut across silos. The French government, for example, has identified 50 life events where you have to interact with government, such as getting married and starting a business, and sought to simplify the process.

   When designing a new service, you have to define the users - then map out the journey. Mapping a service like this can help identify the following: the most important content in the user journey; content gaps; duplicated content; content trying to meet multiple needs; and content covering a user need that's being met by another department. The mapping is done in four stages: scoping, auditing, journey mapping and content mapping. It is a painful process, but one that transforms the service available to the citizen. You may even find that you have to change outdated laws and regulations along the way to enable your new service.

6. **Reassess your appetite for risk**

   The sixth point to remember is to take risks. As the old adage goes, no one ever got fired for saying No. Every day, businesses, particularly innovative ones, take risks, which sometimes lead to failure; yet very few of these lead to commentary in the media. Shareholders and investors tend to understand the need for calculated risks to make a company more efficient or profitable. The situation is very different where public money is involved, where the incentive is often the opposite. Failure often leads to being pilloried in the press, and the stewardship of public money has to be taken seriously. The irony here is that government often wastes catastrophic sums of public money doing things the "right" way – letting large IT contracts to significant, established players, which often run massively over budget and over time. But in those situations, officials can take refuge in the fact that they did the "right" thing. Contrast this with someone who tries to introduce a new process and contract with a small, less well-established supplier. If the project goes wrong, they will be criticised for doing the "wrong" thing.

   Better government, and government transformation, could be helped if we introduced awards for failure – acknowledging and rewarding officials who tried to do something different, as if they were in a business, even if it didn't work out. (Francis Maude always joked that we should hold the Failure Awards to celebrate civil servants who at least tried to do something different.) In digital transformation, this is even more important. It is impossible to get a new service exactly right from the start, but it is essential to get a beta site up and running and test it with real users. The beauty of digital transformation, provided it has been procured appropriately, is that changes can be made on the run, and the service tweaked as it comes into contact with real world users. As the Government Digital Service puts it: "strategy is delivery."

7. **Be data driven**

   The seventh point is the use of data. Data is absolutely vital to the success of digital transformation. A digital process throws up huge amounts of data that is extremely valuable. It allows you to see who is using the service and how they are using it, so that you can continue to improve it.

   One of the interesting projects that emerged from the use of data was the establishment of the Behavioural Insights Team (aka the Nudge Unit), inspired by the science of behavioural economics. The team used data about citizen behaviour to make small incremental changes to government interactions, such as the tone of government letters. It increased compliance – such as paying tax on time – so successfully that it paid for itself 22 times over in first two years.

Another angle that comes from getting government data right is the opportunity for the private sector to establish services that are useful to the citizen. Companies like CityMapper use government (or city) transport data to provide a helpful service to the citizen, by providing route maps for journeys. Companies and applications like these have only emerged since governments have begun to make data available to the private sector. Crucially, government is not the app designer. Nevertheless, they benefit from it, by getting new data on how journeys are actually being made, allowing them to design better transport networks.

8. **Embrace public private collaboration**
   Government needs to keep pushing for partnerships with the private sector, particularly with emerging and startup companies. For example, the British government has set up the GovTech catalyst. This is a fund specifically designed to support companies that want to work with government. The £20 million fund lets small businesses apply to solve a specific challenge. In the last couple of years, it has funded digital solutions to, for example, sequence adult care, use sensors to support the maintenance of public housing or manage autonomous vehicles in traffic. In addition, the Spark programme allows government departments to buy and implement proven and innovative technology, avoiding a long-drawn out procurement programme that favours the big IT incumbents.

BUILDING A TECH ECOSYSTEM

The United Kingdom remains the home of the largest proportion of tech investment in Europe. According to a recent report by European venture capital firm, Atomico, London attracted just over US$11.1 billion in investment in 1300 rounds in 2019. If government is active in adopting technology solutions it creates a halo effect, which signals that the Britain is a good place to innovate and thus attracts the right talent. But there is always more that can be done.

Early on in the Cameron government, we established Tech City (now known as Tech Nation), which acts as a resource centre for British startups and scale-ups. This innovative organisation was again set up outside Whitehall, to give it maximum flexibility. The long-term plan is for it to be self-financing, though it currently receives a small grant from government.

Tech Nation tracks and monitors emerging technology companies and provides a map of the emerging tech scene, which informs policy makers. Its continuous work helps to identify emerging trends, such as agri-tech and fintech, identify the companies that are likely to break through, highlight policy innovation that can better support the tech ecology and provide information on where geographical tech clusters are emerging. It remains a small and nimble organisation, with fewer than 75 employees, but nevertheless acts as a very effective cheerleader for tech investment in the United Kingdom.

Alongside Tech Nation, we also reformed the government grants system. Innovate UK is another government organisation that gives grants to early tech startups. Since 2007, Innovate UK has invested £2.5 billion into 8,500 companies, creating an estimated value of £14 billion. This investment is a mix of match-funded grants and loans, and about three-quarters go to small businesses that would be deemed too high risk to access conventional financing.

The tax system is a further example of how countries can support tech innovation. The Enterprise Investment Scheme (EIS) and the Seed Enterprise Investment Scheme (SEIS), while not specifically designed for tech, have served to encourage the most important level of investment - in high-risk and unproven startups. Since 1994, EIS has attracted some £20 billion of investment into almost 30,000 companies and SEIS since 2012 has attracted about £1 billion into 1900 companies. About a third of current funding goes to what we can define as tech companies, and indeed the scheme is often cited as one of the key building blocks of the startup community in the United Kingdom.

Immigration is a vital factor. The British government, at the behest of bodies like Tech Nation that understand the ecosystem, has promoted entrepreneur visas, which allow tech entrepreneurs from outside the United Kingdom to build their businesses in the United Kingdom. Tech Nation manages the visa process, and looks not just at people with a company, but those that show promise as well.

MY LEADERSHIP JOURNEY

I was appointed a spokesman for technology and culture in 2006 when the Conservative Party was in opposition. I had no particular qualifications for my role – certainly no engineering expertise – but my four years in opposition gave me the opportunity to listen and learn from experts, and to formulate strategies for my various responsibilities.

Once appointed as a minister, after the Conservatives won the election in 2010, I, along with my colleagues, was able to hit the ground running. We were able to implement our priorities very quickly and then see them through. I served as a minister for the entire length of the Cameron administration, and it is important to note that many ministers remained in post for several years, which is unusual in politics. To achieve genuine and sustained change, continuity is vital.

People often ask how I combined the two briefs of culture and technology, which at first sight appear very different. In my view they were actually compatible – technology is ultimately about disruption and creativity, looking at the world with a fresh pair of eyes and asking if things could be done differently. And that is also what great artists do. People also need to appreciate how much technology depends on the arts; great inventions and transformations are first achieved in the imagination. I often say if you want to know what the world will look like in the future, do not speak to an engineer, speak to a science fiction author. After all, the technology that succeeds is the technology that people actually want to use in the real world, rather than the laboratory.

It's interesting to reflect that there is no formal training for a ministerial role. To a certain extent, there is an element of self-selection, with people who have a specific passion, energy and drive making it to the top. You also need good judgement, and the ability to synthesise arguments and different points of view – not something that is easily taught. So, one has to learn on the job. The biggest lesson is never to let your foot off the pedal. We are blessed in Britain by being supported by very effective officials, but at the end of the day the minister is ultimately responsible for the delivery of the policy and must therefore learn how best to pull the levers to ensure it is being implemented. That will involve daily or weekly meetings, the ability to ask tough questions and the need to be flexible. Above all the focus must be kept on the ultimate prize of successful reform, which means accepting mistakes will be made along the way.

Any minister must also work effectively with colleagues. That means providing a clear narrative for what one wants to achieve and showing colleagues that your success will mean success for them as well. In fact, the most effective minister is one who allows others to take the credit for what they have achieved.

RECOMMENDATIONS

Finally, here are my recommendations on how governments need to evolve to thrive in the digital age. The world is changing at a frantic pace, so I have endeavoured to make my recommendations "future-proof".

To government

- Technology is now dominant in all developed countries, and governments across the world must step up their engagement.
- Every government should be looking at transferring its services online and at pace.
- Transformation can only be achieved by an outside-in model – by setting up an agency with real powers to transform government functions.
- The guiding philosophy must be the need of the citizen, not the government.
- Duplication must be avoided, and services built on one platform.
- Digitising a service involves reimagining the analogue service from the ground up.
- Risks must be taken and embraced.
- Data sharing is crucial.
- Digital government must be accompanied by a technology-friendly business environment, which focuses on marketing, taxation, government investment and pro-tech immigration.

To leaders

Governments are only as good as their leaders, so here are some guiding principles.

- Take time to listen to the experts and synthesise their views.
- Have a clear goal that you want to achieve.
- Do not be put off by mistakes or failures along the way.
- Work closely with colleagues – show them how they will benefit if your reforms are successful.
- Live what you do – use the technology that you are recommending for others.
- Try to stay in office for as long as possible to have a chance to achieve the goals you set out to achieve.

SOUTH KOREA

South Korea is one of the four economies that came to be known as the Asian Tigers, with Singapore, Taiwan and Hong Kong. The economic transformation that South Korea underwent between the 1960s and the 1990s is a remarkable one. From being one of the poorest countries of the world in the 1950s, South Korea has emerged as one of the most economically and technologically advanced today.

Between 1910 and 1945, Korea was a colony of imperial Japan. At the end of the second world war, Korea became divided along the 38th parallel, with the north controlled by the Soviet Union and the south by the United States – neither of whom could agree on the terms of Korea's independence. In 1950, the Korean war broke out, culminating in a stalemate in 1953 but no formal peace treaty.

Economically, the Korean war left South Korea in ruins – devoid of capital and natural resources. It remained one of the poorest countries for a decade, with a GDP per capita of less than US$100 until the early 1960s. The country was kept afloat only through foreign aid, which sponsored a staggering 90% of the budget. Largely, South Korea was considered a failed state, with little or no infrastructure in place. The natural resources and industrial infrastructure that had benefited a unified Korea were all in the north. In fact, according to a World Bank report in the early 1960s, South Korea's prospect for development was "anything but bright."

By 2018, South Korea's GDP per capita (PPP) had grown to over US$30,000 – higher than New Zealand, Italy and Spain – placing the country firmly in the top 15 of national income rankings. In 2019, the country ranked 13th in the World Economic Forum's Global Competitiveness Report and fifth in the World Bank's Ease of Doing Business ranking. In terms of human development, South Korea had reached the top 25 of the UN's Human Development Index by 2017.

The extraordinary acceleration of development in South Korea – known as "the miracle on the Han River" - started with a series of five-year plans in 1962. Industrialisation, import-substitution, export-orientation and trade were all positioned as the way forward. However, these plans required funds, which South Korea did not have access to. Foreign aid was just enough to keep it afloat, but no other country wanted to invest, given the complete lack of economic fundamentals.

After receiving some funds from Germany, South Korea started some small-scale industries including textile, wig-making and plywood. By the 1970s these micro businesses had proven to be significantly competitive, allowing the country to progress to a more value-added approach. The first new investment was a steel mill, followed by shipbuilding, car manufacturing, electronics and chemical facilities. This laid the groundwork for the export of heavy industrial products over the next two decades.

In 1990, South Korean manufacturers planned a shift toward high-technology industries. Innovation and technology have played a key role in strengthening its export competitiveness and today, South Korea spends more on research and development than the United States and Japan.

Throughout the economic transformation, the South Korean government worked in close collaboration with the private sector. Under the leadership of Park Chung-Hee, government-protected "chaebols", or family-run conglomerates, became the driving force in manufacturing. Government-selected companies undertook major projects often financed with government-backed loans. Although this policy of "guided capitalism" came under global criticism for the wealth accumulation it promoted, new industrial sectors were created that then tapped into lucrative foreign markets. Exports grew from just 4% of GDP in 1961 to over 40% in 2016, and the chaebol policy laid the groundwork for the global success of South Korean brands such as Samsung, LG and Hyundai.

One of the core engines for South Korea's growth was investment in human capital, and the nation's well-educated labour force has been instrumental in the country's remarkable turnaround. While per capita spending on education has not been high (by global standards), the social emphasis on human capital development - Korean society has traditionally long respected the need and desire for learning - has yielded a high-quality, skilled and productive labour force. The government's low-cost approach to education (including high student-per-class ratios and multiple school shifts) enabled wider access to meet increasing demand.

Teachers are known as nation-builders in South Korea and the favourable rewards and job security teaching offers make it an attractive profession. Teacher training and recruitment is overseen by the government and there are a number of government-funded institutes dedicated to educational research, ensuring the nation's education system is up-to-date and aligned with national objectives. In 2018, South Korea ranked in the top 25 countries of the World Bank Group's Human Capital Index.

South Korea's rapid industrialisation has been spurred on by pro-business policies and incentives for investment in innovation. The role played by the leadership and the political institutions has also been critical. Park Chung-Hee, who seized power in a military coup in 1961 and governed for 18 years, made modernisation a priority and considered the establishment of industrial infrastructure essential to growth. He also recognised the importance of harnessing the support of the people in order to implement reforms effectively. South Korea's economic miracle is a result of collaboration between government, the private sector and the nation's citizens.

Part II

In Part I, we heard from an array of eminent public sector leaders. Part II is an assimilation of their perspectives coupled with my own experiences as both a public sector leader and in my work developing public sector leaders.

I have endeavoured to coalesce these various sources into a set of guiding principles to support leaders in their quest to build responsive and responsible organisations.

In the next four chapters, I will codify both the problems government leaders face and the steps you need to take to transform both personally and organisationally.

Ali Qassim Jawad
Senior Advisor, Diwan of Royal Court (2012 – Present), Sultanate of Oman

The New Realities

7

Government leaders from even the recent past would not recognise the world in its current form. Though unfortunately they would recognise many of the governance models and systems, as would countless predecessors. Consequently, the public sector is broadly failing to serve citizens today because it is based on a model that is optimised for a bygone era.

In this chapter, we will look at the forces shaping the world in which governments today operate. We will then identify the new realities that governments face in the context of these forces. Finally, I will propose three principles that public sector leaders will find useful in driving citizen-centric government transformation.

When I wrote my first book, *Leading Smart Transformation*, my co-authors and I argued that smart transformation could be likened to an onion, with a number of layers that need to be peeled back to create a lasting change. What I have learned since is that real transformation is a continuous, ongoing and never-ending cycle.

That cycle is about to accelerate because the world is shifting gears, both upwards and downwards. Ever-faster technological change is propelling us along at dizzying speed, accelerating social, economic and geopolitical shifts, meaning societies, economies and governments have to reinvent themselves continuously. At the same time, global threats, most obviously the covid-19 pandemic, have sent shock waves around the world, creating further uncertainty.

Taken together, these global megatrends are highly transformative, converging and interacting with each other, and getting ever deeper into our personal space as citizens, but also challenging governments to respond in new ways. The forces driving the new realities can be grouped into five global trends:

1. Technological changes.
2. Social changes.
3. Economic shifts.
4. Geopolitical shifts.
5. Global threats.

TECHNOLOGICAL CHANGES

The first and most immediately visible global trend, readily evident to the general public, government and business alike, is the accelerating speed of technological change. Technological change is highly disruptive but is something that every nation has to face. It constantly raises the question; can we afford to keep up? But the real question for governments is, can we afford to fall behind?

Technological change is being driven by:

- Rapid advances in science and technology, which are changing expectations and even behaviours among populations.
- The maturing of a cluster of technologies that have been dubbed the 4th Industrial Revolution (4IR).

Broadband is now regarded as a basic human right. It is the essential support for a whole raft of activities: conducting science, communication, learning and entertainment; collecting, disseminating and retrieving information; earning a living for countless individuals; operating factories and businesses; running a modern government - and much, much more. And the advent of 5G will bring about another step-change. Some governments may try to hold back the technological tide but restricting broadband access – or not providing sufficient resources to support its expansion and improvement - is not only economic suicide, it also risks causing a social backlash.

The technology trend is incontrovertible and unprecedented in human history. Inventions previously only imagined in science fiction such as virtual and augmented reality, 3D printing, robotics, blockchain, quantum computing, nanotechnology and bioengineering are now a reality - changing how materials, money, products and services are made, exchanged and consumed.

These are the technologies that the World Economic Forum (WEF) has named collectively the 4th Industrial Revolution (4IR) because they represent a new paradigm, changing not just productivity through automation, but the fundamentals of how we live and govern within societies. WEF founder Klaus Schwab described it as a culmination of emerging technologies, arguing that this revolution is different in scale, scope and complexity from any that have come before.

One of the challenges I have been wrestling with in Oman is how to prepare the country for 4IR. The Future of Government initiative I lead, for example, targets senior government leaders (under-secretary level) with the purpose of exposing them to the driving themes and leading practices that will shape and transform the public sector as the 4IR takes hold. That covers the application of a multitude of different technologies, everything from artificial intelligence (AI) and robotics to big data and the Internet of Things (IoT).

And it is not simply digital technology that governments need to consider; biotechnology and nanotechnology are also advancing rapidly and offer huge potential benefits but also raise ethical and environmental concerns.

All of these technological advances offer enormous promise but also present graver dangers than at almost any other time in history. Just like dynamite, nuclear power and the internet, these developments can be used for good and evil. The challenge for policymakers is how to harness the benefits of introducing these technologies into their economies and societies, while at the same time keeping the disruption and damage they cause to a minimum.

As well as preparing their populations for rapid technological change, government itself needs to adapt as it cannot remain separate from the transformational context and world in which it operates. Digital technologies will become integral to the workings of the state.

As Toomas Ilves, the former president of Estonia, explains in Chapter 1, "digitalisation of governance is not just about 'putting government online'. Nor is it merely turning paper records into PDFs. Digitalisation of government ultimately means rethinking and reimagining how governance works."

The potential benefits of such a rethink (or reimagining) outstrip anything we have seen since the beginning of record-keeping several millennia ago.

SOCIAL CHANGES

The second global trend impacting on governments is social change, which is in part enabled by technology. Social changes typically move more slowly and more subtly than technological changes, but they are highly pervasive and nearly impossible to stop. Not only do they spread relentlessly throughout nations, they tend to spread equally relentlessly around the globe.

Social change is being accelerated by:

- The rise of social media and other forms of connectedness.
- Economic volatility.
- Changing demographics.

Social changes are granting new powers to citizens, posing baffling problems for policymakers and governments. People have grown increasingly used to having everything at the touch of a smartphone, for example, which is raising their expectations. Mobile government – the ability to access government information and services from a mobile device – is shifting from being a nice-to-have to an expect-to-have.

The rise of social media

This hyper-connectivity is also creating new forms of social interaction, most notably social media. This is enabling citizens to self-organise and also encouraging the polarisation of views as individuals bypass official news channels and access information through their own personal networks. This puts more pressure on government to interact with citizens via their chosen social channel. Issues can inflate, conflate and ignite within hours or minutes, requiring a rapid response from government, which may not be fully aware of the undercurrents or causes.

Allied to this, another social change is the emergence of tribalism. Personalisation and AI-powered filtering have created increasingly idiosyncratic attitudes, including the rise of what can be described as a tribalistic mindset. Tribalism leads to higher levels of intolerance and of "us versus them" posturing. Connectivity has made it possible for those with a tribalistic mindset to see their grievances reaffirmed and amplified in their own echo chambers. They form groups of like-minded individuals, and organise to take action (against companies, policies and governments).

Connectivity

Connectivity also has great potential for positive social change. Social media can bring individuals together to pool their efforts towards larger goals. Crowdsourcing, crowd funding and other crowd-based activities offer interesting new avenues that governments can explore. For instance, crowdsourcing has created a "leapfrogging" effect, which has enabled many branches of science to discover and validate findings much faster and more cheaply. This approach was particularly useful and relevant for the covid-19 pandemic - to expand the body of knowledge about rates of infection, therapies and clinical trials.

Democratisation of education

Another big social change is in how we learn, leading to more widespread and more intense use of virtual learning. This affects not only elementary and high school education but also higher education and university courses. Students are discovering their own ways of finding information and content creators are devising novel ways to present it. The role of the teacher is becoming less of information-giver and more of problem-solver; the focus is shifting towards learning not teaching, and in educating students on how to think, instead of what to think. Teachers and education systems now need to catch up with their students.

Changing demographics

Demographic changes also play a significant part in global social trends. The population in most developed countries is ageing due to falling birth rates coupled with higher life expectancy. Falling fertility rates mean nearly every country could have shrinking populations by the end of the century. Researchers at the University of Washington's Institute for Health Metrics and Evaluation, for example, found that the global fertility rate nearly halved to 2.4 in 2017, and will fall below 1.7 by 2100.[51] Some 23 nations - including Spain and Japan - are expected to see their populations halve by 2100.

Countries will also age dramatically, with as many people turning 80 as there are being born. By 2035, it is estimated that there will be one billion people over 65 years (that's 13% of the world's total population). At the other end of the spectrum, around 90% of the world's youth now live in developing countries. In India alone, more than a million young people enter the labour market every month. Jobs are not being created fast enough to absorb the new entrants and, as a result, global youth unemployment averages 40% of the total unemployed population.

Urbanisation is another clear trend. Research suggests that nearly two-thirds of the world's population will reside in cities before the end of this decade. Urbanisation increases service delivery, thanks to more concentrated populations, but it also increases the risk of uncontrollable epidemics and puts increasing pressure on infrastructure and resources.

ECONOMIC SHIFTS

The third megatrend covers economic shifts. Once the economic direction of travel seemed relatively predictable but that is no longer the case. At the end of 2019, for example, the economic landscape was changing in a more or less foreseeable way:

- Towards a more service-based than manufacturing-based economy.
- Towards higher efficiency and productivity thanks to global supply chains.
- Towards more dominance of high-tech and more reliance on innovation.

But then along came covid-19, which compounded certain counter trends that were already evident and reversed the course of changes that we once confidently predicted.

At the time of writing:

- Globalisation is stalling and even going into reverse.
- Trade wars and protectionism are on the rise.
- Unemployment is accelerating.
- Global supply chains are fracturing.
- Governments are borrowing huge amounts to fund stimulus packages.

GLOBALISATION IN REVERSE

Globalisation, for example, once viewed as an unstoppable force in the world, is in retreat. The United States, the perennial champion of free trade, is turning its back on closer ties with other nations and has become one of the most protectionist countries in the world. China is now promoting free trade.

The trade war between the United States and China, which has intensified in the last few years, is fragmenting global trade, increasing costs and prices, and reducing investment.

The global pandemic added fuel to that fire, raising trade barriers and encouraging "our country first" attitudes - the scrambling for medical gear, personal protection equipment (PPE), and medicines is a case in point. In June 2020, the United States bought up the world stock of the drug remdesivir, leaving all other countries high and dry.[52]

The pandemic has had other economic effects on industry, too. Companies have realised that the efficiency and productivity gains from global supply chains makes them fragile and vulnerable to global threats. In future, we can expect onshoring as companies and governments try to bring supply chains back home, or at least closer to home, in the name of increasing resilience and also for political reasons. This will lead to regionalisation instead of globalisation.

One of the features of globalisation has been the ability to operate geographically fragmented supply chains. The lean manufacturing techniques first introduced by Toyota and other Japanese companies, for example, used Just in Time (JIT) systems to minimise inventory of raw materials or components. However, recent events have shown how brittle global supply chains can be, with multinational companies such as Apple, Toyota and Hyundai relying on components sourced from China, affected by disruptions in production. As a result, companies are now trying to build greater resilience back into their supply chains, moving away from Just in Time to a model that is described as "just in case".[53]

"Just in case" aims to build in contingencies by using suppliers that are closer to home, so will be national or regional rather than global. Governments will try to boost economic self-reliance and create strategic autonomy. This is likely to come at the price of higher inflation, lower productivity, lower efficiency, and higher prices for intermediate and consumer goods. Decreasing overseas investment will hurt developing economies.

Public debt has been high in most of the world for decades. Now, the massive state support provided to companies and employees as a result of covid-19 has made public debt across the world explode. Radical solutions for over-indebtedness will become a priority, as massive borrowing will be required to stimulate the economy.

Government borrowing is already at unprecedented levels. The IMF predicted that rich countries would borrow 17% of their combined GDP in 2020 to fund US$4.2 trillion in spending and tax cuts designed to keep the economy going. This has led to "a desperate scramble to enact policies that only a few months ago were either unimaginable or heretical", declared a leader in *The Economist* on 25 July 2020: "A profound shift is taking place in economics as a result, of the sort that happens only once in a generation. Much as in the 1970s when clubby Keynesianism gave way to Milton Friedman's austere monetarism, and in the 1990s when central banks were given their independence, so the pandemic marks the start of a new era. Its overriding preoccupation will be exploiting the opportunities and containing the enormous risks that stem from a supersized level of state intervention in the economy and financial markets."

THE CHANGING NATURE OF WORK

In my country, Oman, unemployment will have a disproportionate effect on manufacturing, oil extraction and certain service industries such as travel, air transport, hospitality, retail and office services, pushing many in the middle class down to lower income levels. Business will see widespread changes, with more remote working, and the move to a post-oil world will also have big implications for oil-producing economies.

Taken together, these economic shifts represent new challenges for the governments of the world. The assumed and seemingly relentless drive towards globalisation has suffered a significant setback, making it far harder to predict what will happen next. With calls for greater economic self-reliance, some nations will be tempted towards short-term measures such as protectionism. In reality, however, governments adopting policies that encourage innovation and competitiveness, and that attract talent rather than driving it away, will best serve the interests of their nations.

GEOPOLITICAL SHIFTS

The fourth global trend facing the world's governments is a series of power shifts that are redrawing the political map. The tectonic plates of global politics have been shifting for several years now:

- The unipolarity that prevailed after the collapse of the Soviet Union is no more.
- The relentless economic rise of China has lifted all economies but is now making America nervous.

The institutional architecture that underpinned the world order for 75 years is under severe stress. Add to this the rise of populist leaders and the continuing fall-out from a global pandemic, and the real geopolitical change has begun.

The United States has stepped back from the world stage, which has created a vacuum that is being rapidly filled by Russia on the military front and by China on the economic and "soft power" front. China's Belt and Road Initiative (BRI) will deliver trillions of dollars of infrastructure financing and spread Chinese influence.

In the Middle East, the Gulf Cooperation Council, which includes all the Arab states of the Gulf region except Iraq, is seeking to mitigate the move away from fossil fuels to a post-oil world. The UAE's recent Mars mission attests to this and is a sign of the region's technological ambition. Confidence in the United States' commitments towards its allies is on the wane in the region, however, and oil-producing countries, whether part of OPEC or not, have lost economic and geopolitical clout. The United States' No. 1 producer status makes it less dependent on, and less interested in, oil from Middle Eastern countries. This is contributing to a feeling of insecurity in the region, prompting nations to seek other possible partnerships, and to join China's Belt and Road Initiative, rather than stay in the Western camp.

Technology leadership is also shifting. After decades of dominance, Silicon Valley can no longer assume that it will remain the epicentre of the technological revolution. America is losing its lead in many technological fields, including AI, telecoms and nuclear power (to China) and software development (to India).

Multilateral institutions (the UN, IMF, World Bank, WHO, WTO, ILO, ICJ, IPCC) and alliances (NATO, Japan-United States, South Korea-United States) that were created for mutual assistance are straining. The European Union, a community of shared values and interests that was created to overcome the nationalism that sparked the great wars of the 20th century, is facing the challenges of nationalism once more.

As the superpowers jockey for position, Brexit means that Europe, which through the EU project could have been a superpower in its own right, appears to be fragmenting, and increasingly looks like a failed experiment. Yet there are many who still believe that being European matters, and is the best way to address global challenges. The comments of one of our contributors, John Bruton, bear witness to that:

"Although our problems are multinational," says Bruton, "we haven't created, even in Europe where we have so much in common with one another historically, … a supranational sense of shared identity … and shared destiny. We haven't created that adequately to give the sort of moral and emotional support to politicians who need to do things at a multinational level, which is the only level these problems can be solved at."

Elsewhere, there are tensions between North and South Korea; Russia and the West; Saudi Arabia and Iran; China and India; India and Pakistan; and Israel and the Arab world. Latin America looks increasingly marginalised from North America and will be subject to growing Russian and Chinese influence. The region's reliance on commodity products makes it vulnerable to global price fluctuations, and uncertainty.

In Asia Pacific, as Dr Supachai Panitchpakdi observes in Chapter 4: "Competing geopolitical blocs are dividing Asia as never before… In the coming years, membership of regional power blocs will be vital."

Meanwhile, Africa remains the great unknown. With its natural resources, younger population and growing middle class, it should be a force to be reckoned with. But to achieve its economic, political and social potential, Africa will have to overturn decades of poor governance and overcome the obstacles and scars of its colonial history. The African Union (AU), consisting of the 55 member states that make up the African Continent, was officially launched in 2002 as a successor to the Organisation of African Unity (OAU, 1963-1999), with that as its main objective. Whether it will succeed remains to be seen.

What is clear from the contributors to Part I of this book, however, is that there is no one-size-fits-all development model for all nations. This is even more apparent for countries with multiple ethnicities, where achieving and maintaining social harmony is an important goal in itself.

The power shift from west to east, which some commentators have heralded as the start of an Asian century, will be given additional momentum by technological change and global threats.

DEMOCRACY UNDER PRESSURE

Along with the geopolitical shift to the east, some commentators question the long-term future of established political systems, including the democratic capitalism of the United States. The growing gap between rich and poor is fomenting discontent, says Harvard Business School's Michael Porter, one of the world's leading experts on competitiveness and an adviser to governments. In his 2020 book, ***The Politics Industry****,*[54] *Porter and his co-author Katherine Gehl argue that America's political system does not benefit the citizens it was intended to serve. Instead, the political-industrial complex subjugates the American political system so that special interest groups, lobbyists, big money donors, think tanks, pollsters and consultants are the only winners in the game. By applying his famous Five Forces framework, Porter* *argues that the American political system functions in a similar way to other industries. As such, the problem is a lack of competition caused by a dysfunctional two-party system acting as a duopoly.*

Roger Martin, former dean of the Rotman School of Management at Toronto University, is another commentator questioning the American system. In his latest book, ***When More Isn't Better****, Martin argues that democratic capitalism, in its current form, is unsustainable.*[55] *For the last 250 years and more, he observes, capitalism has been the economic model that America has chosen, and democracy its system of government. And for two-and-a-half centuries those two systems worked together to ensure rising standards of living for the majority of the population. But that consistent economic advance isn't happening anymore – and it hasn't for the longest period in American history.*

In the 23 years from 1953 to the American bicentenary in 1976, the real median family income in America grew at a healthy annual compound rate of 2.4%, meaning that the median family was 72% better off economically in 1976 than in 1953, and was on track to hit a doubling of real income in seven additional years – ie, doubling in one generation (30 years). It was that kind of very long-term growth that made American democratic capitalism so effective in producing broad prosperity during its first 200 years. However, in the 40 years following the bicentenary, growth plummeted to an anemic 0.6% per year, meaning that the median family was only 26% better off – one third the progress in almost twice the time (ie, 40 versus 23 years).

Martin points to a winner-takes-all economy that has developed in the United States, which is fueling inequality and disillusionment. If middle-income voters don't feel democratic capitalism is working for them, they will vote for something else and, Martin argues, they are dangerously close to that point now. The last time this group of voters were as disenchanted as they are today was in the 1930s in the depths of the Great Depression. At that time, voters in many of the world's major developed countries voted for fascism, communism, or socialism over democratic capitalism.

Government that is "for the people" but in reality does not serve its citizens, is not sustainable in the long term, and will have to be reimagined or it will eventually fail.

GLOBAL THREATS

The final megatrend is the incidence of global threats. The covid-19 pandemic has exposed the weakness of our global institutions.

As noted in the introduction, going forwards, governments will have to give greater consideration to discontinuities and unexpected events, especially low-probability, high-impact events – the "black swans" identified by Nassim Nicholas Taleb.[56] The covid-19 pandemic was just such a black swan - an event that was unforeseen (even though a pandemic was widely predicted) but had a huge impact. However, it was just the latest in a string of unexpected but highly damaging events over the last two-and-a-half decades that include the Asian financial crisis in 1997, the dot-com bust in 2000, the SARS crisis in 2002, the tsunamis in 2004 and 2011, the global financial crisis in 2008, the Ebola outbreak in 2014 … the list goes on. Governments are under increasing pressure to be ready to respond to these sorts of unwelcome surprises.

Global threats are compounded by other factors:

- Ideological differences continue to inflame the minds of terrorists.
- Intentional viruses are infecting cross-border cyberspace.
- Anthropogenic effects, such as global warming.

And so far, no cure has been found for any of them.

In his chapter on Thailand's transformation, Dr Supachai Panitchpakdi refers to the state of VUCA (volatile, uncertain, complex and ambiguous) as the new normal. It is my belief that we have been living in a state of "synthetic certainty" for some time. That era is now over; covid-19 has seen to that.

Increasingly, leading government will be about managing uncertainty and ambiguity. This requires creating trust through transparency, and leaders who are prepared to admit that they do not have all the answers or know what will happen next.

To cope with an increasingly complex and unpredictable world, governments need to be more innovative, entrepreneurial and resilient. They also need to be more collaborative with business and private citizens and, on the international stage, with each other, to tackle global challenges. A virus such as covid-19 has no respect for borders. It is only by working together that the governments of the world can prevent more pandemics and tackle other threats such as global warming, terrorism and cyber security.

As John Bruton observed, multinational problems require multinational solutions. Terrorism remains a real and present danger. A massive increase in unemployment in the wake of covid-19 will provide more angry recruits to terrorist movements.

Disinformation, conspiracy theories, fake news and hate-filled feeds will continue to radicalise people. Cyber-attacks are an economic and political form of terrorism and they are on the rise.

Global warming is another underlying threat that respects no borders, recognises no political differences, and can destroy economies and livelihoods on a worldwide scale.

NEW REALITIES FOR GOVERNMENT

The mentioned megatrends – technological, social, economic, geopolitical and global threats - are already impacting on the environments that governments operate in. Taken all together, I believe they add up to seven new realities facing the governments of the world. Each of these new realities represents a crisis of a kind. I summarise them as follows:

1. Social contracts are fraying.
2. Governments have lost the trust of their people.
3. There is a lack of citizen-centricity.
4. Governments appear unresponsive.
5. Governments are failing to harness the potential of the private sector.
6. Government leaders are ill-prepared for an unknowable future.
7. Citizens are behaving as passive recipients.

1. Social contracts are fraying

The fundamental question here is whether the "deal" between a government and the people it serves is a satisfactory and stable one.

The political philosopher Thomas Hobbes defined the social contract as the condition in which people give up some individual liberty in exchange for some common security.[57] A century later, in his 1762 book, *The Social Contract*, Jean-Jacques Rousseau argued that laws are only binding when they are supported by the general will of the people.

Rousseau's famous observation that "man is born free but is everywhere in chains" challenged the perceptions of his time that elites should rule over the common people simply as a right of birth. Instead, Rousseau argued that the will of the people was the most important legitimising factor for any government.

The social contract is what holds a nation together. A set of assumptions, expectations and implicit understandings, it is the glue that binds government, business and citizens to each other. The point about a meaningful social contract is that it is a contract between all three parties with each playing their part. As the social contract frays, so citizens and the private sector become disengaged and are less inclined to invest in maintaining a safe and thriving state.

There will always be a trade-off between the provision of stability, safety and opportunity and the restriction of certain freedoms. But that should not be taken for granted. The strength of the social contract in different countries was tested by the covid-19 crisis.

It is no coincidence that the countries that were most effective at dealing with the first wave of the pandemic were those with a more defined social contract. As Lim Hwee Hua notes in Chapter 3, Singapore's success over recent decades has been built on the strong social contract between government, citizens and business. "The government and people have a common heartbeat and common cause, constantly thinking ahead about the challenges and agonising over how to address them. The way the country responds to crises, including the covid-19 pandemic, is a good illustration of the social contract", she notes.

Few nations have a social contract as strong as Singapore and tensions were exposed in other countries by the coronavirus crisis, especially in the response of citizens to government guidelines on social distancing and other preventative measures. In the United States, for example, people took to the streets to protest about wearing masks. This raises a fundamental question about the trade-off between the needs of the nation (the greater good) and the rights of the individual.

Another question for governments is what to do as traditional jobs become obsolete with the advent of robots, algorithms, driverless cars and other new technologies. There will be growing pressure for some form of universal basic income. This will shine a spotlight on a debate already underway about the future of capitalism. China and some other Asian countries have prospered using a form of state-funded capitalism that is a hybrid of western-style capitalism and national planning. There is a growing mood in the West towards taking a wider view, shifting from narrowly focused shareholder value to a more inclusive view of stakeholder value.

In the next few years, there will be pressure to create more frugal forms of capitalism, and more minimalist lifestyles. The implications for luxury goods and other discretionary product providers are unclear. Similarly, the future of sectors such as travel and hospitality are likely to be very different to what was imagined before the pandemic. As the socio-economic landscape alters, governments will need to find a way to renew the social contract with their citizens.

2. **Governments have lost the trust of the people**
Underlying this tension with the social contract is a related problem - that many governments have lost the trust of their people. Citizens feel that leaders are perhaps only interested in power and have no empathy for their plight. When there is a lack of trust, people will be less forgiving of the government and more reluctant to follow instructions. This in turn makes governance more difficult and less effective. Without trust there can be no meaningful collaboration between citizens, business and government.

It is too often the case that governments introduce measures that make citizens nervous of their intentions. A good example is how London, with over 600,000 cameras, is becoming a surveillance state, without a public debate about the right to privacy. Clearly, the need to counter crime and terrorism is a good reason for the cameras, but only if citizens understand and accept that the technology is there to protect them and not to spy on them.

A government should be prepared to make the case for the intrusion into citizens' privacy. Trust breeds trust and distrust breeds distrust.

The lack of trust in governments is also leading to the rise of identity politics and social movements. As we have seen recently with the Black Lives Matter (#BLM) and the Me Too (#Metoo) movements, demands for social change that are not addressed by government can suddenly burst to the surface, causing protests and social unrest. This may be triggered by a catalysing event, such as the outcry about police brutality towards African Americans following the killing of George Floyd by a police officer in Minneapolis, on 25 May 2020. But it is usually the result of pent-up frustration and resentment dating back many years and, sometimes, generations.

Other movements such as Extinction Rebellion and Green Peace activists rally around environmental issues and are increasingly vocal and focal for their followers.

The dark side of social media is that it creates echo chambers that confirm prejudices and exacerbate tribalism. This has led to a growing culture of rage and resentment, encouraging those who feel disadvantaged or left out to make their voices heard – *en masse*. Governments that ignore these social eddies risk becoming caught in a more serious vortex. The need to combat, or at least challenge, fake news and the threat of foreign governments interfering in the affairs of other governments via social media is all too evident.

Populist politicians are also taking advantage of tribalism to further their own agendas, diminishing the relevance of left versus right. In Britain, for example, Boris Johnson's victory in the 2019 general election was predicated on his appeal to Brexit voters from both sides of the traditional left and right divide. Voters in the former Labour heartland of the north of England broke with tradition to deliver a large Conservative majority.

"A big shift is taking place in global politics," notes Alexander Stubb in Chapter 2. "The rise of populism has seen traditional ideology-based politics being replaced by identity politics. The big ideologies that dictated the course of 20th century politics have become less relevant. Populist movements – Brexit, Trump - are based on identity. And that identity is usually a one-issue identity, such as nationality, the nation state, or the environment."

Adding to the confusion is a torrent of information, misinformation and disinformation. The internet has put the world's knowledge at our fingertips. In 2011, for example, a typical American was exposed to five times the information per day than they would have been 25 years earlier — and this was before most people had smartphones.

Today, the volume of information has more than doubled again. But together with information there is also much disinformation, including fake news, conspiracy theories and crackpot ideas that the earth is flat. Unverified channels have overwhelmed the reporting criteria and best practices of the traditional media, making it increasingly difficult to know who or what to believe. The advent of counterfeit technologies, including deep fake videos and other synthetic media, will make this even more of a problem in the future.

Rebuilding trust in the era of populism, fake news and information overload will be essential.

3. **There is a lack of citizen-centricity**

Another criticism of governments is that the services they provide are not citizen friendly. Private sector organisations have been using the language of customer centricity for many years now, with businesses organised around the needs and experience of individual customers. But most governments have been slow to adopt it in respect of citizens and business.

Services should be structured around the citizen's experience and journey rather than the convenience of government departments. Yet governments often provide services for citizens either begrudgingly or in a highly bureaucratic way, which projects indifference to citizens' needs. For those who feel excluded from it, the system can seem optimised for big corporates or the 1% of people who are the society's elite.

At present, most governments seem unwilling or unable to utilize new technologies to enhance the experience of citizens or even to ensure their safety. The speed with which covid-19 spread highlights the importance of governments using technology - from effective testing to track and trace apps - to increase their situational awareness. The governments that acted decisively and on expert advice were shown to be more effective at controlling the spread of the disease and protecting their citizens. Government leaders who dithered and failed to recognise the seriousness of the threat to public health, or viewed it through a narrow political lens, were found wanting.

Smart cities are another example of how governments can move towards citizen-centricity, with technology and services organised around the needs of the urban populations. Similarly, the adoption of earthquake early warning systems in buildings in Tokyo and other Japanese cities shows what can be achieved when technology is adopted in a citizen-centric way.

In Chapter 1, Toomas Ilves points out that the digitalisation of government is a huge opportunity to create citizen-centric processes for all the important moments of our lives – birth, marriage and death. Yet in most countries registering any of these important milestones is steeped in bureaucracy, which does not serve the citizen. "There is a paradox here." Ilves notes of his time in America. "Despite living in the heart of Silicon Valley, if I need to register a child for school or obtain a driving licence or, indeed, have any interaction with any level of government – local, state or national – I would almost certainly have to travel to a government office. Once there, I would have to wait or stand in line for hours, then fill out forms and applications by hand, stand in line (again) to hand them in and then wait for weeks for it all to be processed."

As Ilves explains, it is beholden on governments to utilize technology to provide the best services to citizens and by extension the private sector. The advent of IoT will provide even greater opportunities.

Governments that fail to adopt and adapt to new technologies will be unable to respond adequately to the demands of their citizens or the private sector and so risk being left behind. If they lag too far behind, they will lose the trust of their people. Just as they demand a minimum level of law, people also expect and demand a minimum service level via the devices through which they increasingly engage with the world. If they do not find the conditions they need to thrive in one country, the most talented members of the population will seek it elsewhere.

Ed Vaizey makes the same point Chapter 6, when he observes: "The fundamental point about the Government Digital Service – and I cannot emphasise this enough - was that it asked one simple, but crucial question: what is the user need? Government is very good at thinking about what it wants, but it doesn't always think about what its citizens want."

This leads us to the fourth new reality or crisis - government in general is too unresponsive.

4. **Governments appear unresponsive**

Put simply, many governments are failing to deliver on their part of the social contract. They do not prioritise or act on what the citizens perceive as important – for example, health and employment. When citizens become disenchanted and resentful of government failings, they are more inclined to explore wild-card options in the form of extreme policies or populist demagogues. If the status quo does not serve their perceived interests, and if government is indifferent to their concerns, they will look elsewhere for alternatives. In particular, governments that do not capitalise on new technologies or do not respond quickly to global threats can seem arrogant and complacent.

There is a growing sense of frustration that governments are too often out of step with the needs of the people they are supposed to serve. It is becoming increasingly clear, for example, that governments need to keep up with the pace of change, be that technological, regulatory, commercial, or social. At present, however, many governments lag behind on the issues facing their citizens and businesses and are constantly having to play catch-up.

A case in point is that the General Data Protection Regulation (GDPR), a major piece of EU legislation related to data protection and privacy, was introduced many years after social media had comprehensively redrawn the boundaries around personal privacy. As a consequence, companies and individuals were faced with new rules, which they had to implement and comply with retrospectively, incurring huge costs. The same catch-up is being played out with regulations governing the use of drones and self-driving vehicles.

In many cases, the government has a bold vision of being a high-tech nation or reducing pollution or some other laudable aspiration, which it proclaims but fails to deliver on. Governments need to find a better balance between vision and execution. Where they do need to respond, governments often react in a flailing and ineffective manner. Given the fast pace of change, government officials no longer have the luxury of a few years to observe how a new technology or trend plays out before devising a suitable regulatory environment to govern it. Today, they need to anticipate and then move at the same pace as those creating the disruption.

Take personal data, for example. Data can be viewed as a national resource; like oil, it can be extracted, refined, and turned into valuable products. Firms such as Apple, Facebook and Google operate a "walled garden" strategy to protect and make revenues from the data they mine. Data, however, is also akin to sunlight, in that it is everywhere, underlies everything, and could be freely accessible for everyone to use, as argued by the open data movements.

Toomas Ilves observes that one of keys to the successful digitalisation of a country is to establish what data must be private and what should be public. Crucially, he says, citizens must be able to see who has accessed their data at any time. As Ilves also points out, a country cannot afford to treat data as merely a legal or regulatory issue, as attitudes to data and privacy vary between cultures. "In Estonia, even before digitalisation anyone could access someone else's property records; in Greece you cannot. You need to design your system to follow your laws but also to meet the cultural expectations of your population."

Yet, despite the clear need for a framework, most governments continue to prevaricate and fudge the issue. Whether you subscribe to the walled garden approach or the free data movement, or something in between, what is undeniable is that data has become a valuable resource and, unlike previously valuable resources like oil that were highly prized because of their limited supply, the supply of data is expanding rapidly.

The global datasphere is growing at a rate of more than 60% per year and is expected to reach 175 Zettabytes by 2025 (one Zettabyte is one trillion gigabytes). It has given rise to the data economy, which includes everything from low-earning data taggers to multibillion-earning data brokers and data-insights traders.

We are witnessing the data-isation of everything. You used to go for a walk, for example; now you do 10,373 steps and burn 430 calories!

The implications for government in terms of adopting new digital technologies whilst protecting the wellbeing and livelihoods of their citizens are huge, and hugely challenging. The rewards for nations that get digital transformation right, however, are equally huge. Responsiveness, of course, needs to be balanced with responsibility. It is important to respond to the changing needs and demands of the nation without losing sight of long-term responsibilities for issues such as financial stability and personal security.

5. **Governments are failing to harness the potential of the private sector**
Business has an important role to play in delivering more responsive government and better social solutions. Governments need to move from being buyers of products and services to being collaborators with business in order to harness the private sector's capacity for innovation. There is ample evidence to suggest that this can work. Consider how business stepped up to help governments cope with shortages during the pandemic, for instance, diverting resources and expertise in innovative ways to fill the public sector's capability gaps.

At present, where government does collaborate with business it tends to be with a handful of mega players – large corporates, who wield a disproportionate amount of power and influence over government policy and contracts. Furthermore, there are still too many examples of cronyism, with government contracts going to friends and family members of government leaders or advisers. Nations need to become more adept at harnessing the capabilities of smaller organisations, where a lot of the real innovation occurs, and collaborating with individual experts and practitioners. This requires government to create the conditions for an innovative and collaborative private sector to develop. This includes both the way governments control the private sector and the need for infrastructure to compete on the world stage. The private sector needs to step up in respect of meeting the needs of all stakeholders and not simply shareholders. It also needs government to take on more risk, backing innovative solutions so that the nation can enjoy more of the rewards that go with taking such risks.

6. **Government leaders are ill-prepared for an unknowable future**

We now live in a more uncertain and volatile world, which makes the future unknowable. Yet government leaders have not adapted to this new reality and seem woefully unprepared for anything out of the ordinary. A recent headline in *The Economist* declared: "Governments routinely ignore seemingly far-out risks. Rocked by a global pandemic, they need to up their game."[58]

Upping their game requires government leaders to be more proactive. Simply trying to keep the ship on an even keel to remain in power is not enough. The five global trends outlined earlier mean there are choppy waters ahead, to put it mildly. The ship needs radical transformation if it is to carry the nation forward into a future that is better than the past. This requires pioneering leadership and not just stewardship. Such leaders need to be comfortable (and responsible) with taking bold decisions, which also requires them to be well informed.

Governments need to be data driven and execute on evidence-based policies. The pandemic illustrated this perfectly: the most effective governments used the best technology and scientific advice to create guidelines to address the crisis, and the vast majority of their businesses (shops and restaurants and factories) and citizens played their part by respecting and abiding by the guidelines.

In some places, however, the advice of experts was spurned and even derided by populist leaders seeking to shift the blame. *The Economist* noted of the Trump administration's attacks on health expert Anthony Fauci: "An administration at war with its own scientific and medical experts in the middle of a pandemic … makes developing a cohesive strategy - one that the public trusts and will follow - challenging, to say the least."

Singapore and other countries in Southeast Asia benefited from their previous experience with SARS and other public health crises. They had better systems in place to cope with the covid-19 outbreak. They were also better at gathering and interpreting data. This involves an understanding among citizens and the business community that they have a commitment to fulfil their obligations and responsibilities toward the state and therefore to their government.

Elsewhere, government guidelines were flouted. The reasons for the dissatisfaction and erosion of trust are many and varied as noted earlier, but the underlying cause is that many citizens perceive that their governments are failing to deliver – whether it is on the level of services they demand, the transparency with which they share information, or on appropriate action to ensure their safety in a crisis. This links to the next point: government is just one part of a national ecosystem - citizens need to step up, too.

7. **Citizens are behaving as passive recipients**
Just as government and business needs to step up, so citizens cannot be passive actors in society; they need to raise their game as well. Individuals have a role to play in maintaining a healthy society and have a responsibility to take on more of the social contract by behaving less like traditional salarymen and more like entrepreneurs.

In particular, citizens need to take responsibility for developing their own marketable skills, rather than simply relying on government to find them a job or guarantee them a minimum income. This is a two-way street, however, and governments need to provide the incentives and means to allow citizens and businesses to engage with and contribute to, their communities. If there is no mechanism for capturing their ideas and enlisting the talents of citizens, they will remain cynical and disengaged.

Government has a responsibility for citizen development and creating the infrastructure for better G2C (government-to-citizen) and C2G (citizen-to-government) communications. The role of crowdsourcing in tracking the spread of covid-19 and informing citizens about spikes in infection, for example, was discussed earlier. In another surprising case, astronomers enlisted volunteer "citizen scientists" to help them examine and understand the universe. Over an eight-month period, 37,000 volunteers combed more than 430,000 images in an online photo library of deep-space and were able to identify 29 locations in the cosmos where gravity was bending light, so-called gravitational lenses, that computers could not.

Similarly, when the conditions for engaging business in a mutually beneficial manner are absent, there is no framework for government to tap into private sector expertise. The new social contract has to be between the three key parts of any modern nation: government, business and the citizens. All three parts of society need to feel that they are contributors to societal health rather than being passive bystanders or, worse still, where they feel no moral imperative to intervene when problems arise.

NAVIGATING THROUGH NEW REALITIES: A WAY FORWARD

These new realities, or crises, point to the pressing need for change. Traditional government is no longer fit for purpose. It cannot cope with a VUCA world, and a failure to adapt to the new realities will lead to more crises.

This brings me to my central thesis and the underlying message of this book: governments need a threefold transformation in order to make them fit for purpose in the modern age.

1. Thriving states require strong and trustful engagement between the primary actors. Governments do not work in isolation. They are part of an ecosystem that includes business, citizens and other governments. I refer to this as the GBC (government, business, citizen) model, and I believe it is universal.
2. Governments need to be more dynamic and entrepreneurial to respond to a rapidly changing world. Governments must become more entrepreneurial in their behaviours and more resilient in their systems. This entails developing a culture that is more innovative and adaptable, with a more nuanced approach to risk management.
3. A new type of government leader is required to transform government appropriately. Leaders who operate effectively in uncertain and volatile environments exhibit common and trainable attributes. These attributes are relevant to all leaders, especially those working in the public sector.

I believe these three principles underpin states optimised to thrive in uncertain times.

The style of leadership required is explored in more detail in Chapter 10. Before that, Chapter 9 will examine the second operating principle – the need for governments to become more dynamic and entrepreneurial. But we begin our solutions journey in Chapter 8 by diving deeper into the ecosystem comprised of the three parts of civil society – government, business and citizen.

The Government-Business-Citizens (GBC) Model

8

In the last chapter, we examined the megatrends that are contributing to the volatile, uncertain, complex and ambiguous world we now live in, and the consequent new realities disrupting governments. I concluded with three principles to guide leaders in how to respond to today's challenges.

In this chapter, we will look at the first of these principles:

Thriving states require active and trustful engagement between the primary actors (government, business and citizens).

I will share with you a model that has helped remind me that government does not exist simply to keep civil servants in gainful employment. As you will discover, there are three primary actors in the societal ecosystem. Given this book's focus on leadership and government transformation, we will focus on government and its interrelationship with both business and the citizen.

BACKGROUND

Something I recognised early on in my career is that governments do not work in isolation. They are part of an ecosystem that includes business and citizens, (as well as other governments). I refer to this as the GBC (government, business, citizens) model, and I believe it is universal.

There is a symbiotic relationship between government, business and the citizenry; together, they form a network of relationships that binds the culture of a healthy nation. But this web of symbiosis is not generally considered. Instead, government (as the authority of the state) is typically seen as separate from the other two parts, providing basic functions such as law and order, physical infrastructure and national security. In its direct interactions with business and citizens, government is seen primarily as a regulator of the former and a service provider to the latter. In both cases, the relationship is predominantly one-way, creating expectations on government that are not reciprocated. As such, business and citizens are largely absolved from their societal responsibilities and, more importantly perhaps, robbed of their agency. As a consequence, government does not benefit from their entrepreneurial dynamism and collective brain power.

In today's increasingly complex and interconnected world, governments cannot hope to have all the solutions or even to know all the questions. What is needed to create a thriving state is intelligent collaboration between the public and private sectors, which also recognises the public duty of private citizens. When all the actors are collaborating effectively, we will have the conditions for a stable, progressive and thriving state.

As we have seen in the previous chapter, citizen discontent is on the increase and this makes rebalancing the ecosystem an imperative. Similarly, a model that views business purely as a supplier of goods and services to government, or worse, a profit maximising capitalist, misses the dynamic interplay and mutuality that should exist between enterprise and the state. For this reason, even though it was clear to me that public private partnerships were a good idea and a necessary way of creating value for a nation, I could see that they were fraught with problems and I was keen to understand how they might work better.

THE GBC MODEL

I have spent the last five years working to understand how the public and private sectors in Oman can collaborate more effectively to co-create value for and with citizens. The GBC model came out of that work; it recognises that in order to thrive the conditions need to be suitable for all three.

Government is sometimes blamed for a nation's ills, but the reality is both more nuanced and more exciting. Viewed through the lens of the GBC ecosystem, the responsiveness and responsibility for a nation's wellbeing rests with all three actors and opens the door to new opportunities.

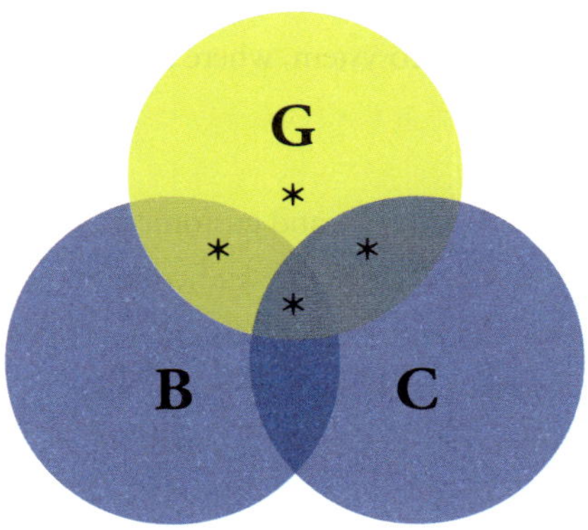

Figure: the government-business-citizens model

We focus here on the government component (G) and the relationships between, firstly, government and business (G2B and B2G); and secondly, between government and citizens (G2C and C2G). The interconnections between business and citizens (C2B and B2C) are also important to the ecosystem (with implications for customer loyalty and talent management) but are largely beyond the scope of this book.

The two-way interactions between government and business and government and citizens are represented by the overlap between the G and B circles and the G and C circles, respectively. But there is also growing scope for three-way collaboration, which is denoted by the asterisk at the centre of the model where all three circles overlap. This three-way GBC "sweet spot" is a particular focus of my interest and work in Oman. It was highlighted during the covid-19 pandemic, when it was vital for all three parts of the ecosystem to work together to combat the threat, as we will see later.

For our purposes, it should be noted that business here also includes the not-for-profit sector, and all organisations that are not funded by the public purse or purely profit oriented. This includes the emergence of social entrepreneurs and impact investors, who play an increasingly important role in many countries and are often powerful engines for progress, addressing social issues such as poverty, homelessness and mental health issues. That said, the most important force for progress is the extent to which the private sector both transforms and engages with government.

COLLABORATION IN ACTION

The next two chapters (9 and 10) will drill down deeper into the G part of the GBC model, but the rest of this chapter focuses on government's interactions with business and citizens (the areas marked with asterisks in the diagram).

As stated before, this is a symbiotic ecosystem, where all three parts rely on each other for their success. For example:

- Business needs citizens as employees and customers, and needs government to create the legal framework, infrastructure and conditions for trade.
- Citizens require meaningful work and goods and services from business, and the personal security and services that the state provides.
- And government relies on the talents of its citizens as civil servants and technocrats, and on a vibrant and profitable private sector to help fund, innovate and support public services.

When the ecosystem works effectively, it's a win: win: win scenario. It is therefore essential that the three component parts of the nation are able to collaborate in productive and purposeful ways. The GBC model is a very modern way of looking at a nation and requires a reimagining of how a society and an economy can and should function. The biggest single obstacle to achieving it lies with the attitudes and mindsets of government, business and citizens.

A QUESTION OF TRUST

Collaboration thrives on trust. Creating trust between government, business and citizens takes time and hard work. It is far easier to create rules and more red tape, which is the default position of most government departments. Fostering trust and collaboration, however, is more effective in the long term than arguing over individual contracts or regulations.

In the previous chapter, we identified the loss of trust in government on the part of business and citizens as a major cause for concern. This manifests itself not only in a growing cynicism towards politicians and government leaders but also in a diminishing trust in the institutions of state. To create a thriving GBC ecosystem, it is essential to reclaim and rebuild that institutional trust. As we shall see in Chapter 10, the ability to engender trust – and to be trustworthy - is a key factor for bringing about government transformation.

Governments have a duty to provide a safe environment for their citizens. The covid-19 pandemic put that responsibility to the test. In nations where trust was low, citizens and businesses were more likely to behave in an irresponsible way, thwarting government efforts. Recent research examined the impact of epidemics on political trust in nearly 140 countries worldwide. It found that epidemic exposure during an individual's "impressionable years" of 18 to 25 has a persistent negative effect on their trust in political institutions and leaders, especially in democracies.[59] The research found that trust is an important factor for limiting the spread of infection and depends on how well the government handled previous health scares. As the authors point out: "This raises the spectre of a circular, self-reinforcing spiral in which poor health policy adherence leads to deeper distrust, further undermining the efficacy of public health policy." In other words, the effectiveness of the response to the next pandemic will be dependent on how well the government handled the previous ones.

There has been some debate, too, over which type of government is more effective in a crisis. Writing in *The Atlantic*, the American political scientist and writer Francis Fukuyama observed: "The major dividing line in effective crisis response will not place autocracies on one side and democracies on the other. Rather, there will be some high-performing autocracies, and some with disastrous outcomes. There will be a similar, though likely smaller, variance in outcomes among democracies. The crucial determinant in performance will not be the type of regime, but the state's capacity to both engender trust and deliver adequate services."[60]

Trust in government, Fukuyama[61] argues, is built on two foundations. "First, citizens must believe that their government has the expertise, technical knowledge, capacity, and impartiality to make the best available judgments. Capacity simply has to do with the government having an adequate number of people with the right training and skills to carry out the tasks they are assigned, from local firemen, policemen and health workers to the government executives making higher-level decisions about issues such as quarantines and bailouts."

"The second foundation is trust in the top end of the hierarchy, which means, in the United States system, the president. Lincoln, Wilson and Roosevelt enjoyed high levels of trust during their respective crises. As wartime presidents, this trio succeeded in symbolizing, in their own persons, the national struggle."

Trust, Fukuyama goes on to say, is something the United States Federal Reserve had in 2008 when it faced the global financial crisis, because its chairman, Ben Bernanke, was a former academic who had studied the Great Depression in depth, and it was staffed with professional economists rather than political appointees likely to favour friends and cronies. But today, he argues, America faces a crisis of political trust.

Yet, some nations and governments have managed to create deep reserves of trust. Singapore's success has been built on the strong social contract between government, citizens and business. As a visiting fellow at the National University of Singapore (NUS), I've spent a lot of time in the country and have been struck by the level of confidence that ordinary people seem to have in their government. On one occasion, I remember talking to a taxi driver on the journey from the airport and being told that although government servants were highly paid, they deserve their high salaries due to their hard work in providing a good standard of living, a quality lifestyle and security.

As Lim Hwee Hua notes in Chapter 3: "A lasting relationship between government and citizens has to be built on nothing less than trust. A social contract that endures the test of time for longer-term macro-economic policies and sustains the nation through crises is founded on the underlying shared values of meritocracy, prosperity through hard work and thrift, and a collective responsibility for - and ownership of - the country's future and wellbeing of its people. To foster these values, the Singaporean government and citizens needed a shared vision – a plan they could work towards together."

A shared vision is an important first step but, unless there is trust on all sides, progress will be difficult. Take business, for example (I will discuss the relationship with citizens later). The traditional tension between government and business makes both sides suspicious, and the failure to pull together makes citizens cynical. The public sector may take the view that its role is to primarily protect the citizens from unscrupulous and greedy profiteers or big corporates in the private sector. Given the traditional private sector focus on making shareholders rich, this is understandable.

Less entrenched but still requiring a change of mindset, is the public sector perception that the private sector simply represents a pool of contractors that works best when heavily directed in respect of requirements. Whilst this can work, it destroys value because the contractor is now focused on minimising costs to maximise profitability, rather than creating new services where all parties benefit in the long term.

So, we need more open attitudes on the part of the public sector, but business also has a big part to play in re-imagining its role and responsibilities to communities and citizens.

COLLECTIVE RESPONSIBILITY

Some traditional businesses were built on the mindset of the merchant, not surprisingly, given the commodity nature of what they traded. This is typically a transactional short-term collaboration to win a deal, rather than a long-term strategic partnership. This is still the case in some cultures, especially in the Middle East. My experiences working with the PPC Task Force trying to bridge the gap, confirmed that the mercantile attitude can be an obstacle to longer-term collaborations. Similarly, if a business is focused too narrowly on shareholder returns and quarterly reports to please traders on the stock markets, then the case for a long-term collaboration is harder to make.

In order to optimise the relationship between the private and public sectors we need businesses to reset their goals. "Rather than shareholder returns being the main aim, firms can re-align their values and mission with a much wider goal: bringing returns to the whole community," say Isaac Getz and Laurent Marbacher, authors of *The Altruistic Corporation*.[62] Over a four-year period, Getz and Marbacher conducted interviews with CEOs, employees, customers and suppliers as well local community members. Their varying case studies include a French cheese company sensitive to the decline of the rural region it occupies, and a large Japanese pharmaceutical lab that focuses its attention on patients and their families rather than on profits. These examples show that business can be reimagined – and remain economically viable.

What is required is a new breed of businesses with a broader focus on all stakeholders, including the communities in which they operate. There are some indications that these new businesses might now be emerging.

Andrew Winston, author of *The Big Pivot*, notes some positive signs. In August 2019, nearly 200 CEOs of large multinationals – all members of the Business Roundtable in the United States - declared an end to the decades-long obsession with shareholder returns.[63] The purpose of a corporation, they said, is "to create value for all of our stakeholders". The rise of so-called B Corporations, which require certification of social and environmental performance as well as the usual financial criteria, is another step in the right direction.

Much of the literature around nation building focuses on the relationship between the public and private sectors. But nations will not thrive in this increasingly uncertain world unless they also recognise and respect the essential role of the citizens in what is a three-way relationship. Done well, the relationship between the three is both a symbiotic and sustainable one.

INTERACTIONS BETWEEN GOVERNMENT, BUSINESS AND CITIZENS

The interaction between government and the private sector is wide ranging and includes a multiplicity of contracts and services. Examples of G2B, for example, include all the services that governments provide by way of the business infrastructure, including the provision of the talent pool and technology infrastructure, and supervision of processes covering everything from registering a company to issuing export and import licences, and providing customs controls at ports and airports. On the other side, B2G activities include any goods or services that the private sector provides to government, anything from building and maintaining government buildings, and government IT projects, to the manufacture of personal protection equipment (PPE) or medical supplies to support hospitals and public health services.

The interaction between government and individual citizens is even broader ranging and is essentially the delivery of the social contract. G2C, for instance, starts with the hospital a citizen is born in, and then extends on through life right up until the registration of their death certificate, and everything the state provides in between – from roads to rubbish collection, and from public health to passports. It also includes the provision of national and personal security through the armed forces and emergency services.

The quid pro quo for the individuals is being a good citizen. So C2G includes citizens abiding by the laws of the land, paying their taxes and following the correct procedures for the purposes of public records.

These interactions between government, business and citizens typically evolve over time. Even though each nation has taken its own unique path to becoming a modern state, they generally share a broad pattern of development.

NATION BUILDING

For a great many liberal economies around the world, initial economic development was almost exclusively government led. From Singapore to the United States, to France, Germany, South Korea and Japan, the hand of the government was strong and ubiquitous throughout the early phases of economic development. Even a country with a strong tradition of minimal government, like the United States, has benefited greatly from government investment, most obviously the military spending on technology and space exploration that helped create Silicon Valley.

There comes a moment in this process, however, where the economy has grown so large and complex that the government can no longer do everything or orchestrate innovation. The institutions and the legislative framework have already been established, the infrastructure created, the provision of services instituted and the main industries set up.

The government's efforts and its investments begin to taper off. That is the time when the private sector should become the government's partner, assuming the role of main economic engine. But a nation's development is not all about economics. The ultimate goal of all regulations and legislation, and economic and institutional development, is the wellbeing of the substance of a nation: its people.

Thus, a modern, thriving state necessarily rests on the three pillars: the government, business and its citizens. In fact, it owes its stability to the simultaneous good health of each of these pillars: just like a three-legged stool, it cannot stand for long if one of them is weak.

An alternative metaphor is of the diligent gardener who having created a fertile environment, then plants some seeds. There comes a point where the gardener has to stand back and let the garden grow. Their role becomes that of nurturing, protecting the ecosystem from harmful pests and weeds, watering the plants if they need it and ensuring the soil remains fortified with the right nutrients for growth. Oman is a case in point.

THE NEW SULTAN'S PRIORITIES

As soon as he took office, after the passing of his revered predecessor, Sultan Qaboos, Oman's new ruler, Sultan Haitham bin Tarik, emphasised that a healthy, stable and thriving state relies on a strong partnership between government, business and citizen. His very first speech highlighted the importance of this three-way partnership for the ongoing development and prosperity of his nation.

Sultan Haitham bin Tarik started out by stressing the importance of the country's youth — "the wealth of a nation… its present and future"— and how he intends to empower it. "Our government will follow up progress in various sectors, including small and medium enterprises, and entrepreneurship, particularly those based on innovation, artificial intelligence, and advanced technology. This is in addition to training and enabling youth to benefit from the opportunities made available in this vital sector, so that it could form a cornerstone in the national economy."

But the Sultan's ultimate concern goes beyond youth: he spoke of "a national framework of recruitment", as another of the fundamental pillars of the national economy; as well as the vital role of the "citizens' partnership in moulding the country's present and future, which is a "basic pillar of national action," he said, hoping that "women will enjoy their rights as guaranteed by law, and that they will work in different fields along with men". These national fundamentals, he underlined, "cannot be compromised".

The second pillar, the government, will be restructured and streamlined, "espousing ... governance, integrity, accountability", while legislation and procedures will be modernised in order to increase efficiency and responsiveness, all in the service of citizens and the private sector.

The third pillar, business, will receive the full attention and support of the Sultan's government, with a special mention of small and medium enterprises. He put particular emphasis on companies based on innovation and advanced technology, to turn them into a "cornerstone of the national economy".

Keenly aware of where his country stands in terms of the phases of economic development, the new Sultan made a point of extolling "the private sector's commendable role in the national development, hoping that this sector will maximise this role".

So, the three-way partnership, the government-citizen-business model, has become firmly established in Oman, as a balanced, stable and solid base to work towards further prosperity.

EMPOWERING BUSINESS

As we have seen from the GBC model, business has a major role to play in a thriving state ecosystem. But as identified in our exploration of the new realities in the previous chapter:

- Governments are failing to harness the potential of the private sector in respect of delivering best value public services.

There are two aspects to this. First, some governments appear unresponsive to creating the necessary regulations and infrastructure to allow domestic businesses to plan and prosper. As a result, private sector leaders feel unsupported.

Second, and allied to the first point, governments are failing to harness the potential of the private sector in respect of delivering best-value public services. This often manifests as an uneasy stand-off. Governments regard business as purely profit motivated, and therefore a necessary evil that needs to be carefully watched and bound up in contractual safeguards. And, on the other side, business sees governments either as draconian or overly cautious, and is therefore unwilling to collaborate on innovative initiatives that could enhance the citizen experience.

Linked to both these points, business often perceives government as ill-prepared for an unknowable future, lacking in both the situation-sensing skills to anticipate changes in the global economy and the operational agility to respond to disruptive forces. In short, business sees government as a behemoth – a dinosaur that doesn't see the meteor approaching.

The challenge for governments is to find ways to overcome that perception and transform their image. In the eyes of business, government needs to evolve from being a ponderous brontosaurus to a nimble gazelle. Similarly, in the eyes of government, business needs to shed its reputation as a cold-blooded raptor and become something more akin to a friendly and supportive dolphin, swimming alongside the ship of state.

Such a transformation is possible, but it requires fresh leadership on both sides. It starts with the explicit recognition that government and business are part of the same ecosystem, so they should be collaborators not combatants. What they have in common is a vested interest in delivering value to the citizens. For both, delivering on the social contract confers a licence to operate, and creates a virtuous circle that serves all.

In my work with the PPC Task Force in Oman, I took part in several discussions with leaders from both the public and the private sectors to further understand the reasons behind the lack of collaboration. Leaders from the public sector stated that they strive to create long term partnerships with the private sector, but business leaders see themselves as contractors for government projects. Public sector leaders also discussed how the government works to protect citizens from the private sector and that businesses need to start giving back to society.

On the other side, business leaders said that the government rarely comprehends the challenges they face and that they focus on developing strategies but are very slow in implementation. It was also mentioned that the culture is very "us versus them" and lacks transparency.

However, there were a number of examples where we were able to foster better collaboration. For example, by inviting business leaders to help with the drafting of the newly promulgated Public Private Partnership Law, which established the Public Authority for Privatization and Partnership, as well as participating in national discussions on the new Foreign Capital Investment Law. We also launched the Oman Business Forum, which has become the main platform for ongoing dialogue between the private and public sectors, airing and discussing ideas and issues, sharing business opportunities and much more.

These are small but important steps towards a more collaborative and dynamic relationship between government and business. Such moves are part of a journey to build trust between public and private sector leaders, as explained below.

GOVERNMENT COLLABORATING WITH BUSINESS (G2B AND B2G)

There are broadly three stages of trust between the public and private sectors:

- Fragmentation: Neither party wants to engage.
- Domination: The public sector sees the value of engaging with the private sector but doesn't trust it enough and so dominates the relationship through harsh contractual terms and policies. The opposite may also occur where large, commercially astute businesses gain the upper hand contractually and thus focus on exploitation, rather than what is good for citizens.
- Collaboration: The public and private sector realise that their destinies are entwined and so they need to cooperate and operate as a genuine partnership. The government no longer awards the contract and sits back; it plays an active role throughout the relationship to ensure success. The focus is on the spirit of the relationship, rather than the contractual framework.

One obvious area of potential collaboration between government and business is in the area of large infrastructure projects.

PUBLIC PRIVATE COLLABORATION

Oman has been a pioneer in the Middle East for public private partnership (PPP) projects especially in the form of independent power producer projects (IPPs) and independent water and power projects (IWPPs). In 1994, Oman saw its first PPP project, the Al-Manah independent power project, and has since regularly used the PPP model.

PPPs enable governments to fund public infrastructure projects such as hospitals, roads, schools and airports, and increasingly telecommunications and other technology infrastructure. But PPPs have had mixed results.

As a publication from the OECD[64] spells out: "A number of failed public-private partnerships in the infrastructure sector attest to the challenges facing policy makers.

Infrastructure investment involves contracts that are by nature complex and of long duration, and that must ensure financial sustainability while meeting user needs and social objectives. The challenges are more acute when foreign investors are involved, as is often the case where the infrastructure project exceeds a certain size."

Despite the challenges with PPPs, this form of collaboration between government and the business sector has much to commend it. Such relationships have to be built on mutual respect and trust. I have spent a lot of time studying best practice with PPPs and led the work of Oman's PPC Task Force.

It is important to keep in mind that PPP is not the goal in and of itself; rather the goal is to create value for the country and its citizens. This becomes more crucial as countries progress along their development journeys.

The idea of the public and private sector collaborating for the benefit of the citizens makes sense. A more innovative and agile public sector will lead to a better citizen experience, which in turn will lead to improvements in infrastructure that will make a country more attractive to employers. So, the citizen gains access to a better employer, which in turn creates an upward-spiralling skills cycle.

Optimising human capital or talent also means making it easy for businesses to hire the best people wherever they come from, something I have been involved in through a number of initiatives to improve the business environment in Oman.

The PPC Task Force's recommendations were presented to the late Sultan HM Qaboos and his ministers and resulted in the implementation of several initiatives such as proposing and designing the National Training Fund (NTF), which aimed at bridging the gap between the education system outcomes and the labour market demands. The NTF has already produced several thousand graduates trained to top international standards.

I participated in national discussions on the labour law which led, among other positive steps, to the lifting the two-year labour ban on foreign workers in June 2020. Effective from January 2021, the new rule replaced a 1996 order that prohibited foreign employees from joining another company for two years after the expiry of their contracts unless they were granted a no-objection certificate (NOC). The change supports the human rights agenda in Oman and means that foreign workers can move freely within the job market, increasing the competitiveness of the Sultanate's private sector.

I have also led a number of initiatives aimed at developing home-grown talent. A clear advantage to upskilling citizens is that these talented workers are part of the symbiotic GBC model and are thus more committed to nation building. For this reason, developing home-grown human capital must be the priority.

OMAN'S PPC TASK FORCE

The notion of a stronger partnership among the main stakeholders of a nation began to take concrete form in 2013, when the Public Private Collaboration Task Force (PPC Task Force) was instituted by the late Sultan Qaboos. The PPC Task Force grouped top government ministers with high-ranking members of the private sector, plus an echelon of further government officials and representatives of all business segments and company sizes. It tasked them with helping to plot a course towards sustainable economic growth for the Sultanate. It proved to be a game-changer. I had the pleasure of leading the work of the PPC Task Force and its initiatives.

Through the Task Force, we identified a number of critical success factors that contribute to a more effective collaborative approach. This led to drafting the now-promulgated Public Private Partnership Law and the establishment of the Public Authority for Privatisation and Partnership, which is empowered as the body to oversee PPP projects. We also launched a number of measures to enhance the ease of doing business, which were well received by the Omani business community and foreign investors. This was also reflected in the Sultanate's ranking in the World Bank's "Ease of Doing Business Index", rising from 78 in 2018 to 68 in 2019. But it goes further than that.

From the outset, the PPC Task Force has operated on the conviction that the bedrock and driving force for Oman's economic and social development is its human capital. Factoring in the primary societal actors, namely government, business and citizens, I led a number of PPC Task Force human capital development initiatives for the government, the private sector and citizens—primarily youth— including:

- *The National CEO Programme (NCP); focused on entrepreneurship, leadership and innovation in the private sector. In addition, the National Leadership and Competitiveness Programme (NLCP) was created to develop the leadership capabilities of senior government officials. Its objective was to instil a competitive and collaborative mindset.*

- *Over 40% of NCP's participants were promoted to more senior positions, including CEOs, within two years of concluding the programme. Likewise, a number of NLCP's participants were recently appointed at under-secretary and minister levels.*

- *We also launched the National Youth Programme for Skills Development aiming to equipping the youth with the right mindset and skills (technical, social and entrepreneurial) to thrive in a digitalised world. The programme was delivered through a blended learning approach. As a result, over 40,000 students participated and 24 startup companies were established.*

This implementation of the tripartite partnership (government, business and citizens) notion in my country has already borne fruit in terms of capability building, policy development and in broader institutional achievements. On top of that, it has also inculcated a new mindset among all partners, so we have established a firmer foundation for Oman to cope with, and emerge from, the social and economic ravages of the covid-19 pandemic and in turn secure its future prosperity.

EMPOWERING CITIZENS

As highlighted earlier, citizens are the third actor in the GBC model, and an essential part of a nation's ecosystem; indeed, they are its *raison d'etre* - without a government and a state there can be no citizens and vice versa. So how do you secure the buy-in of citizens to a three-way socioeconomic model, especially if they are suspicious of government or business? The answer lies with the fairness and quality of the social contract that exists between them. If the contract is skewed in favour of one of the three actors, then the others will be less willing to collaborate. Data management is important in this regard, especially in relation to whether citizens feel respected and empowered. As we saw with Estonia in Chapter 1, transparency of data plays a vital part in establishing trust.

The sheer pace of change, exacerbated by the megatrends outlined in Chapter 7, is making many citizens uneasy. Add to this the recent covid-19 pandemic and other global threats and the world can seem a very uncertain, intimidating and even frightening place. People are anxious and look to their governments for reassurance. However, what they see does not always mitigate their concerns.

As we saw in Chapter 7, the new realities pose serious challenges for the relationship between government and citizens. Whereas one of the new realities relates directly to business (governments are failing to harness the potential of the private sector), the remaining six relate to the citizen:

- The social contract is fraying.
- Governments have lost the trust of the people.
- There is a lack of citizen-centricity.
- Governments appear unresponsive.
- Government leaders are ill-prepared for an unknowable future.
- Citizens are behaving as passive recipients.

Addressing these new realities requires an explicit recognition of the symbiotic relationship that exists between government and citizens. One side of that equation is that government exists to serve its citizens. Just as businesses rely on customer satisfaction to ensure that they remain viable, so government should pride itself on meeting the needs of its citizens. When we think of the individual citizen experience, we should think of something comparable to the consumer experience. The citizens are consumers of government services, and those services should recognise and be designed around the people who use them.

Government needs to improve the way it engages with citizens, taking the lead from business best practice. Ideas such as design thinking, the experience economy, zero distance from customers, organisational agility and the lean startup movement (see next chapter) all have lessons for government. Taken to its logical conclusion this might even mean that every citizen has their own account manager – even if that account manager is an algorithm or AI-inspired bot or avatar.

But the relationship cannot be one-sided. It may be unpalatable for some, but the reality is that, just like business, individual citizens have to take responsibility for their part in the social contract. If the GBC model is correct, and nation building in the 21st century is about creating a dynamic national ecosystem, then citizens must also step up and raise their game. They will need to acquire certain attributes, capabilities and skills to remain economically relevant in an increasingly uncertain and automated world. To do so, they will need the support of their government.

Just as we saw earlier, with the business community, one of the vital roles of governments is to create the conditions under which the other actors can not only thrive but also contribute to the wellbeing of the nation. To do so government must find ways of encouraging citizen engagement and enlisting citizen collaboration.

Citizens need the conditions to stimulate individual entrepreneurialism and be more comfortable with uncertainty. Similarly, citizens need to be inculcated with the attributes, capabilities and skills needed for them to be less reliant on government largesse.

If we look at Singapore as an example of a country following a successful development path, it is clear that the role of Singaporean citizens is not passive. As Lim Hwee Hua notes: "The people of Singapore have been described as paranoid – and with good reason. Their unwillingness to take success for granted or rest on their laurels is integral to the country's remarkable economic transformation. Without the nation's healthy caution, the story could have been very different."

She outlines four elements that are vital to Singapore's success:

- Developing talent within the public sector.
- Equipping human capital for purpose.
- Staying agile with macro planning and execution.
- Showing solidarity in a crisis.

All four of these elements rely on citizens stepping up to their responsibilities. The second element, in particular, puts the onus on individuals to keep their skills current.

"Human capital development is the vital ingredient in Singapore's recipe for economic success,' explains Lim. "This has taken on greater emphasis with shortening business cycles resulting from increasing globalisation and technological disruption. This is of national importance and not limited to the public sector. All stakeholders have to regularly update their skills and be able to create goods and services that meet fast-changing needs, regardless of how long ago they left school. Life-long learning has become a mantra – and taking charge of this responsibility at the individual level is vital to creating a coherent and appropriate collective national response. The value of a pool of human capital that is able to respond in a dynamic manner cannot be over-stated."

The need to create a dynamic pool of human capital has important implications for government, most obviously in terms of education, but also for the sorts of ongoing professional development the state provides. In Oman, the PPC Task Force pointed to the need to develop the right skill sets and mindsets for the future. From this, the National Training Fund was established to identify relevant skills and bridge the gap between the supply and demand.

THE GBC SWEET SPOT

So far, we have explored the two-way interactions between government and business and government and citizens. But there is also growing scope for three-way collaboration – between government, business and citizens.

I believe that government leaders need to be more entrepreneurial and open to risk. As several of our contributors acknowledged, transformational leaders have to walk the talk. When I was given the task of developing a programme for public and private sector leaders, rather than view it as another training programme, I embraced it as an opportunity to develop an engine of national transformation.

The National CEO Programme was launched in 2015, (the same year that Klaus Schwab started using the phrase 4th Industrial Revolution at WEF), and the focus was on preparing Oman's leaders for the new technologies. Recognising there needed to be more collaboration within the ecosystem, we decided to include public and private sector leaders.

Following the success of the National CEO Programme, I took a risk, proposing a youth programme to support the aspirations of the next generation of leaders.

This was even more challenging because it meant finding entities and educational bodies who were experts in developing and designing such programmes. Several of those around me, senior leaders, colleagues and advisers, cautioned me against it. One of the chief concerns was that it was impossible to understand the demands and aspirations of young people living in very different situations. How would I, a middle-aged man, understand the needs of a young person? I was also warned that young students would not be able to relate to my 5Qs leadership model we based the course on. Moreover, they warned me that my reputation would be damaged if the programme failed.
So, what to do? In the end I decided to proceed - with care. I formed an advisory committee (aged from 14 to 24) to help me better understand the context and issues

facing young people and how to design a programme to meet their aspirations. Then I visited Silicon Valley to meet with a number of companies and leaders. This trip reaffirmed my belief in the importance of investing in youth.

When the programme launched, we hoped for 5000 to 6000 registrations. To my great joy (and relief) 14,000 young people registered in the first cohort, and more than 5500 students (around 56%) concluded the programme in just a few weeks. When surveyed, more than 90% of the students said that the modules and educational material were relatable and that they were able to comprehend the 5Qs concepts and scenarios. They also said that the material is relevant to level up their skills for the new 4IR era and the digital economy.

CROWDSOURCING FOR GOVERNMENT

As discussed in Chapter 7, crowdsourcing is a technique that governments can employ to encourage the active participation of citizens; one that is in step with recent technological advances.

In general, gamification, the application of elements of online game playing - point scoring, competition with others, rules of play - also has applications to engaging citizens with government and other public problems.

A 2013 report published by the IBM Center for The Business of Government acknowledged the promise of harnessing the "participatory spirit of citizen engagement" and identified four potential uses for crowdsourcing.[65]

- *Knowledge discovery and management: collecting knowledge reported by an online community, such as the reporting of earth tremors or potholes to a central source.*

- *Distributed human intelligence tasking: distributing "micro-tasks" that require human intelligence to solve, such as transcribing handwritten historical documents into electronic files, or scrutinising images from deep space.*

- *Broadcast search (gamification): broadcasting a problem-solving challenge widely on the internet and providing an award for its solution, such as NASA's prize for an algorithm to predict solar flares.*

- *Peer-vetted creative production: creating peer-vetted solutions, where an online community proposes possible solutions and is empowered to collectively choose among them.*

In the section on social change, we discussed how crowdsourcing is being used for public challenges including scientific research. The Covid Symptom Study app, for example, is a not-for-profit collaboration between health-care science company ZOE and scientists at King's College London, with input from researchers at Lund University, Sweden and Harvard University. It was launched at the end of March 2020 and by July 2020 had become the world's largest study of covid-19, powered by a community of more than 4 million citizen volunteers in the United Kingdom, United States and Sweden.

SUMMARY

Chapter 7 identified three principles that underpin a reimagined citizen-centric government and which I believe governments need to embrace to thrive in this time of continuous crisis. In this chapter we explored the first principle that healthy, thriving states can be thought of as ecosystems that require active and trustful engagement between the primary actors, ie, government, business and citizen (the GBC model).

Increasing uncertainty will change the way citizens live and the way businesses operate. Governments need to transform to better serve their ecosystem, as do businesses and citizens. The alternative is a failed state or the prospect of becoming an economic backwater. Whilst it is beyond the scope of this book, businesses and citizens also need to embrace their responsibilities within the GBC model, and become both more adaptable and more resilient to threats.

In the next two chapters we will drill down into the government element (the G in the GBC model) to explore the remaining two principles. In Chapter 9, we will consider the second principle: how governments need to be more dynamic and entrepreneurial to respond to a rapidly changing world. In particular, we will examine how governments can become more innovative and more entrepreneurial, balancing responsiveness with responsibility.

To do so, however, will require a different sort of leadership, which is the subject of the third principle, and something that we will discuss in Chapter 10.

Entrepreneurial Government

9

In Chapter 8, we explored the first of my three guiding principles on how governments and their leaders need to adapt to the new realities we face today. I introduced my GBC model and we started to explore government in respect of its relationship with business and the citizen.

We now take a deeper dive into how governments need to adapt to provide a more responsive service to their citizens. This is captured in my second principle:

Governments need to be more dynamic and entrepreneurial to respond to a rapidly changing world.

Government can become more responsive without losing sight of its long-term responsibilities. A vision of where a nation aspires to go is inspirational and provides a clear direction, but it is vital to keep an open mind about the path it will follow to get there. Faced with a more uncertain and changeable world, it is no longer possible to provide a detailed route map, or even be sure of the final destination.

In this chapter, I make the case that governments need to behave in a more entrepreneurial manner. This is a radical notion. However, it reflects the far-reaching transformation that governments need to undertake if they are going to be effective in what is essentially an unknowable future.

We start with a look at what is happening in the private sector, where responsiveness to disruption and changing markets has always been important and is becoming more so. In particular, we examine how the twin qualities of innovation and entrepreneurialism are often the difference between success and failure.

In Chapter 1, Toomas Ilves offered strong guidance on the journey towards genuine government transformation. In this chapter, we will hear a similarly radical story from outside the public sector. One that has several valuable lessons for government leaders.

"Innovate or die" has become a mantra in business and we take an illuminating close-up look at a company that epitomizes that spirit. The white goods manufacturer, Haier, is one of the most radically innovative companies in the world. We hear from its CEO about how it has maintained a state of continuous transformation for the best part of two decades and now regards itself as less of a factory and more of an ecosystem for its workers, customers and suppliers. From Haier, we extract lessons for public sector transformation. We also examine lessons from other parts of the business world and consider what entrepreneurial government might look like.

BEYOND STRATEGY

The first point to make is that faced with an unknowable future, there is only so much long-range planning you can do. Gone are the days when public and private sector leaders could formulate strategy and policy and then sit back and turn the handle. There simply isn't time any more to create a complete plan – and even if we had that luxury, the world is too volatile to plan much beyond the present. Today we need a more adaptable approach.

This is evident in business. Strategy as we once knew it and as practised in the planning departments of traditional companies such as General Electric and Ford Motor Company is dead. This reminds me of when IBM was in crisis and its new CEO, Lou Gerstner, was asked what his vision was. He famously replied, "The last thing IBM needs right now is a vision. What the company needed, he later explained, "was a strategy they could immediately execute."

This was brought home to me in a conversation with Mohamed Alabbar, the founder and chairman of Emaar Properties.

Emaar Properties is the largest development company in the Middle East and the company behind the Burj Khalifa and the Dubai Mall. (Downtown Dubai is only one square kilometre but contributes 2% of the whole of Dubai's GDP.) It is government supported, but it runs like a private sector company. Emaar is a byword for entrepreneurialism in the Middle East and Alabbar, who is the founder and director of noon.com, an e-commerce ecosystem, is himself an entrepreneurial brand. When he buys a piece of land, the whole area goes up in value. He is very shrewd and very smart. We were talking about strategy, and I asked him the secret of his success.

"I work with the big consulting firms," he said, "but when you ask them for a strategy to develop a site, they say it will take 12 to 18 months. And I say, no, that's too long. The best they can do, they say, is 6 to 8 months. When I tell them that I want to do it in one month, their response is you can't have a complete strategy within a month. And then I tell them there's no such thing as a complete strategy anymore. A strategy gets completed during implementation. So, by the end of the project, I have the plan - the project is done, and I have the document of how we've done it."

Alabbar is right, there is no such thing as a complete strategy anymore. Even if there ever was, there certainly isn't now. More than that, there is no playbook for getting the sorts of projects done that governments are now faced with. The private sector is similarly struggling with this new world, where the rules of the game are being rewritten daily and where companies and even entire sectors are facing massive disruption. That said, the private sector is adapting and in turn is becoming more innovative and data driven.

In recent years, new cutting-edge philosophies have been adopted by business to cope with the sort of quick-fire change that is a day-to-day reality. These include Agile, Lean Startup and Design Thinking. An interesting recent notion is that a business can be viewed as the hub or at least part of an ecosystem.

FROM EFFICIENCY TO INNOVATION

Probably the biggest shift in business today is the move from competing on efficiency to competing on innovation. In the 20th century, during the industrial era, we saw the super efficiency of mass production manufacturing. Think of Toyota, for example, where the famous Toyota Production System was a watchword for manufacturing efficiency, enabling the company to produce cars with zero defects.

The industrial era offered some predictability. Factories were built with a high degree of confidence that what they would produce would be in demand for a sufficient duration to justify the initial investment. The objective was to make the factories and the production processes as lean and efficient as possible. It was all about competing on economies of scale and minimising waste and reworking. The best quality at the lowest cost won. But today we have no idea what the future holds - situational awareness trumps strategy. Adaptability trumps efficiency.

"If you become too efficient, you lose your flexibility so you can't pivot when the market changes. To stay successful, you need to stay a little loose," Reed Hastings, CEO of the video streaming giant Netflix, says.

Organisations in the 21st century must constantly innovate to survive and thrive. They need to respond to the changing needs of the consumer, to pivot and adapt to the fast-moving business landscape. The same is true of citizens, who must also be able to pivot if their skills are no longer valued in the labour market.

Where they have a choice, and the most valuable citizens generally do, they will migrate to a society where they can thrive. Thus, governments need to up their game in respect of creating such environments. Attracting, developing and retaining the best people will lead to economic growth, which in turn will create a more prosperous, progressive nation. It's a virtuous circle.

Private sector organisations that grew up in the industrial era are struggling to adapt to the new realities they face. Birthed in the industrial era, they are often blind to the changes taking place around them. Because of their insistence on sticking to the strategic plan, they are suffering from sensory deprivation, an inability to sense the disruptive changes that are occurring in their markets. These old school organisations are still very hierarchical, to the point that only a handful of people make all the decisions for everyone else in the organisation. This means that all the cognitive power of their employees is squandered. It also means that their customer facing staff or field operatives have very limited scope to address the needs of their customers.

Take General Electric, for example. Once the hero of a thousand business school case studies, GE has lost its way. In trying to pursue a radically new business model it neglected its core business and stumbled. It is not alone. One by one the great corporate names of the industrial era are fading. Kodak made the opposite mistake to GE. Sticking rigidly to its core business of processing film, it was blindsided by its past successes and missed the big disruption in its market – the move to digital photography. What makes this cautionary tale all the more alarming is that Kodak invented the first self-contained digital camera in 1975 but did not see the need to disrupt its own business.

These old-fashioned firms ignore opportunities or threats that do not fit their traditional model. They are slow to recognise the potential of new technologies or how new players such as Airbnb and Uber can offer a better service using only data and so have no need to make heavy capital outlays. They assume that past successes are indicative of future successes. The "dinosaurs" continue to focus on process management, which is natural when you are trying to create an efficient factory, but potentially ruinous in the post-factory world, where competitive advantage is transient and where continuous innovation is a survival reflex.

The business models of the future will be designed not to maximise efficiency but to be able to pivot from one form of production, service, or product line to another with minimal retooling.

BUILT TO PIVOT

Businesses birthed in the digital age continuously sense the market for opportunity and continuously monitor whether their primary business is growing, stagnating, or in need of tuning. They are built to pivot. They see the value in their people and harness their potential. They create the conditions for their people to thrive. They are strong on culture, often creating a tribe or a tribe of tribes. They generally have a common *esprit de corps*, a united sense of purpose, where everyone has bought into the organisation's success.

Recognising that the organisation needs to be adaptable, digital-age talent is similarly adaptable. Regardless of their seniority or qualifications, they will roll up their sleeves when the survival of the organisation is at stake.

Digital-age organisations devolve decision-making, creating what might be called ubiquitous, or distributed, leadership. Their flat organisational structures reflect this. Businesses born in the digital age are less "inert factory" and more akin to a "sensing, situationally aware living organism". In other words, they are adapted to being part of an ecosystem. Governments cannot simply try to maintain their archaic operating models. Like the private sector they need to change.

There are plenty of examples of successful digital-age organisations. But they do not have the legacy of the industrial era players, such as old IT systems, a stale culture, or entrenched politics. As a result, these shiny young unicorns are not the best reference point for the public sector. Examples of old school organisations transforming to a model more appropriate to the digital age are few and far between. Microsoft has done it. So has John Deere. As mentioned, GE has gone for it in a big way but has so far failed.

Perhaps the best example I have seen in respect of organisational transformation is to be found in China. What makes it all the more impressive is that the company began life as a state-owned factory, controlled by the Chinese government. It demonstrates that innovation and entrepreneurial verve is not the sole preserve of Silicon Valley startups.

FROM "ZERO DEFECTS" TO "ZERO DISTANCE"

"There are no great companies; only relevant companies," says Zhang Ruimin, CEO of Haier. The same principle applies to the skills and training of citizens – and to government itself. Adaptability is required to stay relevant in an increasingly turbulent world.

In Japan in the 1980s, the quality-efficiency revolution revolved around producing products with "zero defects". But Haier champions "zero distance" – getting as close to the end user as possible. The focus has shifted from product to customer. The business model has evolved from mass manufacturing to fulfilling the changing demands of the consumer.

Founded in Qingdao, China, in 1984, Haier evolved from a small, collective factory on the verge of collapse into a leading ecosystem of the IoT era. The company's origins go back much further, to the 1920s, when a refrigerator factory was built in Qingdao to supply the Chinese market. After the People's Republic of China was established in 1949, the factory was turned into a state-owned enterprise. By the 1980s, the factory had accumulated huge debts and was in a state of near bankruptcy. In 1982, the Qingdao government hired a young assistant city-manager called Zhang Ruimin who was responsible for a number of city-owned appliance companies.

Zhang was appointed managing director of the factory in 1984, and Haier was founded as the Qingdao Refrigerator Co. Under Zhang's leadership the company embarked on a radical programme of quality improvement and international expansion.

Today, the white goods company produces everything from refrigerators to air conditioning units, and is a role model for businesses around the world seeking to reinvent themselves by reducing bureaucracy and embracing digital technologies to become entrepreneurial platforms for microenterprises.

Haier has been featured in the *Harvard Business Review*, as a case study in business schools worldwide and in books by management academics Bill Fischer, Gary Hamel and others. Its management model, Rendanheyi, is a Chinese word that fuses the words for employee and user value. With its emphasis on giving people responsibility, using technology to eliminate distance to consumers and developing mutually beneficial ecosystems, Haier is a fascinating example of an industrial-era company that has transformed itself to be fit for purpose in the 21st century.

As management expert Gary Hamel observed: "… new realities are at last producing alternatives to bureaucracy.[66] Perhaps the most promising model can be found at a company that would not, at first glance, appear to be a child of the digital age. Haier, based in Qingdao, China, is currently the world's largest appliance maker. With revenue of US$35 billion, it competes with household names such as Whirlpool, LG, and Electrolux. … Outside China it has 27,000 employees, many of whom joined the company when it bought GE's appliance business, in 2016.

Over the past decade the gross profits of Haier's core appliance business have grown by 23% a year, while revenue has increased by 18% annually. The company has also created more than US$2 billion in market value from new ventures. Those feats are unmatched by any of Haier's domestic or global competitors. This remarkable journey hasn't been entirely pain-free. In recent years Haier dismissed more than 10,000 employees. Yet it has also generated tens of thousands of new jobs in its rapidly expanding ecosystem."

Hamel's enthusiasm for Haier is understandable. Microenterprises are free to form and evolve within the company - with little central direction. The company's remarkable success is the result of a transformation of its once-traditional management model. Seeing bureaucracy as a competitive liability, Zhang Ruimin has built a company where everyone is directly accountable to customers, something he describes as zero distance; employees are energetic entrepreneurs; and an open ecosystem of users, inventors and partners replaces formal hierarchy.

In writing this book I reached out to Zhang to get his insights on the sort of radical entrepreneurship required to create a ground-breaking organisation in this volatile climate. He was generous with his time and his ideas. What follows is a summary of that conversation, which was inspiring and challenging in equal measure. In particular, Zhang's insights on ecosystems and zero distance have profound resonance for reimagining government.

A MANAGEMENT MODEL FOR THE IOT ERA

Under your leadership, Haier has been through huge changes, but despite all the disruptions it continues to grow. What makes the business so successful?

There are no successful businesses, only relevant ones. The only businesses that will survive are the ones that stay in sync with changing times. For companies and organisations everywhere, the question is: are we waiting to be phased out, or are we going to reinvent ourselves?

Can you explain your management model and how it has transformed Haier over the last decade and a half?

We first proposed Rendanheyi in 2005, as a way of managing and organising for the next phase of the industrial revolution – the Internet of Things (IoT). "Ren" means our employees; "dan" refers to our users. We are bringing together ('heyi') our employees and users. In traditional businesses, there are no users: products are simply sold to transactional customers.

Our model reflects an essential characteristic of the IoT. The IoT is about the interconnection of all things for the purpose of improving experiences for people. To me, the IoT is essentially an internet of people. And if you don't get people connected to it, you can't have a successful IoT.

How does the model work in practice?

To achieve it, we believe you need to do three things. The first is creative destruction: throw out the classical management models that are no longer relevant in this information age. The second is creative restructuring: with a radical departure from classical management models, we need to be creative and set up models fit for the IoT era. The third is creative leadership: the ultimate goal is not just to affect a restructure but to create an ecosystem brand leading the IoT era.

How does your approach relate to previous organisational models and theories from the 20th century?

Frederick Taylor, Max Weber and Henry Fayol are three pioneers of classical management theories. Taylor, the father of scientific management, created the highly efficient assembly line that underpins mass manufacturing. However, what we need today is mass customisation rather than mass manufacturing, so we need to put Taylorism aside.

Weber, creator of bureaucracy, said bureaucracy was the best system. But bureaucracy suppresses humanness and creativity so today we must eliminate it. This will help turn information asymmetry to information symmetry, meaning leaders will no longer have more information than their subordinates. In fact, with the personalisation of user needs, the subordinates will have more information than their leaders.

Fayol proposed the general principles of management: planning, coordinating, organising and so on. However, today's markets are not just one-sided, with factories and sales, but multi-sided,[67] *as posited by 2014 Nobel Laureate, Jean Tirole. E-commerce is a multi-sided network, where businesses cannot only rely on their own internal coordination to plan, organise and control, as they did in the past.*

So Rendanheyi requires us to do away with some of the classical management theories of the 20th century. This is the first step towards achieving Rendanheyi: creative destruction. Only then we can begin the second step: creative restructuring.

With Haier, you are talking about reimagining and restructuring a very large organisation. But how do you do that in a creative way?

There are three main aspects to creative restructuring, which is the first step towards Rendanheyi. First, business model restructuring. Business model restructuring has two elements: restructuring the organisation to eliminate bureaucracy and restructuring incentives to better serve users. Our Rendanheyi model, with employees (ren) on the one hand and users (dan) on the other, allows employees to demonstrate their own value by creating value for their users. It's been 15 years since this model was introduced. We hope it will become a third-generation model after Fordism and Toyotism, two world-class management models. From Fordism, which exemplifies the high efficiency of the assembly line, to Toyotism, which embodies lean "just-in-time" manufacturing, we see a transition from single assembly lines to industry-wide supply chains. We hope to go further and build ecosystems.

The American economist James F. Moore proposed the concept of a business ecosystem and defined it as an organism in the business world. Traditional businesses are not organisms, but rigid systems, whereas organisms are federated economies where people and organisations can constantly interact, engage and evolve together in an interdependent way. Businesses everywhere should translate their business models into ecosystems.

Ecosystems are something that governments need to embrace in order to create a harmonious and symbiotic relationship between government, business and citizens. They need to align these stakeholders. What does that mean for Haier?

Rendanheyi is an ecosystem model that achieves two alignments (heyi). The first alignment is between employees and users. This has never been achieved in other businesses: ask a factory worker who their users are, and you are likely to hear "I don't know. All I do is fasten bolts on the shop floor." Ask a finance person who their users are, and you are likely hear "I don't know. All I know is how to do the books." But today, all companies must know who their users are. Only by aligning with their users can each employee realise their own value. And this will transform an employee from mere cog in the wheel into an empowered, autonomous individual.

The second alignment is between value creation and value sharing. This has also never been achieved in the past: employees would not know how much value they created. How much value is created by producing 1,000 products? No one tells the employee; all they know is how much pay they are taking home each month. It is difficult to align the value created by employees with the share of value they get. With Rendanheyi, how much you create is how much you get: value created is aligned with value shared.

Building on the two alignments, we can go on to address two further issues: how to create value and how to distribute it – an essential theme of all economic research and theories. Adam Smith said that it's better to distribute value by creating a mechanism that allows each individual to make their own decisions while pursuing their own interests. In the past, creating such a mechanism was difficult. Now, it is possible through Rendanheyi.

Creating value for business and citizens goes right to the heart of what government is for. What is the second element of creative restructuring?

The second aspect is restructuring to eliminate bureaucracy. At Haier, there used to be 12,000 middle managers. We gave them two choices: either to become an entrepreneur or to leave. Today, with no middle management departments and no middle managers, we have transformed our business into an entrepreneurial platform for numerous independent microenterprises, each with eight to ten people. These microenterprises are empowered with three CEO privileges: the power to hire people, to make important decisions and to set remuneration.

So how can other organisations, including governments, get started if they want to emulate Haier's entrepreneurial model?

More than 10,000 companies visit us at Haier every year, and many business leaders have asked me that question. I would say, you need to give those three CEO powers to your microenterprises.

A microenterprise with the three powers becomes a decentralised autonomous organisation (DAO) that unites various community capabilities and resources. For example, they can seek human resources from anywhere because "the world" is their HR department. They can also seek capital from the wider business community, which allows them in turn to invest in their own microenterprise. And so, our business has become a myriad of startups.

Transforming into a group of startups, however, is not our ultimate goal. Our goal is to create an ecosystem of emerging entrepreneurs. At present, Haier's innovation and entrepreneurship platform is home to more than 4,000 microenterprises, including three listed companies, two unicorn companies and twelve gazelle companies. Several hundred venture capitalists have invested in these microenterprises. Entrepreneurs who have secured venture capital investments can follow with their own investment and become shareholders. In this process, the most important thing is openness. We are not asking all employees to become entrepreneurs. Instead, we are encouraging all entrepreneurs to join Haier's global platform for innovation and entrepreneurship. Our company is not a traditional bureaucratic enterprise, but a global entrepreneurial platform. As Joseph Schumpeter, the Austrian economist, said, only those engaged in innovative activities can become entrepreneurs. A business owner is not necessarily an entrepreneur. Innovation is key to the emergence of entrepreneurs. Anyone who makes an effort can become an entrepreneur, even if they are just ordinary employees.

There is an urgent need for governments to be more entrepreneurial, too. So, what is the third part of creative restructuring?

The third aspect to creative restructuring is the restructuring of compensation and incentives so that the employee is paid by the user, not the employer. Compensation used to be set by the employer, based on criteria such as seniority, competence, or stock options, but in this system the value created by the employee is not linked to the value they receive.

That sounds radically different to the traditional models. Can you give an example of how this works in practice?

Take Haier's Yunxi washing machine, which has gone through six R&D iterations in the two years after it was initially launched.

Previously, the company would dictate what kind of products to develop. Now, our R&D, manufacturing, sales and other microenterprises spontaneously form an ecosystem micro-community (EMC) to work together to address user needs. Previously, each product iteration used to take between six months to six years. Today, the Yunxi washing machine is updated every two or three months, to meet the evolving individual needs of users. With these shorter iteration cycles, the teams working behind Yunxi have been rewarded handsomely. The value they have received is based on the value they have created for users. All teams share risk, and everyone has to share any losses, which means everyone is motivated to create value.

The ecosystem is a much more organic model compared to the mechanistic language of the last hundred years. It sounds like you are rewriting the rules of economics, too, moving away from zero-sum thinking to a different sort of mindset?

Yes, Rendanheyi changes the economic foundations. W. Brian Arthur, a founder of the science of complexity, put economics into three categories: classical economics, which represents the agricultural civilisation; neoclassical economics, which represents the industrial civilisation; and complexity economics, which represents the information civilisation.

He believes that complexity economics has the following characteristics. First, the structure and model of complexity economics is proactive self-organisation, unlike bureaucracy, which is passive organisation by others. Second, complexity economics is characterised by increasing marginal returns, because there are not only product revenues but also service revenues. Traditional product revenues suffer from price wars and diminishing marginal returns. Third, in a complex economic environment, new species can be created through evolution, which we call "win-win evolution." In this system, a lot of new things that have never been imagined before can emerge. For instance, Haier used to make only white goods but today, it is involved in a wide variety of fields, offering not just products but also scenario-based services.

The third step you said is creative leadership; can you explain this a little more?

Creative leadership is about creating a leading ecosystem brand.

First, we need to create an EMC [ecosystem micro-community] contract, which serves a cluster of enterprises in the same ecosystem. An EMC contract has an x-axis and a y-axis. The x-axis represents solution-oriented microenterprises creating products and services that users need. The y-axis represents experience-oriented microenterprises exploring the needs of users and communities. In an EMC, there are no functional departments, only a large number of microenterprises. The two can be united through self-organisation. Traditionally, corporate functional departments worked in silos. Now, they can be brought together with the user and use-case scenarios at the centre.

Secondly, we need to build scenario-driven ecosystems, which are the foundation of ecosystem brands. I personally believe that 5G and IoT are ultimately about use-case scenarios when it comes to applications. Without use-case scenarios, there wouldn't be IoT. And without IoT, there wouldn't be any ecosystem brand.

Our experience store in Shanghai is not about selling appliances at all. Instead, it presents a set of household solutions based on scenarios. Behind our refrigerators is an ecosystem - an Internet of Food – connecting hundreds of organic food suppliers; behind our washing machines is an Internet of Clothing. I believe there is no way out if your sole focus is on making products, because there won't be a perfect product in the future. All you can do is to keep up with dynamically changing user needs and focus on scenario iteration and evolution. In the IoT era, all companies will eventually work on scenarios.

So, how would you define the Haier strategy and goals?

Ultimately, our goal is to create ecosystem brands. The Rendanheyi model and EMC contracts have served as a catalyst for business model transformation and, in turn, for the creation of business ecosystems.

Our industrial internet platform, which led the creation of an international standard for mass customisation, has empowered many companies to transform themselves. With our industrial internet we have helped to transform small and medium-sized businesses across many industries, including construction, ceramics and agriculture. Through the Rendanheyi model, the IoT has the potential to transform many more industries.

What are the entrepreneurial lessons from Haier?

I want our company to become a place for entrepreneurship, where everyone can realise their value and create infinite value for their users.

The opening words in James P. Carse's book, ***Finite and Infinite Games****, are as follows: "There are at least two kinds of games. One could be called finite, the other infinite. A finite game is played for the purpose of winning, an infinite game for the purpose of continuing the play. Because an infinite game cannot be brought to an end, it cannot be repeated." Most companies today are still playing a finite game to win, wanting to be number one in their industry. Meeting the personal needs of users is an infinite game without an end: all user needs are different, and there is no end to dynamically changing user needs.*

Today, the Rendanheyi model is being applied in various industries around the world. In Haier subsidiaries such as GE Appliances in the United States and Candy in Europe, and Sanyo in Japan to Fisher & Paykel in New Zealand, Rendanheyi has produced great results. Across different industries, putting users at the centre and creating best-in-class user experience is a universal truth.

At the core of Rendanheyi is a belief in the maximisation of human value and in the immeasurable value of every individual. That is why it works in every industry and every country.

WHAT THE PUBLIC SECTOR CAN LEARN

What can we learn from Haier? It is a company that started life as a workers' collective and very few people would have given it any chance whatsoever of making the transformation from an industrial-era factory (and not even a very good or efficient one) into a world-beating global giant. The fact that it started life and to some extent is still in the public sector makes it an inspiring and instructive story.

Famously, in 1985, after a customer complained about a faulty refrigerator, Zhang went through the entire inventory of 400 refrigerators looking for a replacement only to discover that nearly 20% were defective. Zhang promptly had the 76 sub-standard refrigerators lined up on the factory floor and joined employees in demolishing them with sledgehammers. The point was made - Haier had to match or exceed the highest quality standards. The incident became a signature story about Zhang's quest for quality and garnered some much-needed publicity for the company. Visitors to the Haier cultural centre at its HQ in Qingdao can still see the original sledgehammer he used that day, preserved in a glass case.

The lessons from Haier include sensitivity to the market, the recognition that the fortunes of the employee and the customer experience are entwined, the need for continuous innovation and risk-taking, and the belief that there is no steady state or end goal. Rather, continuous improvement and ongoing transformation are a natural consequence of the infinite game we are all caught up in, as individuals, businesses and governments.

Haier's zero distance policy is a lesson in how governments could and should view their relationships with citizens. It demonstrates how an old-style government organisation, under exceptional leadership, can recognise and respond to its changing environment and transform itself to be not just fit for purpose in the IoT era but a world leader. Haier is "business reimagined".

If a company like Haier, operating in one of the most competitive markets in the world, can reimagine itself, why not government?

In the altered landscape created by the new realities outlined in Chapter 7, it is beholden on governments to not only follow trends but to lead the way. The global megatrends we examined create new threats but also present new opportunities for the governments of the world, but only if they are prepared to address some issues raised in previous chapters, namely:

- How can government become more responsive?
- How can government be more innovative?
- How can government engage with business and citizens to create purposeful collaborations?

It is telling that we don't currently have an accepted word that captures this idea. I call it Gov-preneurship. The term may seem a little contrived, but it describes a new way of thinking and being.

The nations that will flourish in the decades ahead will be those that create a harmonious balance between government (which protects and enables), business (the wealth creation engine) and the citizen (who contributes their skills and loyalty). These three parts of society are in a symbiotic relationship and must function collaboratively. To do so, however, government leaders will have to find ways to foster trust and cooperation between all three.

A good example of this occurred in Thailand recently with the setting of the country's 20-year national plan. As Dr Supachai Panitchpakdi explained in Chapter 5, the six pillars that form the basis of the national plan, and the priorities identified with them, were arrived at after a process of national consultation involving the public sector, business and private citizens from all walks of life. To ensure that the plan is adhered to, it was also enshrined in constitutional law. In future, I would expect to see governments doing more of this sort of "sense taking" and "sense making".

What does all this mean for government innovation? The implications are two-fold. First, public sector innovation is essential to reimagining government. It is not enough to simply do what governments have always done in the same old ways. Secondly, the people who work in government need to become more entrepreneurial if they are to innovate in a way that has impact and creates new value for individual citizens and for the nation.

"Entrepreneurs are simply those who understand that there is little difference between obstacle and opportunity and are able to turn both to their advantage," Niccolò Machiavelli observed.

Once the connection is made between reimagining government on the one hand, and entrepreneurialism on the other, all sorts other potentially useful connections follow. One way to reimagine important public initiatives, for example, is to liken them to startups in the private sector. In this regard, the Lean Startup and Agile movement that has become popular in the business world has much to offer in the government context – if public sector leaders are open to new ways of working.

WHAT MIGHT AN ENTREPRENEURIAL GOVERNMENT LOOK LIKE?

One might argue that unlike Haier, the public sector doesn't have competition. Monopolies are typically client indifferent and inefficient. But as citizen mobility increases, citizens will seek societies that give them the best lifestyle return on their taxes. Consequently, the best governments will attract the best people, which will in turn attract the best employers. This creates a demand for more hotels and restaurants, which in turn stimulates tourism.

Conversely those governments that are citizen-contemptuous or indifferent will turn their country into an economic backwater, which in turn creates the perfect conditions for civil unrest. Governments must behave as if they are in a very competitive situation because they are. The consequences of thinking otherwise are already playing out across the world in the form of protests, riots and uprisings.

So, what can government do to encourage innovation and entrepreneurial behaviours? Here are seven suggestions, based on learnings from the private sector.

1. **Adopt a different mindset**
   This is critical to reimagining government. To become more entrepreneurial, government leaders must think differently. We will explore this in Chapter 10. Governments need to realise that governance is an infinite game.[68] Unlike a finite game which is based on an unchanging set of players and rules, an infinite game is one involving known and unknown players, where the rules are changeable, and the objective is not to win but to keep playing. When you pit a finite player against another finite player the result is stable, but when you pit a finite player against an infinite player, the finite player will struggle as their strategic decisions will be motivated by very different aims. With an infinite game the goal is simply to stay in play.

2. **Zero distance to citizens – as championed by Haier**
   It is vital that governments develop a better understanding of the needs of the citizens through better G2C and C2G connections. There should be no boundary. Zero distance should be the government mantra.

3. **Adopt Design Thinking**
   Design thinking is an innovation technique popular in entrepreneurial businesses today. Design thinking puts the human being and their needs – the user experience - at the centre of the design process. It looks for the human root of a problem – social, cultural, environmental, or economic – to solve real needs. Government services should be designed around the citizen journey, rather than on the needs of department leaders, or outdated bureaucratic processes.

4. **Reward citizen satisfaction**
   The private sector recognises the importance of performance-related remuneration. Such practices have been slower to catch on in the public sector. Yet there is no reason why remuneration of civil servants should not be correlated with the satisfaction of the citizens in respect of the associated service. Such rewards do not have to be financial. It could be in the form of access to professional development opportunities (courses) or time off, or even recognition (for example, a leader-board of citizen satisfaction in different government services).

   As noted in the previous chapter, the vision for government services might even include the idea that every citizen has an account manager. This account manager might well be an algo-driven avatar, but because government is so well integrated and manages its data so well, it can offer citizens a highly personalised experience.

5. **Recognise and reward risk-taking**
   Make it clear that sensible risk-taking is to be encouraged. Celebrate success and failure. Companies such as Netflix recognise that celebrating failure – "sunshining" in the Netflix parlance - is a good way to encourage risk-taking. Risk and reward need to be shared. Today when government takes the risks, in PPP projects, for example, the private sector generally takes the rewards. Governments need to drop the fortress mentality – the notion that we are on the inside and citizens are on the outside.

6. **Use expert sourcing**
   Democracy done well is an exercise in crowdsourcing. A subset of crowdsourcing is expert sourcing. Government should not be limited to using large corporations or global consulting firms. Having access to the best and brightest individuals should be simply an extension of the government's operating model.

7. **Make government purposeful and therefore aspirational to work for**
   Government at its best has a very necessary and noble purpose. This is a powerful way of attracting and retaining innovative and entrepreneurial talent. As talented people increasingly reflect on the emptiness of working for organisations focused solely on profits, the opportunity to work for the public sector might well become more attractive. In the past, the best talent would have drifted into the private sector, but governments would be wise to snap up the best people. Scholarship programmes like the one in Singapore described in Chapter 4 can create an ethos of civic duty and social status in serving the government.

SUMMARY: CREATING ENTREPRENEURIAL GOVERNMENT

It might seem like a radical idea to think of government in entrepreneurial terms but, as we are seeing, there is little choice if we are to meet the evolving needs of the citizens in an increasingly volatile and uncertain world.

Most importantly, it is a requirement for maintaining a stable and thriving state.

The Haier interview shows us it is possible to turn even the most unlikely, seemingly market-indifferent organisation into a continuously evolving world-leading one. But Zhang Ruimin is an exceptional leader. His restless and radically challenging example is what drives Haier's continuous transformation.

There will be little chance of government transforming to something more entrepreneurial if you don't have the appropriate leadership. That is the topic of the next chapter, where we analyse the leadership attributes public sector leaders need to reimagine government.

A New Type of Leader

10

Developing an entrepreneurial government that engages symbiotically with both business and citizens is unlikely to happen unless the associated government leaders undergo a parallel transformation.

In the previous chapters, we discovered that thriving states require active and trustful engagement between the primary actors (Principle 1) and that governments need to be more dynamic and entrepreneurial to respond to a rapidly changing world (Principle 2). In this chapter, we will explore the final principle, which underpins principles 1 and 2:

Transforming the government as the world transforms itself calls for a new breed of leaders.

Such leaders exhibit certain attributes that will enable them to be effective in what are increasingly tempestuous conditions. In this chapter, I will present my research into the attributes that these transformative government leaders need to acquire or develop to be able to lead a responsive and responsible government in these uncertain times. We will explore each of these attributes in detail, including how we develop them and what we must guard against in respect of their downsides.

Over the last 300 years, government has taken its lead from the private sector in that it has developed into a machine where the role of the leader was simply to maintain or refine it. Process efficiency was the goal. However, unlike in the private sector where the market punishes inefficiency, the public sector has generally been granted a licence to plod along sluggishly with a broadly indifferent approach to its client base ie, the citizens. Monopolies are rarely good for the consumer.

Societal tensions brought about by the trends we covered in the new realities chapter are on the rise in both the developing and developed world. Governments cannot afford to ignore this tension. This is not a phase that governments can ride out. People talk of a post-covid world as if covid-19 is a brief societal interruption and all will return to normal soon enough. The bad news is that there is no "normal", "new normal" or "next normal" at the other end of the tunnel. There is only a kaleidoscope of abnormal waiting for us.

My first principle reflects that the interaction between the primary actors in society needs improvement. My second principle reflects that governments need to move from sluggish plodders to situationally aware living organisms. These changes can only happen with leaders who possesses the attributes for this new dynamic.

In many respects, Principle 3 is the most important factor in government transformation. Given that this is new territory, I asked our esteemed contributors to this book, all former high-profile public sector leaders, to help formulate a set of attributes future government leaders must possess. In this chapter, I will share with you the approach we have taken and then I will present each of the key attributes.

Please note that I have looked at attributes, rather than skills. Without doubt, skills are needed to get the job done. However, given the uncertain nature of what lies ahead, it is impossible to predict job specifics. Attributes are more durable. With the right attributes, skill acquisition is simply a formality.

ATTRIBUTES VERSUS SKILLS

Skills are learned through practice; by repeating an action we form mental and physical muscle memory that allows us to perform the task without thinking. Attributes are more inherent; we are born with certain qualities or characteristics, such as patience, resilience and courage, which inform our behaviour and how we show up in situations. Some people are more naturally disposed to certain attributes, but we can cultivate character in terms of our attributes by the choices we make. For example, we might be born with a tendency to be impatient, or fragile or fearful, but we can choose to modify our natural behaviourial tendencies to become more patient or resilient or courageous.

Skills direct behaviours for known situations; for example, how to ride a bike or drive a car. But when we are faced with an unknown, an uncertain or unpredictable situation, skills don't apply; instead we lean on our attributes.[69] This is the difference between a finite game-minded person and someone who is infinite game minded. Finite-minded players fear the unknown and uncertainty; they practice their skills over and over again to ensure they are ready for any situation (any known situation, that is). Think of how an athlete prepares for the Olympics or how the military trains its personnel. The finite-minded player has already done their thinking in the past, so under pressure they rely on what has become a muscle memory skill. You will hear people say, "I didn't have to think, I just relied on my training".

The problem is that skills training only works for expected and predictable events. The infinite-minded player, on the other hand, embraces uncertainty. Rather than simply rely on training and past thinking, they start to think when the situation changes to present them with something they have not experienced before. At that point, they lean on their attributes, their meta behaviours, which dictate how they approach the new situation. Skills are good for a finite environment, but attributes are what it takes to build an infinite mindset.

This notion is not as modern as you might think. Aristotle was an early advocate of attribute cultivation. He believed that people were born with certain characteristics – good and bad - but that they could cultivate them in such a way that they modified them through rational choice. By choosing to act in a certain way, he said, you create a habit, which eventually results in an active condition which he called a "virtue". Over time our thoughts and feelings start to align and when that occurs it creates a virtue. As leaders we can cultivate virtues. Someone who is frightened of public speaking, for example, but forces themselves to overcome their fear will, in time, become more comfortable with giving speeches: a phenomenon also referred to as "faking it until you make it".

Importantly, too, it is our attributes that build trust in others. A belief is simply an emotion justified and rationalised. We cannot make someone trust us; we can only behave in such a way that allows them to make a decision to trust us. It is our attributes that people identify us with. This applies to government leaders.

THE APPROACH

The attributes identified here are not the result of personal musing. I consulted the contributors because they understand first-hand what makes a successful leader through their own experiences and through their exclusive exposure to other leaders globally.

From a process perspective, each contributor was asked to suggest the leadership attributes they believe leaders need to possess in these increasingly uncertain and volatile times. The inputs from each leader were aggregated to generate a shortlist of six attributes.

This was not an easy task because the contributors were unconstrained in their submissions. They were not offered a long list of possible attributes, for example, each with a robust and unambiguous definition. This was to ensure there was no "leading the witness" in the exercise.

Consequently, I received a variety of attributes that in some cases overlapped with other attributes or could be considered sub-attributes. Surprisingly, despite the unconstrained nature of this research, the variety of responses could be converged down to six attributes, namely:

- Solution architect.
- Trustworthy.
- Resilient.
- Innovative.
- Visionary.
- Erudite.

You will note that these six attributes spell the word "Strive", which is itself an attribute. According to the *Cambridge Dictionary*, to strive is to try very hard to do something or to make something happen, especially for a long time or against difficulties.[70] (As an aside, this might be considered the most important attribute of all because without it we would never do what is required to develop the other attributes and become the leader that our societies require.)

Just to clarify what I mean by an attribute: the term attribute is defined as a particular characteristic that can produce a particular type of behaviour. Attributes might be considered as meta-skills. In other words, they can be applied to more than one specific task. Bricklaying or programming are examples of skills. They are needed to deliver an output, for example to build a wall or create an app. Arriving at work unable to lay bricks but being visionary will not get the job done. However, attributes, particularly positive attributes, are the catalysts that turbocharge performance, assuming the person has the necessary skills.

THE ATTRIBUTES

We will look at each attribute in turn. Specifically, we will:

- Explore the attribute in respect to public sector leadership.
- Consider how one might cultivate the attribute.
- Flag concerns associated with the attribute.
- Show the link between the attribute and my first and second principles, namely:
    - Principle 1: Thriving states require strong and trustful engagement between the primary actors.
    - Principle 2: Governments need to be more dynamic and entrepreneurial to respond to a rapidly changing world.

1. SOLUTION ARCHITECT

The notion of solution architect might seem controversial. Is it not more of a role than an attribute, particularly when viewed in the context of its IT sector origins?[71] It's not sufficient to be simply solution oriented. Whilst it captures the creation of the solution, it fails to embrace the implementational and operational aspects of the solution. Grand announcements are not enough; citizens need services. In this broader context, a solution architect is someone who identifies and frames a problem, develops a solution and oversees the implementation and execution of that service.[72]

The framing of the problem is critical. It is not enough to understand what is required, but why it is required and what the associated implications are. Will the associated solution bring about a better future? What are the underlying assumptions? Do these assumptions still hold true as the world becomes more uncertain?[73]

Solution architects might well be applauded by their peers for the elegance of their solution, but they will be trusted and respected by the citizens based on the value it delivers, too.

Today, with issues such as increasing economic uncertainty, citizen disengagement and ecological challenges, public sector challenges might be better described as "wicked problems".[74,75] Such problems are complex and do not have a definitive solution. The problem is interdependent with other such wicked problems. These problems are dynamic. There is no end point. In such circumstances, government and society are best perceived as infinite games.[76]

Solution architecture covers policy design, citizen services design and government reengineering. A dilemma that modern leaders must face is whether to transform government "policy by policy" or by rearchitecting government as a whole. Context will drive the decision.

Let's look now at the specific characteristics of a solution architect. As mentioned, the ability to frame the problem is critical. Careful scoping is required and meeting the needs of all stakeholders will require the ability to communicate and "sell" the proposed solution.

In a rapidly changing world, evidence-based policy making is also critical. Solution architects must study the data to understand where the problem lies and resist picking the most media-attractive or interesting problems to solve. Such leaders need to have an openness to learning. Wicked problems do not neatly sit within one discipline or department, so a detailed understanding of all aspects of government is important. The ability to "zoom in" on the details of the solution, whilst retaining a "zoom out" strategic perspective is essential. Despite the increasing complexity of society and the wider world, government leaders must strive for simplicity. Modular design enables their solutions to be adapted in harmony with the evolving needs of citizens with minimal disruption to the overall solution. Design is a skill and leaders need to learn it.

A solution can look elegant on paper, but its success will be determined by the extent to which both the operators of the service and the consumers, ie, the citizens, accept it. Therefore, solution architects need to be cognisant of the anthropological and sociological implications of the emergent services. In some cases, new solutions may have social contract implications and so this needs to be handled with care.[77]

Failure can be a career-ending event in government. However, the likelihood that the initial theoretical solution will be identical to the operational solution is remote in a rapidly evolving world. Leaders need to be open to experimentation and prototyping, moving forward in small steps at pace but with flexibility, so that they can adapt the solution to both local and global forces. Balancing radical change with increasing volatility and "time to value" is a challenge. Openness to experimentation and a willingness to adapt does not imply a lack of ambition. Certainly, it does not suggest that governments today are simply in need of minor adjustments. Incremental change at pace equates to radical change. Tightrope walkers take small steps for a reason! This will require some degree of trial and error and in turn some degree of failure. Government leaders need to create an environment where enquiry, experimentation and prototyping are encouraged. This requires a culture of trust both within government and between government and the citizens.[78]

Solutions to wicked problems are rarely free. Finding a balance between financial, political and time cost is important. There is not always a correlation between the level of spending and successful outcomes.[79] Solutions must be easy to understand, or they will be difficult to maintain. Beware of third parties who are motivated more by contract size than citizen experience and therefore offer unnecessarily elaborate solutions.

Solution architects are the first to realise how emerging technologies can be applied to create better citizen services. Public sector leaders therefore need to be tech-savvy. Of course, the weight of the solution cannot be loaded onto one set of shoulders. Leaders need to engage with a diverse set of players, ranging from market leading behemoths through to independent experts. To ensure the solutions are fit for purpose, leaders would be wise to include representatives of the service consumers as part of the solution team. Taking the stance that "government knows best" doesn't cultivate citizen trust and is often misguided.[80]

Solution architects in the public sector are encouraged to focus more on outcomes and less on process. Having developed an architectural design, allow the civil servants and private sector to exercise their own innovative powers to arrive at the desired outcome. Whilst there will be many stakeholders involved, it is important that the number of objectives the solution is intending to address is kept to a manageable number. If the key performance indicators for the solution cannot be captured on one page or less, it is unlikely that the solution will meet any of its objectives. It will also make institutional performance opaquer.[81]

Whilst there is pressure to make confidence-inspiring promises to the public, it is important not to rush announcements. The feasibility, cost effectiveness and the adaptability of the solution need to be thoroughly evaluated beforehand. This is not to suggest that we adopt the traditional "big bang" linear approach where there is extensive analysis and strategic planning and where the delivery of anything useful is very late in the project lifecycle.

However, whether we take this traditional "waterfall" approach or embrace a more agile way of working, we must not set sail until we are certain that the journey is feasible. Announcing a forthcoming service that involves the use of technologies that are not fully understood will erode public confidence when the budget runs out of control and the initiative is eventually abandoned. In the United Kingdom, for example, Prime Minister Boris Johnson announced that a "world-beating" contact tracing app was being developed to mitigate the pandemic crisis, only to abandon the app in June 2020 after spending millions of pounds on it.

Furthermore, as the solution architect you need to remain involved in the programme throughout the implementation stage and into the operational value realisation stage. These latter two phases are perhaps less exciting and less glamorous, but the solution architect's involvement is key to a successful outcome.

Traditional government is typically not architected to solve today's problems. To ensure proper governance in respect of a new solution it may be necessary to create a task force to govern it over the full lifecycle. From a broad leadership perspective, the increasingly complex environment requires a more adaptable and resilient form of programme management. This will necessitate large-scale re-skilling of government leaders at all levels along with civil service programme and project managers.

Leaders need to factor in the importance of rapid value realisation. Long-fuse, big-bang projects are ill-suited to a world where situational awareness trumps strategy. Even large infrastructure solutions need to deliver positive change at the earliest opportunity. As a solution architect, you must not fall foul of the sunk cost fallacy.[82] Be prepared to halt a project should it start to deviate from government and citizen priorities. Pivoting might be an option, but society is ill-served by keeping an irrelevant programme on life support.

Attribute acquisition:
Here are some suggestions to set you on the path to becoming a solution architect:

Understand the details of your government machinery, particularly the processes and how policy is formed in practice. What is the wider policy-making ecosystem in which the government operates? Keep in mind that where people are involved, solutions need to be mindful of social and political factors.

Build a network of advisers whom you can call upon. Understand their capabilities beyond what they present to the market. For example, your economics adviser might well have a hobby where the associated skills are pertinent to the problem at hand. The secret to creating impressive solutions lies in knowing how to get the best from your team. This is not just in respect of their capability but also in how you emotionally engage them.

Develop your planning skills and scrutinise the plans presented to you. People have a tendency to be overly optimistic in respect of what can be realistically achieved, failing to factor in potential risks. You need to be able to "pressure test" the plans your people and third parties submit for your approval. Consider whether the intended outcome stacks up against the associated costs and risk. Be clear on the criteria for success. Minimising the chance of failure is always important, but also factor in what will be learnt even if the project is not an overall success. Just because the future is largely unknowable it does not mean we can be lazy in respect of planning. You want to know that these submitted plans have been created with an appropriate level of rigour. This, of course, also applies to your plans.

Whilst solution architects will likely "hand off" the implementation of projects to a projects office, it is important that you develop a nuanced sense of each project's overall societal benefit. Think in terms of a project portfolio. The aim is that you have an appropriate balance of projects that are operational (keep society running) and transformational (radically improve society). And within these, aim to have a portfolio that ranges from low risk to "moonshot" in nature.

Develop the ability to ask the right questions. This is more art than science. The point here is to be sensitive to what the question means to the respondent in respect of their own career path. They may feel less inclined to give a response that eventually automates them out of a job. Similarly, the questions must not presume an intended solution. In other words, you must not be simply looking for evidence to support your preconceived notion.

Understand the potential of new technology in delivering effective solutions. Develop an understanding of the relationship between risk and value. Be clear on all risks, including those associated with government reputation and societal stability.

Beware:
Frame the problem carefully. While it is gratifying to come up with the solution, particularly one that might work in theory, there is a danger of rushing to a solution without due consideration of the problem or the unintended consequences of the proposed solution. This is a particular risk given how the speed of society is accelerating alongside ever-increasing uncertainty and volatility.

The media and the public will expect solutions. Smart leaders will give the problem due consideration before making solution-related announcements. As the United States Navy Seals point out – "slow is smooth and smooth is fast", or to put it another way, "less haste, more speed".

I have noticed from my work in the Middle East that one of the systemic problems we face is how glamourous solutions are often favoured over the most effective solution. Public announcements of this nature enable politicians to shine. It can also lead to an indifference towards implementation and, worse still, operation. I believe this is a global problem and one that leads to a sub-optimal experience for the citizen, and to further erosion of trust.

Principles relevance

Principle 1: The needs of citizens and the private sector are continuously evolving. As social contracts globally are put to the test, we need solutions that are perceived as high value by the citizens yet are low cost in respect of delivery. So, government leaders need to be solution oriented.

Principle 2: We need leaders who can develop a sufficiently grand design that reflects the government's long-term responsibilities yet can adapt to the current realities. Great solutions deliver value quickly and are designed to maximise re-use if new opportunities or threats require a change of direction.

2. TRUSTWORTHY

According to the *Oxford Handbook of Positive Organizational Scholarship*, being trustworthy is a key leadership attribute and one of the most critical qualities that leaders should possess to set goals and achieve them.[83] Trust becomes particularly important in the government or public sector context.

Government leaders, especially those leading national transformations, need to be seen as credible, dependable and responsible, as they need to gain buy-in from large groups of the populace, often for decisions that are unpopular. Citizens who trust their government and their national leaders are more likely to be forgiving of mistakes. Such trust is a currency that can be kept in reserve and used in times of crisis. The covid-19 crisis, for example, has shown the importance of trustworthiness amongst leaders. In countries where the government and leadership trust quotient was high, citizens demonstrated limited pushback and complied with measures that would be otherwise be considered extreme in a non-crisis situation (such as lockdowns and the curbing of civil liberties and online privacy).[84]

In addition, leaders not only need to be able to become trusted, they need to create a culture of trust within their government. In respect of transformation, trustworthiness is an important determinant of implementation success. Defined as the capacity to be relied on as honest and reliable, trustworthiness influences the degree to which followers are ready to accept the accuracy and correctness of information they receive from their leaders.[85] In the government leadership context, these followers include not only the general populace, but also the stakeholders who are mandated with executing or implementing the transformation. Examples of these stakeholders include government departments and officials. According to research presented in *Leadership Quarterly*, in a context where these stakeholders consider their leaders trustworthy, they:

- Are motivated to go the extra mile.
- Put in greater effort in ensuring that the transformation exercise sees the light of day.
- Attempt and accomplish difficult tasks.
- Make sacrifices to ensure that targets and goals are achieved.
- Live up to the expectations of their leaders.[86]

Therefore, trustworthiness can generate positive and constructive behaviours and outcomes in transformational contexts. Trustworthiness is contagious, which means that public sector leaders need to be role models if they are to create a trusting culture within both government and society at large.

Research shows there are four main pillars of trustworthiness in leadership, namely ability, benevolence, integrity and predictability.[87] While ability refers to the knowledge, skill and professionalism of leaders, benevolence pertains to the demonstration of interest, empathy, approachability and the recognition of individual needs. Integrity, which is the third pillar of trustworthiness, encompasses the adherence to moral and ethical standards, and is the fundamental value that followers typically seek in their leader. Integrity is more pertinent for government leaders than leaders in any other sector, as the public only trust leaders who act in the interest of their country and people.[88] Lastly, predictability is also a pillar of trustworthiness that most scholarly research identifies. Critical elements of predictability are consistent behaviour and reliability. Integrity and predictability are particularly important for government transformation leaders, as they are often faced with crisis situations where their honesty, sincerity and ability to keep their commitments are put to the test.[89]

Attributes acquisition:
Trust can be broken down into several sub-attributes:

- Credibility – Can you do what you promise?
- Reliability – Do you do what you promised when you promised it?
- Familiarity – Do people have a sense of knowing you or do you like to keep your distance?
- Humility – Do you listen to others and regard them as your equal, putting yourself at their service?
- Selflessness – Are you focused on the needs of others or are you always acting in self-interest?

Becoming trustworthy is about taking every opportunity to galvanise these sub-attributes. This is best practised at the one-to-one level. You build trust with individuals. But over time your reputation as a person to be trusted will spread. The adage that trust is hard to acquire and easy to lose is spot on. If you are generally perceived as untrustworthy, you will have to work hard to regain that trust.

In terms of building a trustworthy team, you need to reward behaviours that build trust and be ruthless about any behaviours that might cultivate distrust between team members or between the government and its citizens. It is worth mentioning that having a humble and modest disposition goes far in respect of cultivating selflessness: typically, there is an inverse correlation between ego size and trustworthiness.

Beware:
Trust is to some extent a nebulous term. It needs context to have meaning. Whilst I might trust a leader to negotiate the best trade deal for the nation, I may not trust them in respect of their intentions towards citizens living below the poverty line. Trust is both an attribute and a key element of personal brand management. Without clear signalling, the citizens will make their own judgements about what motivates their leaders. Smart public leaders continually remind others of their value system and their focus on serving the public.

Trust can be considered as a combination of confidence and competence. Some leaders engender trust by exuding confidence, but their ability to execute is lacking. So, being trustworthy is not simply a brand veneer.

Principles relevance
Principle 1: States run better if the primary actors trust each other. True partnership with business and citizens is underpinned by trust. Government leaders need to signal trust in both their communications and their actions. Trust is a delicate flower and so needs to be handled with great care.

Principle 2: Organisational trustworthiness starts from the top. Your colleagues will not buy into the radical transformation required if they do not trust you. This significantly more dynamic approach to government requires everyone to "up their game". Similarly, the citizens need to trust their leaders. A radically new approach to government might well be viewed with suspicion. If trust is not in place, the government will find itself swimming against the tide.

3. RESILIENT

All transformational leaders are likely to be faced with challenging and disruptive situations. Resilience is a key leadership attribute that helps leaders adapt under pressure, whilst maintaining high energy and leading with confidence. Rooted in the Latin word *resiliens*, which refers to the elastic quality of a substance, resilience has been defined in many ways. According to Michael Rutter, a psychiatric risk researcher, resilience is the positive tone of individual differences in people's response to stress and adversity.[90] Similarly, professor of child psychology Bruce Perry describes resilience as the capacity to face stressors without significant negative disruption in functioning.[91] It has also been used interchangeably with positive coping, adaptation and persistence. Irrespective of how it is defined by individual scholars, all researchers essentially believe that resilience is concerned with the individual's reaction to risk and how they bounce back from adversity, frustration or misfortune.[92]

In respect of leadership, the ability to thrive and hardiness are two critical elements of resilience. The ability to thrive, which emerged from the study of coping paradigms, is based on an individual's positive transformation resulting from the experience of misfortune or adverse circumstances.[93] Psychologist Charles Carver defined thriving as a constructive growth experience, in that it results in decreased reactivity to, and faster recovery from, subsequent stressors, ultimately leading to a consistently higher level of functioning.[94] To illustrate, when faced with adversity, most individuals go through all or some of the stages of a resilience cycle that was conceptualised by professors Jerry Patterson and Paul Kelleher.[95] These stages comprise a deteriorating phase, an adapting phase, a recovery phase and a growing phase.[96] In a transformation context, effective leaders are thrivers who not only continue to function by surviving or coping with the adversity, but also reach the growing stage and achieve a new equilibrium characterised by a new level of functioning (ie, strengthened resilience level).

The second element - hardiness – is similar to thriving, but with the additional ability to make the best of difficult circumstances. According to Bonanno, hardiness is a multi-dimensional concept and comprises:

- The commitment to finding a meaningful purpose in life.
- The conviction that one has an impact on one's surrounding and the outcome of events.
- The belief that both positive and negative life experiences can enable one to learn and grow.[97]

In the transformation context, hardiness is a crucial element of resilience, as it serves as a buffer when an individual is exposed to extreme stress. It enables individuals to appraise potentially trying situations as less hostile, thereby minimizing the distress and shock caused by them. Therefore, leaders who effectively navigate challenging socio-economic realities are not only thrivers, but also have a high degree of hardiness which allows them to remain objective and pragmatic, make the necessary decisions (even if they are unpopular) and help the populace steer through difficult circumstances.

In the government transformation context, their resilience has a positive impact on organisational resilience, as transformational leaders typically foster the resilience capacity of their teams by encouraging a culture of open communication, risk-taking, recognition and shared decision-making.[98] They build teams with personnel who are agile and adaptable and who react quickly and positively to change.[99]

In a similar vein, research also examines the impact that the leader's resilience has on their team during stressful situations. In his review of the research on the relationship between transformational leadership and subordinate reactions to stress, Professor Bernard Bass, the famous transformational leadership scholar, notes that transformational leaders have the ability to reduce stress and burnout amongst their team by reframing crises into developmental challenges and opportunities for growth.[100] Such leaders provide the intellectual stimulation within their team to encourage the identification and uptake of thoughtful and creative solutions as opposed to reactive and hasty ones.

Resilient transformational leaders are also inspirational, in that they exude coping behaviours such as confidence, optimism and enthusiasm, and engender respect and pride amongst their team members. This reduces panic and helplessness in stressful times, replacing these emotions with a sense of positivity, security and belonging.[101]

Attribute acquisition:

Resilience can be thought of as a muscle. When we go to the gym, we start with light weights and through muscular adaptation we become stronger and thus able to work with heavier weights. So ideally, we would develop a resilience progression programme that scales gradually, from handling the trivial reality that the restaurant is out of your favourite dish, to leading your nation through a world war.

Such a programme is difficult to architect. Focussing on personal discipline at every opportunity is a daily practice that will build your resilience muscles. Resilience is to a great extent a lifestyle choice that boils down to your approach to decision-making. Do you tend to act based on what yields a favourable outcome now against what would yield a favourable longer-term outcome? Here are a couple of examples:

- Poor resilience: enjoy the dessert now and run the risk of having heart problems in the years to come.
- Strong resilience: fight on today even though you are weary, with the aim of securing freedom for the next generation.

Beware:
The image of the dogged mountaineer, face covered in ice ascending to the peak, is uplifting. However, having lost their fingers and toes on the ascent, they are unable to make the trickier descent.

Human brains have certain cognitive "bugs". These served us well in ancient times but are counterproductive today. In respect of resilience, the "sunk costs fallacy" comes to mind: our belief that, because we have invested so heavily in a particular pursuit, we cannot give up, and thus we invest further even though the pursuit is a lost cause.

Stubbornness is at the unproductive end of the resilience spectrum. Your ability to know when to throw in the towel or change direction is a key facet of resilience. Your ability to keep your ego out of the decision-making process is similarly important.

Principles relevance
Principle 1: Citizens might not take so well to the need for them to "step up". Their dissatisfaction might be expressed in ways that encourage the abandonment of this model. Unfaltering leadership is required and so resilience is imperative. It is worth mentioning that it is not just government leaders who need resilience. The road to citizen resilience needs to start in the home and be further inculcated in the education system.

Principle 2: The transformation journey from a factory to an entrepreneurial model will not be smooth. There will be setbacks and there will be forces looking to undermine such a transformation. Your ability as a leader to grind forward is critical. A trusting ecosystem will ameliorate this, but that may not necessarily be the case at the outset of the transformation.

4. INNOVATIVE

Successful transformations require innovative leadership. Defined as the process of introducing new ideas to improve organisational performance, innovation is a cornerstone for managing large-scale transformations, which involves gaining the confidence of multiple stakeholders and often convincing these stakeholders that change is possible. Given the multi-dimensional challenges that leaders face today - from climate change to global pandemics - innovation is critical for shaping new solutions to old problems as well as tackling complex unprecedented challenges.

However, it is important to note that while creative solutions are a means to this end, innovation extends beyond creativity. Creativity pertains to the conception of new and groundbreaking ideas, but innovation extends beyond idea generation. It concerns the work required to make an idea viable. Innovative leaders continuously manage their creative resources to design and implement suitable solutions. In this regard, the adoption of an innovative mindset, or "opportunity mode", is a critical success factor.[102] Effective leaders are passionately alert to possibility and to the excitement of transforming vision into reality.[103] They proactively think ahead of the curve, and assess and interpret trends and changes to turn them into new opportunities, even amid genuine fear.[104] Furthermore, they are adept at building the buy-in from various stakeholders, which is essential for widespread change to take place.[105]

Innovative leaders typically exercise six behaviours, as noted in the Deloitte Gov Lab document "Transforming the Public Sector: Delivering successful public sector transformation through innovation"[106], namely agile integration; quiet transparency; social media mastery; horizon scanning; rapid prototyping; and rebel rousing. Leaders who develop these competencies are better at engaging, building agile teams who can respond quickly to rapidly changing environments, and establish platforms to ideate and test new solutions to meet citizen expectations.

The first behaviour is agile integration. Innovative leaders who are agile integrators are able to be responsive, to connect people, information and resources, and work with multiple inter-sectoral stakeholders to solve complex problems that break organisational and sectoral silos. Agile leaders are situationally aware and have the skills to adapt to a rapidly changing environment by exercising flexibility and foresight about real and imagined threats and opportunities.

The second behaviour is quiet transparency. An innovative leader is aware they haven't got all the answers and is willing to question and adapt. Quiet transparency is key to building trust and fostering engagement with teams and stakeholders.

Social media mastery is the third behaviour. It refers to the use of digital media and platforms to gain insight into attitudes and to establish influence and increase motivation. This is an innovative behaviour that has become particularly important in the last two decades. In the government transformation context, digital media mastery becomes particularly important, as leaders must understand the pulse of the citizens as well as stakeholders who implement the transformation. Effective leaders can leverage online platforms to establish trust, create feedback loops, gain buy-in and motivate people.

Fourth, effective leaders typically scan the horizon, in that they analyse patterns across contexts and disciplines, while also testing assumptions about future scenarios and current trends. They ask the right questions and use a range of hypotheses to test those questions.

The fifth behaviour that effective transformational leaders exercise is rapid prototyping. Rapid prototyping allows leaders to explore different potential solutions and to pilot them to see which ones are feasible and scalable. They demonstrate courage by accepting uncertainty and bearing real risk of loss, adhering to the principle of doing "the harder right instead of the easier wrong."[107]

Finally, effective leaders are also rebel rousers, in that they seek out and encourage individuals who question and challenge the status quo, and create a safe and flexible environment for alternate perspectives to be heard and experimented with.[108] Bass refers to this as "intellectual stimulation" or the act of challenging assumptions, taking risks and soliciting team members' inputs and ideas. Furthermore, innovative leaders do not fear failure, and instead instil a safe space for bottom-up innovation. They encourage their teams to ideate, have open conversations and voice diverse perspectives – all with the objective of creating greater value and attaining the objectives of the broader transformation.[109] In a transformation context, innovative leaders inspire creativity among their followers and their implementation teams who are responsible for actioning large-scale change. Several studies suggest that transformational leaders play a key role in creating a conducive climate that promote employee creativity.[110]

It is important to note that leaders today are also faced with a maelstrom of data and analysis tools. Using this treasure trove of data effectively is another dimension of innovative leadership, as it can enable leaders to identify trends and have actionable insights, which can generate effective and sustainable solutions and guide decision-making. In the public sector context, this is particularly important, as it allows leaders to transcend political pressure and lean towards evidence when making critical decisions.[111] Furthermore, in a world where 4IR technologies are enabling society to move forward in quantum leaps, innovative leaders harness the potential of new technologies to explore new concepts and solutions, review their success, revolutionise implementation processes and improve performance.

However, leveraging data and technology cannot be achieved in silos, especially in government. The challenges that states have to tackle, especially in a transformation context, are so fundamental and complex that they require leaders to rethink the traditional demarcation between sectors and explore new and more integrated forms of collaboration (for example, consultative decision-making, joint design and delivery of public sector services, outsourcing). Innovative leaders disrupt typical public-private partnership models and open new frontiers of collaboration by enabling the private sector and citizens to access public sector resources such as data and funding to accelerate innovation and co-create transformation.[112]

Attribute acquisition:
You might consider yourself an analytical person who does not feel very at ease when it comes to unconstrained creativity. Keep in mind that constrained creativity often leads to the best solutions. Silicon Valley is known for its innovation. However, it is awash with venture capital, so there is tremendous waste and perhaps even a lack of deep thinking given that money is no object. We only have to look at how people in impoverished societies innovatively use their limited resources to achieve the outcomes they need. Frugal or constrained innovation can yield the best solutions.[113]

From *Through the Looking-Glass* (Lewis Carroll):
Alice laughed. "There's no use trying," she said: "one can't believe impossible things." "I daresay you haven't had much practice," said the Queen. "When I was your age, I always did it for half-an-hour a day. Why, sometimes I've believed as many as six impossible things before breakfast."

Whilst you may be constrained by budget, you are not constrained by your imagination. Develop the ability to see the world differently. Spend time daydreaming. Develop knowledge in disciplines unadjacent to your own core expertise. Similarly, take counsel from experts in unrelated fields from the problem at hand. Innovation often emerges in the gaps between the traditional pillars of expertise.

Beware:
There is rarely a problem with improving things. However, if one spends too much time on the solution's design, it may miss the window of exploitation. Voltaire was correct – "Perfect is the enemy of the good." Similarly, the anticipated value associated with an innovation must justify the risk and investment to be made. Again, there is a danger from the sunk cost fallacy.

The best innovations are elegant and simple. Beware of complicated innovations that will be difficult to explain, implement and maintain. The fewer moving parts the better. (Note that simple is not the same as simplistic.)

Avoid invention and the urge to be original. If the innovation already exists, use it or repurpose it as required. Don't take all the praise. If you intend to develop an innovative culture, give praise where it is due. Acknowledging your innovators will stimulate further creativity and thus keep your "ideas well" from running dry.

Principles relevance
Principle 1: Governments often need the private sector to provide innovative solutions. But governments need to take a collaborative approach to innovation rather than just relying on the brainpower of the private sector. Government leaders must play an active role in developing innovative solutions. In general, consultants must support rather than lead the government. This is necessary in respect of developing in-house innovative capacity. Keep in mind that citizens are an important source of innovation. Calling upon this significant brain trust will also promote deeper citizen engagement.

Principle 2: Entrepreneurs are natural innovators. This must be woven into the government fabric. This requires a culture that supports experimentation and doesn't lambast failure. Your leadership team and the civil servants will take their cue from your behaviour.

5. VISIONARY

Thinking beyond the existing operating model is a critical attribute of transformational leaders. This requires the ability to consider the big picture, how it will evolve over time and what this requires in respect of a future operating model.[114] In organisational leadership theory, Marshall Sashkin describes this deep understanding as the vision or ideal image of an organisation and its culture.[115] It links the present and the future state, energises people, provides purpose for action and serves as a standard or target that performance can be assessed against.[116] Breakthrough leadership in government and large-scale transformation can only be realised if a leader has a well-thought out and clearly articulated vision.

Given the unprecedented and increasingly complex challenges societies face, government leaders need to envision new operating models that are somehow resilient to increasing uncertainty.

It is also important to understand that vision-setting seeks to establish direction and must not be confused with the planning function, which is a deductive managerial exercise aimed at generating orderly results as opposed to change. According to Professor John Kotter, vision-setting is a more inductive process whereby leaders consider a variety of data, patterns and relationships to identify a long-term goal for the future.[117]

Their vision serves as a leader's north star. It guides planning, day-to-day decision-making and the subsequent activities. In order to be effective, this vision must be crafted whilst keeping a multi-dimensional and a multi-stakeholder context in mind. This is particularly important in the government arena, where buy-in from a wide range of stakeholders is critical for any vision to be realised successfully.[118] Developing a vision that attracts commitment and stimulates stakeholders into action is critical. But at the same time, the vision must not be set in stone. The trends identified in Chapter 7 are interrelated and thus unpredictable in respect of their future impact. Leaders need to have the flexibility of mind to "course correct" as the future unfolds.

Successful leaders construct a vivid vision underpinned by a lucid philosophy and then identify how it will be realised. However, such leaders must also be realistic. A vision that is too challenging to achieve can in fact demotivate those responsible for implementing it. Similarly, the future is not static, so situational awareness is imperative to ensure the vision stays relevant. Such awareness needs to be built into the leadership model.[119] This ensures that the vision or the ideal state is not only desirable, but also attainable.

Again, visionary leaders must not only proactively examine their environment, but also be cognisant of changing factors, both within and outside of the public sector. In today's world of accelerating change and unprecedented interconnectedness, the capability to anticipate change and conduct effective scenario planning is critical. This anticipatory capability ensures that the leader is perceptive, prepared for a variety of eventualities and responsive to the continuously evolving dynamics that characterise the world today. Today's leaders must continuously scan the horizon for potential challenges and opportunities. In turn, they need to regularly fine-tune their strategy and adjust the resources needed to maximise success accordingly.[120]

Success in a public sector context means fulfilling the needs, and ideally the wants, of the citizens. This is a challenge, given the increasingly unpredictable environment within which governments operate today. Moreover, public sector leaders must work within the "givens" of the government model, which typically comprises the government's regulatory and political framework, as well as the customs of their national and local context.[121]

Once the vision and the associated goals are established, it is time to articulate the vision to the larger stakeholder community. Here the leader is a government spokesperson. They prudently use a range of media channels to ensure their message reaches all stakeholders.

A visionary leader not only sets the course, but also inspires the stakeholders to follow and support the construction of this desired future.[122] As well as keeping the vision front of mind for all stakeholders, the visionary leader guides those tasked with building it, much like the architect who regularly visits the building site.

A key aspect of turning vision into reality is the importance of choosing a capable team with a shared *esprit de corps*. Most importantly this vision must be built on a platform of trust.

Attribute acquisition:
Visionaries are naturally futurists. They make predictions about the future based on what they know about the past and the present. Given its recurrent nature, it would be wise to study history. Keeping on top of globally significant events and trends, as we covered in the new realities section in Chapter 7, will enable you to recognise patterns that others do not see.

Of course, there are infinite futures and not all trends carry equal weight, so developing the ability to identify significant trends and in turn anticipate the consequences of their interactions will help you develop a more refined vision. Exploring different scenarios, through war gaming, for example, will help in this respect.

This is as much an art as a science, so play around with scenarios, for example:

- What are the implications for your country in a world where every home has a 3D printer and China's Belt and Road initiative is fully operational?
- How do you maintain law and order when there is a high unemployment rate? Or, as might be the case in the near future, where the economy no longer requires the involvement of people in the workplace?
- If the space industry is in the ascendency, what could your nation do to become a major player?
- What would be your response if your neighbours formed an alliance with a hostile nation?

A great way to "pressure test" your thinking is to write and speak regularly on such matters. It will force you to think deeply, and the feedback you receive will further refine your perspectives.

Beware:
All vision and no execution is simply a way to kick the can down the road.

Multi-year visions are highly risky, particularly if they require high capital outlay up front with no prospect of value realisation until late in the project. What seems like a smart move today, such as a highspeed rail link between two major cities, might not be such a great idea if people increasingly conduct most of their lives from home, replacing all business travel with video conferencing. Covid-19 is rewriting social norms. Similarly, building multiple hospitals based on today's medical solutions and levels of illness may result in expensive overcapacity in ten years' time when the focus moves from illness to wellness.

Principles relevance

Principle 1: We need visionary leaders in government, business and society. The move towards a greater focus on stakeholders, as opposed to shareholders, will necessitate leaders from all three domains coming together to develop a shared vision.

Principle 2: A visionary leader is required to ensure that there is not a reversion to the old factory approach when bumps in the road or obstacles are encountered.

6. ERUDITE

Government transformation is a complex pursuit. Those that lead government transformation require great knowledge. This knowledge needs to include who and what will be impacted and how to develop and sell a solution that has the buy-in of all stakeholders. On top of that, government leaders need to understand how to affect successful transformation.

The *Merriam-Webster Dictionary* defines erudite as "having or showing knowledge that is gained by studying". *The Cambridge English Dictionary* extends this definition to "having a lot of knowledge that is known by very few people". The latter definition perhaps highlights that successful leaders happen to know more than those that follow them. Invariably, being at the top of the organisation, senior leaders will develop a unique, synthesised end-to-end perspective on its workings. The trend towards data-driven organisations will reinforce this.[123]

However, knowing is not enough, so I am advocating what might be called "applied erudition". Leaders need to turn what they know into value. Erudition can be subdivided into several sub-attributes. These include curiosity, elegance, astuteness, communication, statesmanship and political awareness.

To build knowledge in the first place, leaders need to be naturally curious.[124] As an aside, they need to build curiosity into the culture of the organisation.[125] Curiosity can be used beyond simple knowledge acquisition - for example, by posing challenging questions to the leadership team or by exploring how a new technology could be applied to improving the citizen journey. Erudite leaders need to think like data scientists, looking for weak signals that may be early indicators of emerging threats or opportunities.

Curiosity requires cognitive bandwidth. For this reason, elegance is important.[126] Developing a leadership style that is low on effort and high on impact provides the headspace needed to be curious. Harried leaders constantly playing catch-up will have little time to pay attention to what is happening in government or society. In such circumstances the government is "flying blind".

Turning knowledge into value requires astuteness. This ability to accurately assess situations and thus make better decisions is critical to a well-functioning government. Astuteness can be applied to both making strategic government decisions and to how one responds in the moment to a fellow leader's controversial remark at an official engagement. In both situations, poor judgement might turn out costly. Conversely, astuteness in diplomatic matters is an accelerant in respect of finding common ground - a key step in reaching a mutually agreeable outcome.

The ability to communicate is important to the role of leadership.[127] Using conceptual models, often drawn from a variety of disciplines, turns communication into influence. Erudite leaders are thought leaders. They put time aside to assimilate what they have learned, and they develop models that capture the audience's attention and move their mind. Articulate delivery of well-crafted messages can be intoxicating.[128]

Statesmanship is a characteristic of admired government leaders. Whilst it may sound antiquated, perhaps elitist and even gender-insensitive, the need for ethical leaders who conduct themselves well on the world stage has never been greater. We need more stateswomen, too. (Interestingly, initial research found evidence that women leaders handled the covid-19 crisis better than their male counterparts.) When under pressure, the urge to take the most expeditious option is tempting. Ethical leaders have the knowledge and intellectual capacity to create options that do not compromise their morals. Citizens want leaders that they can admire and can trust to act in their best interests.[129]

Nevertheless, it is not sufficient to be knowledgeable, influential, admired and a master government helmsman. There are people both within and beyond government who do not have the leader's best interests at heart and are looking to thwart their progress. Consequently, political awareness is an important aspect of erudition. To manage society and manage one's enemy takes knowledge and skill. Citizens prefer to see their leaders occupied in moving society forward. However, the media loves a political feud or bloodbath. Erudite leaders through skill and elegance handle their opponents both inconspicuously and effectively.[130]

In summary, erudite leaders are needed to tackle complex and novel government problems. There is often little support for new ministers. Given their relatively short tenure and the steep learning curve that goes with leading a new department or government, there is a strong probability that they will spend most of their high-profile public life in a state of incompetence. Thus, we need erudite leaders who are quick learners and who can thus shorten their "time to value".[131]

Attribute acquisition:

The value of erudition comes in its application, particularly in respect of how you engage with others. With that in mind, develop your vocabulary. Weave newly acquired words into your communications. The skill here is not to dumbfound or confuse others, but to maximise the resonance of your message. The aim is to be so clear and nuanced in your communications that you can readily move the minds of those you seek to influence.

Study topics adjacent to your primary focus. Similarly, be curious and explore unadjacent topics. Great insights come from seeing the link between disparate topics. For example, what can nature tell us about conflict resolution? Or what can Zen Buddhism teach us about building smart cities?

Again, take every opportunity to write and speak. These activities require focused thinking, which in turn further builds erudition. Find every opportunity to engage with other erudite people, particularly those who have opposing world views to yours.

Beware:

Not everyone is erudite, so occasionally you will need to "dial down" the erudition so as not to embarrass or confuse the other party. Using your erudition in the same manner as a proud peacock might display its plumage is a signal to all that that insecurity and narcissism feature prominently in your character. Humility is the perfect frame for displaying erudition. Being humble, highly articulate and interesting is a potent mix.

Avoid erudition becoming your identity to the point that you disdain the counsel of others, or insist on pursuing your own recommendations, despite the evidence pointing to the fact that they are failing. Like a martial artist, erudition is a never-ending journey of self-development. There is always room for improvement.

Principles relevance

Principle 1: Citizens respond well to effective orators. Businesses are less likely to misinterpret their commitments if the communications of government leaders are unambiguous. Citizens are bombarded with information from the moment they wake up. Government communications need to be such that they are not only heard but also resonate deeply with the people.

Principle 2: Effective communications is key to running a startup and erudition is key to effective communications. Stakeholders will maintain faith in this approach if the messaging conveys that the government leaders are taking an intelligent approach.

FURTHER OBSERVATIONS

Having explored the six attributes, it is significant that they each have a role to play in support of both the GBC ecosystem and gov-preneurship. This concurs with my thirty-plus years of experience working for and with public sector leaders.

We also asked the contributors which of the six attributes they thought were the most relevant to the challenges governments are facing now and in the foreseeable future. The following were perceived as the most critical attributes:

- Trustworthiness.
- Vision.
- Resilience.

You will have no doubt already picked up on this as you read through the ministerial submissions in Part 1 of the book.

It is very easy to understand why these are considered the most valued attributes. As the world becomes more tempestuous, citizens need leaders they can trust, who appear to have a sense of direction and have the grit necessary to "stay the course".

BEYOND STEADY STATE

The days of running a factory or a government department in a steady state environment are over. The pace of change is on the increase and this requires a new type of government and a new type of leader. These new leadership attributes reflect the increasingly real-time, "always on" nature of modern society.

Again, we must find the balance between responsibility and responsiveness. Whilst the accelerating pace of change necessitates a shift from strategic planning to a more real-time response, government leaders must keep the long-term implications of their day-to-day decisions in mind. I believe these attributes reflect the importance of managing this tension.

In this book, you have heard from several eminent public sector leaders. We considered their perspectives in the context of global trends and identified several new realities that government are facing today. In response to these realities, I proposed three principles that government leaders might embrace to enable their societies to thrive going forward. In the concluding chapter, I will recap on the problems that have led to the need to reimagine government. I will summarise the proposed principles (for easy future reference) and I will make some final remarks on the changing nature of leadership.

Conclusion

11

In this final chapter, we are going to briefly reconnect with the contributors. We will then recap on the new realities and the principles that I believe governments need to embrace to thrive in this new and uncertain world. I will also take a deeper dive into leadership to provide you with a framework on which to build your own leadership approach.

This book has been a fascinating journey, certainly for me and hopefully for you, too. The overarching theme was the need for governments to be both responsive and responsible: that is to be able to respond to the immediate threats and opportunities that present themselves in an increasingly volatile world, whilst also being responsible for the long-term wellbeing and custodianship of the state and future generations of citizens.

In **Part I**, we were fortunate to have as our guides some outstanding past government leaders.

- In Chapter 1, Toomas Ilves, the former president of Estonia, provided a compelling rationale and roadmap for the digitalisation of government, surely one of the most pressing transformations facing any modern government today. As Ilves says: *"digitalisation of governance is not just about 'putting government online.' Nor is it merely turning paper records into PDFs. Digitalisation of government ultimately means rethinking and reimagining how governance works."*

- In Chapter 2, Alexander Stubb, former prime minister of Finland, shared a fascinating account of his country's Nordic miracle, and how Finland was able to weather the storms of change. Transformations, he says, need a trigger. *"As people, we usually only change when we are forced to: a sudden diagnosis of a health condition, for example, triggers a change in lifestyle. It is that moment of realisation or diagnosis that triggers the change. Nations are no different."*

- In Chapter 3, Lim Hwee Hua, the first woman to serve in Singapore's cabinet, explained how her country, with no obvious natural resources and severely restricted for space, reinvented itself as a global hub and powerhouse, creating an enduring bond of trust between government, citizens and business. *"A social contract that endures the test of time for longer-term macro-economic policies and sustains the nation through crises is founded on the underlying shared values of meritocracy, prosperity through hard work and thrift, and a collective responsibility for - and ownership of - the country's future and wellbeing of its people."*

- In Chapter 4, former Irish prime minister (taoiseach) John Bruton took us on an exhilarating ride on the Celtic roller-coaster, describing Ireland's transformation from a poor and largely agrarian economy into one of the most prosperous states in Europe. Looking forward through the lens of the pandemic, he also reminds us that: *"multinational problems require multinational solutions."*

- Chapter 5 looked at Thailand, and we heard from former deputy prime minister Dr Supachai Panitchpakdi how that kingdom has followed its own transformational development path based on the King's Principles embedded in his Sufficiency Economy Philosophy, and positive engagement between the government, business and citizens. *"To have a good, happy, strong nation you need to have what Mencius, a disciple of Confucius, called a benevolent government," he says. "A benevolent government understands development in a benevolent way."*

- In Chapter 6, Ed Vaizey, Britain's former minister for culture and technology, described his experiences of building a tech nation and fostering his country's creative industries. Above all, he argued for the need for governments to be more "citizen-centric", placing the user need at the centre of what the state does, and recognising that technology is now driving change. *"Technology is now dominant in all developed countries, and governments across the world must step up their engagement."*

Finally, in Chapter 9, we heard from another expert contributor, Zhang Ruimin, chairman and CEO of the Haier Group, about how an old-style organisation, under exceptional leadership, can recognise and respond to its changing environment and transform itself to be fit for purpose. *"There are no successful businesses, only relevant ones. The only businesses that will survive are the ones that stay in sync with changing times. For companies and organisations everywhere, the question is: are we waiting to be phased out, or are we going to reinvent ourselves?"*

Part II is an assimilation of our contributors' perspectives coupled with my own experiences, as both a public sector leader and in my work developing public sector leaders. I have endeavoured to coalesce these various sources into a set of guiding principles to support leaders in their quest to build responsive and responsible organisations.

In Chapter 7, we examined the megatrends – technological, social, economic, geopolitical and global threats – that are already impacting on the environments that governments operate in. I argued that together they present seven new realities facing government today. They each represent a crisis of a kind.

1. **Social contracts are fraying**

   The social contract holds a nation together, it is the glue that binds government, business and citizens to each other. But in many nations, there are signs that the social contract is coming unglued, with citizens taking to the streets to protest and businesses behaving in monopolistic and profiteering ways, creating instability and resentment. Governments need to re-establish the social contract by engaging in collaborative dialogue with the other actors.

2. **Governments have lost the trust of the people**

   Allied to the problem with the social contract, many governments have lost the trust of their people. As a consequence, citizens and businesses are suspicious of government intentions and less compliant with policies. Governments need to restore trust through greater transparency and ethical leadership.

3. **There is a lack of citizen-centricity**

   The third crisis facing governments is that the services they provide are not citizen friendly. Citizens and businesses feel they are hamstrung by unnecessary red tape and bloated bureaucracy. Governments need to design services around citizens not the other way round as is too often the case at present.

4. **Governments appear unresponsive**

   This links to the fourth new reality, or layer of crisis: governments are not responsive to the needs of citizens or business. They do not prioritise or act on what the people or the private sector perceive as important – for example, health and employment, or infrastructure. Governments need to become more attentive to their stakeholders and more proactive in their responses; at present they are reactive.

5. **Governments are failing to harness the potential of the private sector**

   Business has an important role to play in delivering more responsive government and social solutions, but governments typically regard themselves as buyers of products and services rather than collaborators. This means they miss out on creative solutions. In order to harness the private sector's capacity for innovation, governments need to create the conditions to allow an innovative and collaborative private sector to develop.

6. **Government leaders are ill-prepared for an unknowable future**
   Most governments cling to the synthetic certainty of the past, even though the world is increasingly uncertain and unpredictable. As a result, governments are ill-prepared for shocks to the system when they occur. Government leaders need to adopt a more proactive and open-minded approach to anticipate what might happen in the future. This requires pioneering leadership and not just stewardship.

   The pandemic illustrated this perfectly: the most effective governments used the best technology and scientific advice to create guidelines to address the crisis, and the vast majority of their businesses (shops and restaurants and factories) and citizens played their part by respecting and abiding by the guidelines. This links to the next point: government is just one part of a national ecosystem and citizens need to step up, too.

7. **Citizens are behaving as passive recipients**
   Citizens have a role to play in maintaining a healthy society, but many are shirking their individual responsibilities. This means that the social contract is broken on their side, and they adopt an attitude of learned helplessness. In particular, citizens need to take responsibility for developing their own marketable skills, rather than simply relying on government to guarantee them a minimum income.

I have endeavoured to codify these various sources into three guiding principles to support leaders in their quest to build responsive and responsible organisations. These are:

Thriving states require active and trustful engagement between the primary actors (government, business and citizens) - Principle 1.

Governments need to be more dynamic and entrepreneurial to respond to a rapidly changing world - Principle 2.

Transforming the government as the world transforms itself calls for a new breed of leaders - Principle 3.

In Chapter 8, we examined Principle 1 and saw that there are three primary actors in the societal ecosystem: government (G), business (B) and the citizen (C). Viewed through the lens of the GBC ecosystem, the responsiveness and responsibility for a nation's wellbeing rests with all three actors and opens the door to new opportunities.

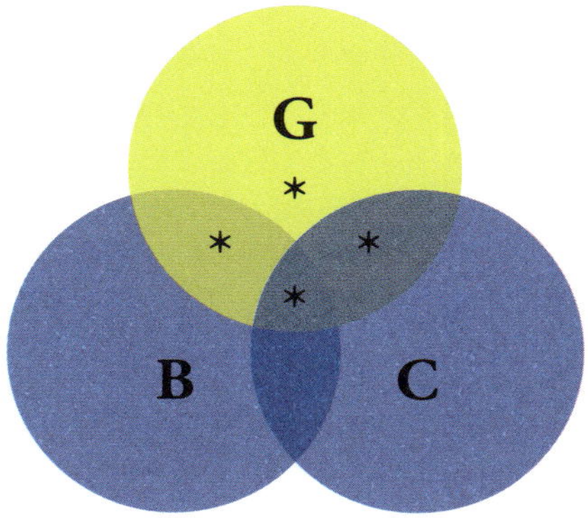

Figure: the government-business-citizens model

This is a symbiotic ecosystem, where all three parts rely on each other for their success. For example:

- Business needs citizens as employees and customers, and needs government to create the legal framework, infrastructure and conditions for trade.
- Citizens require meaningful work and goods and services from business, and the personal security and services that the state provides.
- And governments rely on citizens to play their role in maintaining a thriving and stable state, bring their skills and talents to work, and guide the government's focus.

But with citizen discontent on the increase and governments failing to engage with the business sector, rebalancing the ecosystem is an imperative. It is important to recognise, though, that the strength of the social contract is the priority as it binds the three parts of the ecosystem together.

We focused on the government component (G) and the relationships between, firstly, government and business (G2B and B2G) and secondly, between government and citizens (G2C and C2G). The interconnections between business and citizens (C2B and B2C) are also important to the ecosystem (with implications for customer loyalty and talent management) but lie largely beyond the scope of this book. Our primary focus is on the interconnectedness of all three dimensions G, B and C, and the need to create a harmonious and judicious balance between them.

The GBC model is a very modern way of looking at a state and requires a reimagining of how a country and an economy can and should function. When the ecosystem works effectively, it's a win: win: win scenario. It is therefore essential that the three primary actors can collaborate in productive and purposeful ways. The root of the problem and in turn the source of the solution lies in the attitudes and mindsets of citizens and government and business leaders.

In Chapter 9, we took a deeper dive into how governments need to adapt to provide a more responsive service to its citizens. This is captured in my second principle:

Principle 2: Governments need to be more dynamic and entrepreneurial to respond to a rapidly changing world.

Governments need to behave in a more entrepreneurial manner. Hence my introduction of the term *gov-preneurship*. This is a radical notion. However, it reflects the radical transformation that governments need to undertake if they are going to be effective in what is essentially an unknowable future.

We examined the new imperatives facing the private sector, specifically the need to compete on innovation and resilience rather than efficiency and certainty. To illustrate the radical new models that are emerging, we heard from expert contributor, Zhang Ruimin, the CEO of the Chinese company, the Haier Group.

Haier's zero-distance approach is a lesson in how government could and should view its relationship with citizens. It demonstrates how an old-style organisation, under exceptional leadership, can recognise and respond to its changing environment and transform itself to be not just fit for purpose in the IoT era but a world leader. Haier is "business reimagined".

If a company like Haier, operating in one of the most competitive markets in the world, can reimagine itself, then governments can, too. But only if they are prepared to address some issues, namely:

- How government can become more responsive.
- How government can become more innovative.
- How government can engage with business and citizens to create purposeful collaborations.

In short, how government can become more entrepreneurial. I call this gov-preneurship. The term describes a new way of thinking and being.

The states that will flourish in the decades ahead will be those that create a harmonious balance between government (which protects and enables), business (the wealth creation engine) and the citizen (who contributes their skills and loyalty). These three parts of a state are in a symbiotic relationship and must function collaboratively. To do so, however, government leaders will have to find ways to foster trust and cooperation between all three.

So, what can governments do to encourage innovation and entrepreneurial attributes and behaviours?

1. **Adopt a different mindset**
   This is critical to reimagining government. To become more entrepreneurial, government leaders must think differently. They need to realise that governance is an infinite game.[132]

2. **Zero distance to citizens – as championed by Haier**
   It is vital that governments develop a better understanding of the needs of the citizens through better G2C and C2G connections. There should be no boundary. Zero distance should be the government mantra.

3. **Adopt design thinking**
   Design thinking is an innovation technique popular in entrepreneurial businesses today, which puts the human being and their needs – the user experience - at the centre of the design process.

4. **Reward citizen satisfaction**
   There is no reason why the reward of civil servants should not be correlated with the satisfaction of the citizens in respect of the associated service. Such rewards do not have to be financial. It could be in the form of access to professional development opportunities (courses) or time off, or even recognition (for example, a leader board of citizen satisfaction in different government services).

5. **Recognise and reward risk-taking**
   Make it clear that sensible risk-taking is to be encouraged. Celebrate success and failure. Risk and reward need to be shared. Today when government takes the risks, in PPP projects, for example, the private sector generally takes the rewards.

6. **Use expert sourcing**
   A subset of crowdsourcing is expert sourcing. Government should not be limited to using large corporations or global consulting firms. Having access to the best and brightest individuals should simply be an extension of the government's operating model.

7. **Make government purposeful and therefore aspirational to work for**
   Government at its best has a necessary and noble purpose. This is a powerful way of attracting and retaining innovative and entrepreneurial talent.

   It might seem like a radical idea to think of government in entrepreneurial terms, but as we are seeing there is little choice if we are to meet the evolving needs of the citizens in an increasingly volatile and uncertain world. Most importantly it is a requirement for maintaining a stable and thriving state.

   It should be noted here that people who are more entrepreneurial in their approach are typically mission driven rather than job driven; this also applies to government leaders. They see their role in government not as filling a job but fulfilling a mission. Whereas doing a job focuses on completing routine tasks, achieving a mission focuses on achieving specific objectives. The second big difference between job and mission is time. Missions have a time frame, a beginning and an end. Leaders who recognise this do not get too attached to their positions or resist change because they want to achieve their goals. Entrepreneurial government leaders are not "time servers" but focus on how to complete their mission in the time available. As such, they appreciate the importance of being efficient and time sensitive.

In Chapter 10 we looked at a new type of leader. There will be little chance of government transformation to something more entrepreneurial if you don't have the appropriate leadership. That is the topic of Principle 3.

Principle 3: Transforming the government as the world transforms itself calls for a new breed of leaders.

Chapter 10 presented the attributes that government leaders need to acquire or develop to be able to lead a responsive and responsible government in these uncertain times. We consulted the contributors to understand first-hand what makes a successful leader through their own experiences and through their exclusive exposure to other leaders globally.

We chose to focus on attributes rather than skills because skills training only works for expected and predictable events. Rather than simply rely on training and past thinking, government leaders need to be flexible when the situation changes to present them with something they have not experienced before. At that point, they lean on their attributes - their meta behaviours - which dictate how they approach the new situation. Skills are good for a finite environment, but attributes are what it takes to build an infinite mindset.

Aggregating the inputs from each contributor generated a list of six attributes:

- Solution architect.
- Trustworthy.
- Resilient.
- Innovative.
- Visionary.
- Erudite.

These six attributes spell the word "strive", which is itself an attribute. According to the *Cambridge Dictionary* to strive is to try very hard to do something or to make something happen, especially for a long time or against difficulties.

The six attributes are the first of three important dimensions of leadership; the other two being mindset and intelligences, which we examine in the next two sections. These attributes represent one important dimension of the new style of leadership required.

MINDSET

If we think of leadership attributes (the strive model) as the first dimension of government leadership, then leadership mindset is the second. Innovative and trustful collaboration lies at the heart of a resilient society. To optimise the government-business-citizen partnership, we need a new breed of multi-dimensional leader who not only sees the value in collaborating with their peers across the public-private fence but is also competent enough to collaborate successfully. If all three parties adapt accordingly, then the conditions are set for a safer, more satisfying and a more connected state.

The challenge is one of mindset. American psychologist Carol Dweck identified two different mindsets.[133] In a fixed mindset people believe their basic qualities, like their intelligence or talent, are simply fixed attributes. But in a growth mindset, people believe that their most basic abilities can be developed through dedication and hard work—brains and talent are just the starting point. A fixed mindset is characterised by rigid thinking and the belief that you are a victim of circumstances and there is no point trying to adapt or transform. A growth mindset, on the other hand, is characterised by the belief that you can develop and evolve, and is essential for a leader operating in unpredictable conditions.

It is worth keeping in mind that transformation is less a programme and more an operating model. Consequently, each new day comes with its own unique set of challenges. A growth mindset is essential for operating in such unpredictable conditions.

INTELLIGENCES REVISITED

Attributes and mindset make up the first two dimensions of government leadership. Now, before I conclude, we will explore the third.

My research with Professor Andrew Kakabadse of the Henley Business School in the United Kingdom indicates that the next generation of leaders need to exhibit five dimensions of intelligence to achieve effective transformational change.

We referred to these as the 5Qs: cognitive intelligence (IQ); emotional intelligence (EQ); political intelligence (PQ); resilience intelligence (RQ): and moral intelligence (MQ). Much as DNA's constituent nucleic acids create the substance that works as the framework for human life, these 5Qs come together to inform every aspect of leadership.

Distilled to their essence:

- IQ is a leader's ability to acquire knowledge, reflecting their deductive/rationalist abilities and drawing together contrasting strands of information to emerge with a compelling argument that entices.
- EQ is a leader's ability to understand and manage both their own emotions and those of others.

- PQ is a leader's ability to navigate a way forward through diverse stakeholders' agendas while ensuring continued engagement with critical players.
- RQ reflects the capacity of a leader to emotionally sustain high performance under continued pressure and adversity.
- MQ is a leader's ability to understand their own value system and draw on this to determine the moral boundaries of individuals, teams and of the organisation.

These intelligences represent the unconscious and conscious controls on the actions we take to shape our response to external demands. Our studies tested these concepts on elite leaders including ministers, top civil servants, C-level and board executives in the United States, United Kingdom, India, Australia, Europe, Russia, Asia and the Gulf region.

3D LEADERSHIP

So, we now have three perspectives on leadership, namely:

- Attributes.
- Mindset.
- Intelligences.

As suggested, these might be considered as the three dimensions of leadership.

FINAL THOUGHTS

At the start of this book, I explained my reasons for writing it. I wanted to capture the learnings from real transformational leaders who had experienced the challenging realities of change. I wanted to share my own experiences and insights on leading government projects and initiatives. Above all, I wanted to inspire and help prepare the next generation of government leaders for the road ahead.

Even in the time that I have been working on the book, the world has altered beyond all recognition with the covid-19 pandemic taking a heavy toll on citizens, business and government. Yet, along with the enormous and sometimes tragic events that we have witnessed and continue to witness, we have also seen glimmers of hope and unparalleled opportunity.

We have seen the three parts of a society - government, business and citizens – working together in new ways. Look at the way citizens throughout the world have complied with social distancing guidelines or participated in testing and crowd-sourced tracking systems. Or the way that businesses have stepped up to fill gaps in the production of personal protective equipment. Or how governments have responded decisively to protect their people. Governments took measures and changed regulations, which usually take months, in days and weeks. These are examples of genuine collaboration within the GBC ecosystem, which demonstrate the symbiotic relationship that exists between them and shows what is possible.

That is why I am optimistic that we can reimagine government in a responsive and responsible way. We have reached the end of our journey together, but hopefully it is just the beginning of a new journey for you.

As Scott Anthony, expert on disruptive innovation and senior partner at the consulting firm Innosight, observes:

"To start the journey of becoming the next version of yourself, ask three deceptively simple questions: Who are we today? Who will we become tomorrow? How do we start making the change? Remember, the biggest risk is not the action you take, it is trying fruitlessly to cling to the status quo as the world changes around you.

Leaders that catch disruptive changes early and respond appropriately will have the ability to thrive in the years to come. Those that don't, well, Darwin has a way of taking care of them."

Anthony sums up the challenge and the opportunity not just for government and business leaders but also for all of us as individuals and citizens.

I wish you well on your journey.

APPENDIX A:
BIBLIOGRAPHY

Bibliography (Case Studies)

1. Aiyar, Swaminathan S. Ankleseria. "Twenty-Five Years of Indian Economic Reform: A Story of Private-Sector Success, Government Failure, and Institutional Weakness", Policy Analysis, 803, CATO Institute, (October 2016)

2. Atkinson, Paul, "New Zealand's Radical Reforms", The OECD Observer, 205, April-May 1997

3. BBC News, Vietnam's "stunning" rise in school standards, accessed from: https://www.bbc.com/news/business-33047924, 2015.

4. Bass, Bernard M., Bass and Stodgill's Handbook of Leadership, 3rd Ed, New York, NY: Free Press. 1990.

5. Bass, Bernard M., Transformational Leadership: Industrial, Military, and Educational Impact, Mahwah, NJ: Erlbaum, 1998.

6. Bass, Bernard M., "The Future of Leadership in Learning Organizations", Journal of Leadership & Organizational Studies, 7, 18, 2000

7. Bonanno, George A., "Loss, trauma, and human resilience", American Psychologist, 59, 20-28, (2004).

8. Bryson, John and Barbara C. Crosby, Leadership for the Common Good: Tackling Pubic Problems in a Shared-Power World, San Francisco, CA: Jossey-Bass Publishers, 1992.

9. Burke, C. Shawn., Dana E. Sims., Elizabeth H. Lazzara, and Eduardo Salas., "Trust in leadership: A multi-level review and integration", The Leadership Quarterly, 18, 606–632, (2007).

10. Cameron, Kim S., and Bradley Winn., "Virtuousness in organizations" in Cameron, Kim S., and Gretchen M. Spreitze (eds)., The Oxford Handbook of Positive Organizational Scholarship, 231-243, Oxford: Oxford

11. Carver, Charles S., "Resilience and thriving: Issues, models, and linkages", Journal of Social Issues, 54, 245-266, (1998).

12. Centre for Creative Leadership and Continuum, Innovation Leadership How to use innovation to lead effectively, work collaboratively, and drive results, 2014. White paper accessed from: https://www.ccl.org/wpcontent/uploads/2015/04/InnovationLeadership.pdf

13. Chang, Ha-Joon, Kicking Away the Ladder: Development Strategy in Historical Perspective, London: Anthem, 2002.

14. Conway, Paul. and Adrian Orr., "The Process of Economic Growth in New Zealand", Reserve Bank of New Zealand Bulletin, 63, 1.

15. Cummings, Anne., and Greg. R. Oldham, "Enhancing creativity: Managing work contexts for the high potential employee", California Management Review, 40: 22–38, 1997; Scott, Susanne G., and Reginald A. Bruce, "Determinants of Innovative Behaviour: A Path Model of Individual Innovation in the Workplace", The Academy of Management Journal, 37, 3, 580-607, 1994.

16. Daft, Richard L., The Leadership Experience (6th Edition), Stamford, CT: Cengage Learning Press, 2014.

17. Dirks, Kurt T., and Donald L Ferrin, "Trust in leadership: Meta-analytic findings and implications for research and practice", Journal of Applied Psychology, 87,4, 611–628, (2002).

18. Edelman, Edelman Trust Barometer, 2019

19. Gaspersz, Jeff,. "The Search for Innovation Leadership", The European Business Review, March April 2012.

20. Global Investment Center USA, Vietnam Economic and Development Strategy Handbook Volume 1 Strategic Information and Plans, Washington D.C: International Business Publications, 2014.

21. GovLab Deloitte, Transforming the Public Sector Delivering successful public sector transformation through innovation, 2018

22. Harper, Stephen C., The Forward-Focused Organization: Visionary Thinking and Breakthrough Leadership to Create Your Company's Future. New York, NY: AMACOM, American Management Association, 2001.

23. Hassan, Arif., and Forbis Ahamed., "Authentic Leadership, Trust and Work Engagement", International Journal of Human and Social Sciences, 6, 3, 164-170, (2011).

24. Janas, Monica., "Build resiliency", Intervention in School and Clinic, 38, 117-122, (2002).

25. Jones, Will. and Sally Murray., Consolidating Peace and Legitimacy in Rwanda, LSE-Oxford Commission on State Fragility, Growth and Development, Accessed from: https://www.theigc.org/wp-content/uploads/2018/04/Rwanda-report.pdf, 2018.

26. Kim, Kwang-Suk and Michael Roemer., Growth And Structural Transformation in Korea: 1945-1975. Cambridge: Harvard University Press. 1979.

27. King, David C., Cultures of the World: Oman. New York: Marshall Cavendish Benchmark, 2009.

28. Klump, Rainer, and Thomas Bonschab., Operationalising Pro- Poor Growth: Case Study Vietnam, A joint initiative of AFD, BMZ (GTZ, KfW Development Bank), DFID, and the World Bank, 2004.

29. Kokko, Ari, "Growth and Reform since the 8th Party Congress", In McCargo, Duncan (Ed), Rethinking Southeast Asia, London: Routledge Curzon

30. Kotter, John P., "What Leaders Really Do", Harvard Business Review, May-June 1990.

31. Krugman, Paul R., "The Myth of Asia's Miracle," Foreign Affairs, 73, 6, (1994): 62-78

32. Lalwani, Ashok., This is how India can become the next Silicon Valley, India Economic Summit, World Economic Forum, 2019.

33. Lee, Jong-Wha., The Republic of Korea's Economic Growth and Catch-Up: Implications for the People's Republic of China, ADBI Working Paper Series, 571, (April 2016).

34. Malunda, Dickson, and Serge Musana. "Rwanda Case Study on Economic Transformation", Report for the African Centre for Economic Transformation (ACET), Institute of Policy Analysis and Research – Rwanda (IPAR), 2012.

35. Mayer, Roger C., James H. Davis., and F. David Schoorman, "An integrative model of organizational trust", Academy of Management Review, 20, 3, 709–34, (1995).

36. McDoom, Omar Shahabudin., "Rwanda's Exit Pathway from Violence: A Strategic Assessment". World Development Report 2011, Background Case Study, 2011.

37. McKinsey & Company, Leadership in innovation needs innovation in leadership, 2017.

38. Mehta, Pradeep S. (ed), A Functional Competition Policy for India, New Delhi: Academic Foundation, 2006.

39. Myers, Joe., India is now the world's 5th largest economy. World Economic Forum. Accessed from: https://www.weforum.org/agenda/2020/02/india-gdp-economy-growth-uk-france/. 2020.

40. Nanus, Burt., Visionary Leadership: Creating a Compelling Sense of Direction for Your Organization, San Francisco, CA: Jossey-Bass Publishers, 1992.

41. Nghiep, Le Thanh., "Measuring the Impact of Doi Moi on Vietnam's Gross Domestic Product", Asian Economic Journal, 14, 3, (2002): 317 – 332.

42. Nishikawa, Yvette., Thriving in the face of adversity: Perceptions of elementary-school principals, La Verne, CA: University of La Verne, 2006.

43. Norman, Steven M., Bruce Avolio, and Fred Luthans., "The impact of positivity and transparency on trust in leaders and their perceived effectiveness", Leadership Quarterly, 21, 350-364, (2010).

44. New York Times, "Sultan Qaboos, 79, Is Dead; Built Oman Into Prosperous Oasis of Peacemaking". Accessed from: https://www.nytimes.com/2020/01/10/world/middleeast/sultan-qaboos-79-is-dead-built-oman-into-prosperous-oasis-of-peacemaking.html. 2020

45. Overseas Development Institute, Viet Nam's progress on economic growth and poverty reduction: Impressive improvements, 2011.

46. Oxford Business Group. The Report: Oman 2017. 2017.

47. Patterson, Jerry L., and Paul Kelleher., Resilient school leaders: Strategies for turning adversity into achievement, Alexandria, VA: Association for Supervision and Curriculum Development, 2005.

48. Perry, Bob., "How children become resilient", Scholastic Parent & Child, 10, 2, 33-35, (2002).

49. Peterson, J. E., "Oman: Three and a Half Decades of Change and Development", Middle East Policy Council, 10, 2, (2004).

50. Panagariya, Arvind, "India in the 1980s and 1990s: A Triumph of Reforms", Working Paper WP/04/43, International Monetary Fund. (2004).

51. Pires, Innes and Thomas Sladko, Soft Diplomacy: Modelling Global Interactions, Brussels: Innovation in Diplomacy Network, 2019.

52. Rama, Martin., "Making Difficult Choices: Vietnam in Transition", Working Paper 40, Commission on Growth and Development. 2008.

53. Rand Corporation, Oman and the World: The Emergence of an Independent Foreign Policy, 1995.

54. Rutter, Michael., "Psychosocial resilience and protective mechanisms", American Journal of Orthopsychiatry, 57, 316-331, (1987).

55. Rodrik, Dani, and Arvind Subramanian, "From Hindu Growth to Productivity Surge: The Mystery of the Indian Growth Transition", Working Paper, International Monetary Fund, (1 May 2004).

56. Sashkin, Marshall., "Visionary Leadership", in Rosenbach, William E., and Robert L. Taylor, (Eds), Contemporary Issues in Leadership, 2nd Edition, Westview Press, 1989.

57. Schick, Allen., The Spirit of Reform: Managing the New Zealand State Sector in a Time of Change, Report prepared for the State Service Commission and the Treasury, New Zealand, Wellington, 1996.

58. Scott, Graham C., Government Reform in New Zealand, Washington DC: International Monetary Fund, , 1997.

59. Sitapati, Vinay., Half - Lion: How P.V. Narasimha Rao Transformed India, Haryana, India: Penguin Books. 2016.

60. The Arab Weekly, Smooth transition in Oman after the passing of Qaboos. Accessed from: https://thearabweekly.com/smooth-transition-oman-after-passing-qaboos, 2020

61. The Economic Times, 25 years of reforms: How a PM with zero knowledge of economics scripted India's biggest turnaround story, Accessed from: https://economictimes.indiatimes.com/news/politics-and-nation/25-years-of-reforms-how-a-pm-with-zero-knowledge-of-economics-scripted-indias-biggest-turnaround-story/articleshow/53309051.cms, 2016

62. Tucker, Robert., Six Innovation Leadership Skills Everybody Needs To Master, Accessed from: https://www.forbes.com/sites/robertbtucker/2017/02/09/six-innovation-leadership-skills-everybody-needs-to-master/#66d297965d46

63. UNDP, Human Development Report 2010: The Real Wealth of Nations: Pathways to Human Development, 2010.

64. VOA News., PV Narasimha Rao Remembered as Father of Indian Economic Reforms, Accessed from: https://www.voanews.com/archive/pv-narasimha-rao-remembered-father-indian-economic-reforms. 2009.

65. Wallis, Joe. and Brian Dollery., Market Failure, Government Failure, Leadership and Public Policy, London: Macmillan Press Ltd

66. World Bank, Oman: Transformation of an Economy. Volume 1: Main Report, 1977.

67. World Government Summit, and Pricewaterhouse Coopers, Inspire and Orchestrate: Innovation-Driven Government (IDG), 2018.

68. Oman case study – References:
UNDP. (2010). Human Development Report 2010: The Real Wealth of Nations: Pathways to Human Development.

J. E. Peterson. (2004). Oman: Three and a Half Decades of Change and Development. Middle East Policy Council, Vol 10 (2).

New York Times. (2020). Sultan Qaboos, 79, Is Dead; Built Oman Into Prosperous Oasis of Peace-making. Accessed from: https://www.nytimes.com/2020/01/10/world/middleeast/sultan-qaboos-79-is-dead-built-oman-into-prosperous-oasis-of-peacemaking.html

Rand Corporation. (1995). Oman and the World: The Emergence of an Independent Foreign Policy

Pires, Innes and Thomas Sladko. (2019). Soft Diplomacy: Modelling Global Interactions. Brussels: Innovation in Diplomacy Network

World Bank. (1977). Oman: Transformation of an Economy. Volume 1: Main Report.

Oxford Business Group. (2017). The Report: Oman 2017.

David C. King. (2009). Cultures of the World: Oman. New York: Marshall Cavendish Benchmark.

The Arab Weekly. (2020). Smooth transition in Oman after the passing of Qaboos. Accessed from: https://thearabweekly.com/smooth-transition-oman-after-passing-qaboos

Recommended reading list

- Ali Qassim Jawad et al, Leadership Intelligence: The 5Qs; Leading Smart Transformation: A Roadmap for World Class Government; Redefining Wellbeing in Nations and Organizations
- Banerjee, A. and Watson, T.F. (2011) Pickard's manual of operative dentistry. 9th edn. Oxford: Oxford University Press.
- Maister, D.H. (2002) The Trusted Advisor. New edn. ??: Simon & Schuster UK
- Leuchtenburg, W.E (2013) Franklin D. Roosevelt and the New Deal
- Failed States: The Abuse of Power and the Assault on Democracy - https://www.amazon.co.uk/Failed-States-Abuse-Assault-Democracy/dp/0141023031/.
- Fixing Failed States https://www.amazon.co.uk/Fixing-Failed-States-Framework-Rebuilding/dp/0195398610/
- The Great Transformation: The Political and Economic Origins of Our Time Paperback https://www.amazon.co.uk/Great-Transformation-Political-Economic-Origins/dp/080705643X/
- Grit: Why passion and resilience are the secrets to success: https://www.amazon.co.uk/Grit-passion-resilience-secrets-success/dp/1785040200/
- Ten Types of Innovation: The Discipline of Building Breakthroughs - https://www.amazon.co.uk/Ten-Types-Innovation-Discipline-Breakthroughs-ebook/dp/B00DZLBHU8/
- Vivid Vision: A Remarkable Tool For Aligning Your Business Around a Shared Vision of the Future Paperback - https://www.amazon.co.uk/Vivid-Vision-Remarkable-Aligning-Business/dp/1544508123
- Mental Models: 30 Thinking Tools that Separate the Average From the Exceptional. Improved Decision-Making, Logical Analysis, and Problem-Solving - https://www.amazon.co.uk/Mental-Models-Exceptional-Decision-Making-Problem-Solving/dp/1093915684/
- The Art of Grace: On Moving Well Through Life: https://www.amazon.co.uk/Art-Grace-Moving-Well-Through/dp/0393353184/

APPENDIX B: CONTRIBUTOR BIOGRAPHIES

Toomas Ilves served as the fourth president of Estonia from 2006 to 2016. Ilves is notable for making Estonia one of the most digitally-advanced nations. During his time in government, he introduced progressive initiatives towards digital governance, creating government e-services in voting, banking, health care, transportation and education. The Estonian Parliamentary Election of 2007 was the world's first nationwide vote where part of the voting was carried out in the form of remote internet voting. (Internet-based voting was offered for the first time in Estonia's municipal elections in 2005.)

Born in Sweden to an Estonian refugee family and educated at Columbia University, New York, Ilves used his time in office to integrate Estonia into both the European Union and NATO and to strengthen the country's ties to the United States.

He held several prominent government positions, serving as Estonia's ambassador to the United States, Canada and Mexico from 1993 to 1996. In 1996 he became the minister of foreign affairs; a post he held until 1998, and again from 1999 to 2002.

Ilves' political career advanced when he was elected to the Riigikogu, the Estonian national legislature, in 2002, and to the European Parliament in 2004. He ran for the presidency of Estonia as the joint candidate of the Social Democratic, the Conservative and Liberal parties and was elected in 2006.

Post-presidency, since November 2016, Ilves has co-chaired the Global Futures Council on Blockchain Technology, a working group set up by the World Economic Forum that focuses on how blockchain technology can be used to improve the security of the internet. He is a distinguished visiting fellow at the Hoover Institution, Stanford University and a member of the Munich Security Conference Advisory Board.

Alexander Stubb served as the prime minister, finance minister, foreign minister, and trade and Europe minister of Finland. He was an MEP from 2004 to 2008, in national government from 2008 to 2016 and was the chairman of the National Coalition Party from 2014 to 2016.

Prior to entering politics in 2004, Stubb enjoyed a distinguished career as an academic, which included authoring and editing 18 books, mostly on the EU. He also worked in the Finnish civil service at the ministry for foreign affairs, the EU permanent representation in Brussels and in President Romano Prodi's team at the European Commission, where he was involved in negotiating institutional transformation such as the Amsterdam Treaty, the Nice Treaty and the Constitutional Convention.

From 2017 to 2020, Stubb was vice-president of the European Investment Bank - the lending arm of the EU and the biggest multilateral financial institution in the world – during its period of transition to the Climate Bank of the European Union.

In 2020, Stubb was nominated director and professor of the School of Transnational Governance at the European University Institute in Florence, Italy.

He holds a PhD from the London School of Economics and Political Science. His expertise includes European and international affairs, foreign and security policy, the euro and the global economy.

His current interests are global affairs, the 4th industrial revolution and health. He chaired the Finnish National Commission on Sustainable Development, which is responsible for promoting national and international sustainable development goals and works to encourage society's commitment to and involvement in sustainable development.

Aside from politics, Stubb is passionate about "mind, body and happiness". He believes that the inextricable link between the three should impact our lifestyle. As an avid athlete and Ironman competitor himself, Stubb advocates the view that a healthy body is essential to a healthy mind, with happiness and the success of all of our other endeavours stemming from this bond.

Stubb sits on the 12-member World Happiness Council, convened by Sheikh Mohammed bin Rashid Al Maktoum, the vice-president and prime minister of the UAE and ruler of Dubai.

He is currently working on a book entitled *Digital Democracy or Digital Dictatorship: The Struggle for Global Power between China, the US, and Europe.*

Lim Hwee Hua became the first woman to serve as a full minister in Singapore's cabinet when she was made second minister for finance and concurrently second minister for transport in 2009. In public office from 2004 to 2011, she was responsible for designing regulatory policies and maintaining international standards and best practices in areas such as accounting, corporate governance and finance for small enterprises.

Lim held multiple positions within the Singaporean government. Elected as a member of parliament from 1997 through 2011, between 2002 and 2004 she was the deputy speaker of parliament and chairman of the Public Accounts Committee. In 2004 she was appointed minister of state for finance and transport.

In 2011, following her retirement from politics, Lim was appointed as an independent director at Jardine Cycle & Carriage and as a senior adviser at the global investment firm, Kohlberg Kravis Roberts. In the same year, she was also appointed an independent member of Ernst & Young's Global Advisory Council. She was the honorary chairman of the Securities Investors Association, Singapore, from 2013 to 2017.

Lim's book, *Government in Business: Friend or Foe?* was published in 2013. It sets out the arguments for and against government involvement in business.

Lim's academic journey started at the Raffles Institution. She was awarded a scholarship to Cambridge University where she read mathematics and engineering, graduating in 1981. She earned her MBA, majoring in finance, from the Anderson School of Management at the University of California, Los Angeles (UCLA).

Lim received the Her World Woman of the Year award in 2009 and was inducted into the Singapore Council of Women's Organisations' (SCWO) Singapore Women's Hall of Fame in 2014. She is currently co-chairman at private equity firm, Tembusu Partners Pte Ltd.

John Bruton is a former taoiseach (prime minister) of Ireland, where he held office from 1994 to 1997. Bruton was instrumental in helping transform Ireland into one of the world's fastest-growing economies. As taoiseach, he was also deeply involved in the Northern Irish Peace Process, which led to the signing of the Good Friday Agreement in 1998. In 1996, he presided over a successful Irish EU presidency and helped finalise the EU Stability and Growth Pact.

From 1999 until 2004, Bruton was one of ten vice-presidents of the European People's Party. He was appointed EU ambassador to the United States from 2004 to 2009.

Bruton held several positions within government. He was first elected to the Irish parliament in 1969, at just 22 years. He served as the minister for finance from 1981 to 1982 and 1986 to 1987; minister for industry and energy from 1982 to 1983; minister for trade, commerce and tourism from 1983 to 1986; and was parliamentary secretary from 1973 to 1977.

From 2010 to 2015, Bruton was chairman of IFSC Ireland, a private sector body set up to develop the financial services industry in Ireland. He is a distinguished fellow at the Centre for Transatlantic Relations in Washington DC and a visiting fellow at the European Institute in the London School of Economics.

His interests revolve around European and Irish economic developments and the importance of the EU-United States relationship in matters of trade, counterterrorism, public health, energy and the environment; and the promotion of peace, democracy and human rights around the world. He acts as an adviser to Fairobserver, focusing mainly on the areas of politics, finance and economics, as well as on issues pertaining to Europe.

Supachai Panitchpakdi served as deputy prime minister of Thailand from 1992 to 1995 and 1997 to 2000. From 2002 to 2005 he was director general of the World Trade Organisation (WTO) - the first to be appointed from a developing country - and between 2005 and 2013, he was twice the secretary general of the United Nations Conference on Trade and Development (UNCTAD).

Dr Panitchpakdi began his career as an officer of the Bank of Thailand, before he became deputy finance minister, commerce minister and then twice deputy prime minister. In between, he assumed the presidency role of a commercial bank and chairman of several private corporations, including an international insurance company. At present he is a board member of the Institute for Cultural Diplomacy in Berlin and a founding member of the Asia-New Zealand Foundation.

As deputy prime minister, Dr Panitchpakdi was actively involved in international trade policy and in shaping regional agreements, including the Asia Pacific Economic Cooperation (APEC), the Association of Southeast Asian Nations (ASEAN) and the

Asia Europe Meeting (ASEM). In 2012, he was honoured with the Grand Prize at the ASEAN Asia Cosmopolitan Awards, as the individual making the "most distinguished achievements in economic, social science or cultural fields".

Dr Panitchpakdi's interests revolve around the importance of international cooperation through sub-regional, regional and global frameworks; how to successfully conduct international trade negotiations; and how to develop new markets. He completed his doctoral dissertation on Human Resource Planning and Development in 1973 at the Netherlands School of Economics (now known as Erasmus University) in Rotterdam, under the supervision of Jan Tinbergen, the first Nobel Laureate in economics.

Ed Vaizey (Lord Vaizey of Didcot) was the longest-serving minister for culture and technology in the United Kingdom, from 2010 to 2016.

During his time in office, Vaizey oversaw the successful roll out of a £1 billion rural broadband expansion programme; the implementation of 4G; and the introduction of tax credits for theatre, orchestras, film, television, animation and video games, which helped to make the creative industries the fastest growing part of the British economy. He was responsible for attracting the Star Wars franchise to film in the United Kingdom, and consequently received a credit in Star Wars: The Force Awakens.

Vaizey also protected free admissions to museums; presided over a radical overhaul of English Heritage; and published the first white paper on cultural policy for more than 50 years.

Taking responsibility for the digital industries from 2014 to 2016, Vaizey played a key role in attracting inward investment to the British tech economy. He continues to champion the creative and digital sectors and is a trustee of two national charities: the National Youth Theatre and the Documentary Society. He sits on the advisory board of Common Sense Media, the largest not-for-profit in the United States that campaigns for safer tech for children.

He is vice-chair of the British Esports Association, sits on the advisory board of the London Festival of Architecture, and is an honorary fellow at the Royal Institute of British Architects and of the Radio Academy. Vaizey is a visiting professor for the creative industries at the University of Newcastle. He was made a life peer in 2020.

APPENDIX C:
ABOUT THE AUTHOR

Dr Ali Qassim Jawad is recognised internationally as an expert on public sector transformation and leadership. He has held a number of senior positions within governments in the Middle East, including in his home country, the Sultanate of Oman. *Government Reimagined* is his fourth book.

Before entering government, Dr Jawad worked with the consulting firm, Booz Allen Hamilton and as a government adviser. From 2007 to 2010 he served as strategic adviser to the Department of Economic Development in Abu Dhabi, UAE.

In 2010, Dr Jawad was appointed as scholar in residence at the INSEAD Innovation and Policy Initiative and his research on leadership mindsets formed the foundation for his book, *Leadership Intelligence: The 5Qs* (Bloomsbury, 2019). Dr Jawad is also the co-author of *Leading Smart Transformation: A Roadmap for World-class Government* (Palgrave MacMillan, 2011); and *Redefining Wellbeing in Nations and Organisations* (Palgrave MacMillan, 2016).

Since 2012, Dr Jawad has served as senior adviser for studies and research and head of the Think Tank Unit at the Diwan of Royal Court in Oman. He is vice-chairman of the Institute for Capability Development (ICD) and the founder and chairman of the Oman Business Forum (OBF). Prior to starting the OBF, he played a transformative role in bringing together government and private sector leaders under a national Public Private Collaboration (PPC) Task Force, which was instrumental in creating the Public Private Partnership (PPP) Authority, PPP Law and Public Private Initiatives (PPIs).

Between 2015 and 2019, Dr Jawad established and chaired an integrated national initiative approved by His Majesty the Sultan of Oman. Multiple programmes focused on increasing the readiness of leaders from both the private and public sector to navigate through the digital age.

He was also instrumental in initiating and leading programmes to support youth development through "tech-entrepreneurship". Covering leadership, collaboration and readiness, the programmes were implemented in partnership with Oxford University,

Cambridge University and Nanyang Technological University, Singapore.

Dr Jawad holds a PhD in management of information technology from Cranfield University and a BSc in electrical engineering from Washington University, St. Louis, Missouri. A former visiting fellow at the Yale School of Management, Yale University, he is currently a visiting fellow at the National University of Singapore and Henley Business School, United Kingdom.

Dr Jawad sits on a number of boards, including the School of Business of the American University in Cairo (AUC), Egypt; the Oman 2040 Technical Committee; the National Training Fund, Oman; and the International Culture Communication Centre, China.

His current interests focus on government transformation and innovation, including the impact of digitalisation, leadership mindsets and the need for greater resilience to combat global disruption. He is developing a digital learning platform for upskilling ministers and senior civil servants.

In 2015, Dr Jawad received the Oman Civil Order from His Majesty Sultan Qaboos bin Said, in recognition of his outstanding contributions. In 2020, he received the same award from His Majesty Sultan Haitham bin Tariq bin Taimur Al-Said.

"...we can reimagine government in a responsive and responsible way."

Ali Qassim Jawad,
Senior Advisor, Diwan of Royal Court (2012 – Present), Sultanate of Oman

REFERENCES

1 The acronym VUCA was introduced by the US Army War College to describe the more volatile, uncertain, complex and ambiguous world which resulted from the end of the cold war, Kissinger & Walsh, 2012.

2 Taleb, Nassim, Nicholas, Fooled by Randomness, (Random House, 2001.)

3 Leading Smart Transformation: A Roadmap for World Class Government (Palgrave Macmillan, 2011).

4 Goldsmith, M., What Got You Here Won't Get You There, (Profile Books, 2008).

5 https://www.heritage.org/report/the-estonian-economic-miracle

6 https://data.worldbank.org/indicator/NY.GDP.PCAP.PP.CD?locations=LT-UA-LV-EE

7 https://data.worldbank.org/indicator/NY.GDP.PCAP.PP.CD?locations=LT-UA-LV-EE

8 https://www.bbc.com/future/article/20171019-could-estonia-be-the-first-digital-country

9 "Trump's businesses are full of dirty Russian money. The scandal is that it's legal." Craig Unger, The Washington Post, 29 March 2019.

10 "How a cyber-attack transformed Estonia", by Damien McGuinness, BBC News, Tallinn, Estonia, 27 April 2017.

11 https://www.medrxiv.org/content/10.1101/2020.05.15.20103655v1.full.pdf

12 "Even small differences in timing would have prevented the worst exponential growth, which by April had subsumed New York City, New Orleans and other major cities, researchers found." New York Times

13 Thinking, Fast and Slow, Daniel Kahneman, (Farrar, Straus & Giroux, 2011).

14 Juvénal Habyarimana

15 https://www.pewresearch.org/fact-tank/2019/03/18/the-share-of-women-in-legislatures-around-the-world-is-growing-but-they-are-still-underrepresented/

16 Global Peace Index – Institute for Economics and Peace.

17a https://www.weforum.org

17b https://www.transparency.org/en/cpi

17c https://envirocenter.yale.edu/2020-environmental-performance-index

17d https://worldhappiness.report

18 Mission for Finland: How Finland will demonstrate its strengths by solving the world's most wicked problems, Country brand report, 25/11/10

19 "Mission for Finland: How Finland will demonstrate its strengths by solving the world's most wicked problems", Country brand report, 25/11/10

20 https://www.bbc.co.uk/news/business-32028693

21 https://www.bis.org/review/r150807b.htm

22 http://graphics.wsj.com/singapore-50th-anniversary

23 http://statisticstimes.com/economy/projected-world-gdp-capita-ranking.php

24 https://data.worldbank.org/indicator/HD.HCI.OVRL

25 http://www3.weforum.org/docs/WEF_TheGlobalCompetitivenessReport2019.pdf

26 https://www.heritage.org/index/country/singapore

27 https://data.gov.sg/dataset/total-land-area-of-singapore, Singapore Land Authority, accessed 28 March 2020

28 https://www.psc.gov.sg/docs/default-source/psc/2018-psc-annual-e-report.pdf 31 December 2018, excluding scholarships extended by the other Ministries, Statutory Boards and Companies

29 Three of the most recent efforts are the Economic Review Committee chaired by DPM Lee Hsien Loong in 2001-2003, The Economic Strategies Committee chaired by DPM Tharman Shanmugaratnam in 2009-2010, and the Committee on the Future Economy chaired by Minister for Finance Heng Swee Keat in 2016-2017.

30 Changi Airport has won over 620 awards since its opening, including 28 best airport awards in 2019 alone

31 Sources for Changi airport box
https://eresources.nlb.gov.sg/infopedia/articles/SIP_130_2005-01-22.html
https://eresources.nlb.gov.sg/infopedia/articles/SIP_574_2004-12-23.html
The Straits Times, 10 February 1981
The Straits Times, 17 March 1946
https://www.worldairportawards.com
https://www.changiairport.com/corporate/about-us/awards-and-accolades.html

32 From 1953 to 1967 the currency in Singapore was the Malaya and British Borneo dollar.

33 The Irish Economy in a Comparative Institutional Perspective, Dublin; NESC 1992.

34 A separate body, the CTT, founded in 1959, was responsible for helping Irish-based firms, whether foreign owned or not, to expand into overseas markets. Like the IDA, it had a network of offices overseas. And there were other organisations that existed to help Ireland's food industries to export. All were assisted by the existence of populations of Irish origin all over the world.

35 https://www.enterpriseireland.ie

36 https://www.sfi.ie
37 https://isif.ie
38 Mastercard Global Destination Cities Index 2019 https://www.businessinsider.com/most-visited-cities-around-the-world-ranked-2019-9?r=US&IR=T#1-bangkok-2278-million-19
39 https://www.bangkokpost.com/travel/1803964/medical-tourism-report-released
40 Paul Streeten from Oxford, Albert Hirshman from Harvard, Saburo Okita from the Japan Centre for Economic Research, Hla Myint from London School of Economics, Suparp Yossundara from the Bank of Thailand and other Asian scholars
41 www.un.org/sg/en/content/sg/statement/2006-05-26/secretary-general39s-address-high-level-panel-his-majesty-king-and)
42 http://hdr.undp.org/sites/default/files/pr1-hdr10-overview-e-rev6.pdf
43 In 2020 that population had surpassed five million.
44 Global Peace Index - Institute for Economics and Peace
45 Global Terrorism Index - Institute for Economics and Peace
46 https://www.omanobserver.om/global-competitiveness-report-oman-tops-among-arab-countries/
http://www3.weforum.org/docs/WEF_TheGlobalCompetitivenessReport2019.pdf
47 War in Human Civilization – Azar Gat, Oxford University Press, 2008, p519
48 https://commonslibrary.parliament.uk/research-briefings/sn02787/
49 https://www.information-age.com/biggest-tech-hubs-uk-right-business-123472568/
50 https://www.youtube.com/watch?v=GY-NpWFyu8w
51 "Fertility, mortality, migration, and population scenarios for 195 countries from 2017 to 2100", The Lancet, July 14 2020, Prof Stein Emil Vollset, Emily Goren, Chu-Wei Yuan, Jackie Cao, Amananda E Smith, Thomas Hsiao et al. https://www.thelancet.com/journals/lancet/article/PIIS0140-6736(20)30677-2/fulltext
52 https://www.euronews.com/2020/07/01/us-buys-up-world-s-stock-of-key-covid-19-drug-remdesivir
53 "Moving from Just in Time to Just in Case", Lauren Pittelli, Industry Week, May 27, 2020.
54 The Politics Industry: How Political Innovation Can Break Partisan Gridlock and Save Our Democracy, Katherine M. Gehl and Michael E. Porter, (Harvard Business Review Press, 2020).
55 When More Isn't Better: Overcoming America's Obsession with Economic Efficiency, Roger Martin, (Harvard Business School Press, 2020).
56 Nassim Nicholas Taleb, Fooled by Randomness, (Random House, 2001)

57 Leviathan, Thomas Hobbes (1651).

58 "The next catastrophe", The Economist, June 27th, 2020.

59 Aksoy, C G; B Eichengren and O Saka, (2020) The Political Scars of Epidemics, CEPR Discussion Paper 14879.245

60 Francis Fukuyama, "The Thing That Determines A Country's Resistance To The Coronavirus", The Atlantic, March 30, 2020

61 Francis Fukuyama, "The Thing That Determines A Country's Resistance To The Coronavirus", The Atlantic, March 30, 2020

62 The Altruistic Corporation: Growing Richer by Giving Everything, Isaac Getz and Laurent Marbacher (Albin Michel, 2019).

63 Andrew Winston, The Big Pivot: Radically Practical Strategies for a Hotter, Scarier and More Open World, Harvard Business Review, 2019.)

64 Public Private Partnerships in the Middle East and Africa: A Handbook for Policy Makers, OECD

65 "Using Crowdsourcing in Government", by Daren Brabham, University of Southern California.

66 "The End of Bureaucracy", by Gary Hamel and Michele Zanini, HBR Nov-Dec 2018.

67 A two-sided market is also called a two-sided network and is an intermediary economic platform having two distinct user groups that provide each other with network benefits. The organisation that creates value primarily by enabling direct interactions by two or more distinct types of affiliated customers is called a mult-sided platform. Haigu, Andrei; Wright, Julian, (October 2011), "Multi-sided Platforms", Working paper 12-024. Harvard Business School.

68 Carse, James, Finite and Infinite Games, (Free Press, 2013)

69 Commander Rich Diviney, former US Navy Seal, in conversation with Simon Sinek.

70 https://dictionary.cambridge.org/dictionary/english/strive

71 1 - "Solution architect", Wikipedia, Wikimedia Foundation, https://en.wikipedia.org/wiki/Solution_architecture

72 2 - Fairhurst, Gail T.. Reframing the art of framing: Problems and prospects for leadership (Sage Journal, 2005)

73 Gottlieb, Hildy, Creating a Better World Means Asking Better Questions, (Stamford Social Innovation Review, July 2020), https://ssir.org/articles/entry/creating_a_better_world_means_asking_better_questions

74 3 - Horst W. J. et al, Dilemmas in a general theory of planning (Springer Science and Business Media, 1973)

75 4 - Churchman, C. West., Guest editorial: Wicked problems." (Management Science, 1967)

76 5 - Sinek, Simon, The Infinite Game: How Great Businesses Achieve Long-Lasting Success, (Portfolio Penguin, 2019)

77 Heifetz, Ronald A., Leadership Without Easy Answers, (Harvard University Press, 1994)

78 D'Emidio, Tony et al, The global case for customer experience in government, (McKinsey, 2019), https://www.mckinsey.com/industries/public-sector/our-insights/the-global-case-for-customer-experience-in-government

79 Campion-Awwad, Oliver et al, The National Programme for IT in the NHS: A Case History, (Unoversity of Cambridge, 2014), https://www.cl.cam.ac.uk/~rja14/Papers/npfit-mpp-2014-case-history.pdf

80 Campion-Awwad, Oliver et al, The National Programme for IT in the NHS: A Case History, (University of Cambridge, 2014), https://www.cl.cam.ac.uk/~rja14/Papers/npfit-mpp-2014-case-history.pdf

81 Awad El Araby, Mohamed et al, Dilemma of institutional performance assessment in governmental sector: A proposed KPIs model, (Journal of Humanities and Applied Social Sciences, 2020), https://www.emerald.com/insight/content/doi/10.1108/JHASS-08-2019-0026/full/html

82 "Sunk cost", Wikipedia, Wikimedia Foundation, https://en.wikipedia.org/wiki/Sunk_cost

83 Cameron, Kim S., and Bradley Winn., "Virtuousness in organizations" in Cameron, Kim S., and Gretchen M. Spreitze (eds)., The Oxford Handbook of Positive Organizational Scholarship, 231-243, Oxford: Oxford University Press, 2012.

84 Edelman, Edelman Trust Barometer, 2019

85 Norman, Steven M., Bruce Avolio, and Fred Luthans., "The impact of positivity and transparency on trust in leaders and their perceived effectiveness", Leadership Quarterly, 21, 350-364, (2010).

86 Burke, C. Shawn., Dana E. Sims., Elizabeth H. Lazzara, and Eduardo Salas., "Trust in leadership: A multi-level review and integration", The Leadership Quarterly, 18, 606–632, (2007).

87 Hassan, Arif., and Forbis Ahamed., "Authentic Leadership, Trust and Work Engagement", International Journal of Human and Social Sciences, 6, 3, 164-170, (2011).

88 Mayer, Roger C., James H. Davis., and F. David Schoorman, "An integrative model of organizational trust", Academy of Management Review, 20, 3, 709–34, (1995).

89 Dirks, Kurt T., and Donald L Ferrin, "Trust in leadership: Meta-analytic findings and implications for research and practice", Journal of Applied Psychology, 87,4, 611–628, (2002).

90 Rutter, Michael., "Psychosocial resilience and protective mechanisms", American Journal of Orthopsychiatry, 57, 316-331, (1987).

91 Perry, Bruce., "How children become resilient", Scholastic Parent & Child, 10, 2, 33-35, (2002).

92 Janas, Monica., "Build resiliency", Intervention in School and Clinic, 38, 117-122, (2002).

93 Nishikawa, Yvette., Thriving in the face of adversity: Perceptions of elementary-school principals, La Verne, CA: University of La Verne, 2006.

94 Carver, Charles S., "Resilience and thriving: Issues, models, and linkages", Journal of Social Issues, 54, 245-266, (1998).

95 Patterson, Jerry L., and Paul Kelleher., Resilient school leaders: Strategies for turning adversity into achievement, Alexandria, VA: Association for Supervision and Curriculum Development, 2005.

96 Patterson, Jerry L., and Paul Kelleher., Resilient school leaders: Strategies for turning adversity into achievement, Alexandria, VA: Association for Supervision and Curriculum Development, 2005.

97 Bonanno, George A., "Loss, trauma, and human resilience", American Psychologist, 59, 20-28, (2004).

98 Nishikawa, Yvette., Thriving in the face of adversity: Perceptions of elementary-school principals, La Verne, CA: University of La Verne, 2006.

99 Bass, Bernard M., "The Future of Leadership in Learning Organizations", Journal of Leadership & Organizational Studies, 7, 18, 2000

100 Bass, Bernard M., Bass and Stodgill's Handbook of Leadership, 3rd Ed, New York, NY: Free Press. 1990.

101 Bass, Bernard M., Transformational Leadership: Industrial, Military, and Educational Impact, Mahwah, NJ: Erlbaum, 1998.

102 Gaspersz, Jeff,. "The Search for Innovation Leadership", The European Business Review, March April 2012.

103 Tucker, Robert., Six Innovation Leadership Skills Everybody Needs To Master, Accessed from: https://www.forbes.com/sites/robertbtucker/2017/02/09/six-innovation-leadership-skills-everybody-needs-to-master/#66d297965d46

104 McKinsey & Company, Leadership in innovation needs innovation in leadership, 2017.

105 World Government Summit, and Pricewaterhouse Coopers, Inspire and Orchestrate: Innovation-Driven Government (IDG), 2018.

106 GovLab Deloitte, Transforming the Public Sector Delivering successful public sector transformation through innovation, 2018

107 McKinsey & Company, Leadership in innovation needs innovation in leadership, 2017.

108 Centre for Creative Leadership and Continuum, Innovation Leadership How to use innovation to lead effectively, work collaboratively, and drive results, 2014. White paper accessed from: https://www.ccl.org/wpcontent/uploads/2015/04/InnovationLeadership.pdf

109 Bass, Bernard M., Transformational Leadership: Industrial, Military, and Educational Impact, Mahwah, NJ: Erlbaum, 1998.

110 Cummings, Anne., and Greg. R. Oldham, "Enhancing creativity: Managing work contexts for the high potential employee", California Management Review, 40: 22–38, 1997; Scott, Susanne G., and Reginald A. Bruce, "Determinants of Innovative Behaviour: A Path Model of Individual Innovation in the Workplace", The Academy of Management Journal, 37, 3, 580-607, 1994.

111 Borins, Sandford., "Leadership and Innovation in the Public Sector", Leadership and Organization Development Journal, 23, 8, 467-476, 2002.

112 World Government Summit, and Pricewaterhouse Coopers, Inspire and Orchestrate:Innovation-Driven Government (IDG), 2018.

113 Shaw, William, Frugal innovation: adapting local tech where top-of-the-range is out of reach, (Wired Magazine, April 2013),https://www.wired.co.uk/article/frugal-innovation

114 Nanus, Burt., Visionary Leadership: Creating a Compelling Sense of Direction for Your Organization, San Francisco, CA: Jossey-Bass Publishers, 1992.

115 Sashkin, Marshall., "Visionary Leadership", in Rosenbach, William E., and Robert L. Taylor, (Eds), Contemporary Issues in Leadership, 2nd Edition, Westview Press, 1989.

116 Daft, Richard L., The Leadership Experience (6th Edition), Stamford, CT: Cengage Learning Press, 2014.

117 Kotter, John P., "What Leaders Really Do", Harvard Business Review, May-June 1990.

118 Harper, Stephen C., The Forward-Focused Organization: Visionary Thinking and Breakthrough Leadership to Create Your Company's Future. New York, NY: AMACOM, American Management Association, 2001.

119 Sashkin, Marshall., "Visionary Leadership", in Rosenbach, William E., and Robert L. Taylor, (Eds), Contemporary Issues in Leadership, 2nd Edition, Westview Press, 1989.

120 Harper, Stephen C., The Forward-Focused Organization: Visionary Thinking and Breakthrough Leadership to Create Your Company's Future. New York, NY:

121 AMACOM, American Management Association, 2001.
Bryson, John and Barbara C. Crosby, Leadership for the Common Good: Tackling Public Problems in a Shared-Power World, San Francisco, CA: Jossey-Bass Publishers, 1992.

122 Nanus, Burt., Visionary Leadership: Creating a Compelling Sense of Direction for Your Organization, San Francisco, CA: Jossey-Bass Publishers, 1992.

123 Gourévitch, Antoine, Data-Driven Transformation: Accelerate at Scale Now, (Boston Consulting Group, 2017), https://www.bcg.com/en-gb/publications/2017/digital-transformation-transformation-data-driven-transformation

124 Ready, Douglas A., In Praise of the Incurably Curious Leader, (MIT Sloan Management Review, 2019), https://sloanreview.mit.edu/article/in-praise-of-the-incurably-curious-leader/

125 Gino, Francesca, Why curiosity matters, (HBR, 2018), https://hbr.org/2018/09/curiosity

126 Buchanan, Leigh, How to Be an Elegant Leader, (Inc. Magazine, 2012), https://www.inc.com/magazine/201203/leigh-buchanan/matthew-e-may-how-to-be-an-elegant-leader.html

127 Shambaugh, Rebecca, To Sound Like a Leader, Think About What You Say, and How and When You Say It, (HBR, 2017), https://hbr.org/2017/10/to-sound-like-a-leader-think-about-what-you-say-and-how-and-when-you-say-it

128 Toogood , Granville N., The New Articulate Executive: Look, Act and Sound Like a Leader, (McGraw-Hill, 2010)

129 Overeem, Patrick Overeem and Bakker, Femke E., Statesmanship Beyond the Modern State, (Taylor and Francis, 2017)

130 Greene, Robert, The 48 Laws of Power, (Profile books, 2020)

131 Davison, Nehal, Supporting politicians to lead in government, (Institute for Government, 2015), https://www.instituteforgovernment.org.uk/sites/default/files/publications/Supporting%20politicians%20to%20lead%20in%20government_FINAL.pdf

132 Carse, James, Finite and Infinite Games, (Free Press, 2013)

133 Dweck, C. S. (2006). Mindset: The new psychology of success. New York: Random House.